THE JU

THE JUMANOS

HUNTERS AND TRADERS OF THE SOUTH PLAINS

NANCY PARROTT HICKERSON

UNIVERSITY OF TEXAS PRESS
AUSTIN

To the spirit of Juan Sabeata

Requests for permission to reproduce material from this work should be sent to Permissions, University of Texas Press, Box 7819, Austin, TX 78713-7819.

∞ The paper used in this publication meets the minimum requirements of American National Standard for Information Sciences—Permanence of Paper for Printed Library Materials, ANSI Z39.48-1984.

Library of Congress Cataloging-in-Publication Data

Hickerson, Nancy Parrott.
    The Jumanos : hunters and traders of the South Plains / Nancy Parrott Hickerson. — 1st ed.
        p.   cm.
    Includes bibliographical references and index.
    ISBN 0-292-73083-7 (alk. paper) — ISBN 0-292-73084-5 (pbk. : alk. paper)
        1. Jumano Indians—History—Sources.   2. Jumano Indians—Social life and customs.   3. Ethnohistory—Southwest, New.
    4. Ethnohistory—Mexico—Chihuahua (State).   I. Title.
    E99.J9H53   1994
    978'.004974—dc20   93-39838

CONTENTS

MAPS AND ILLUSTRATIONS

PREFACE

My interest in the Jumanos, an early historic Plains people, began more than a decade ago during a symposium sponsored by the Texas Tech University Museum. The subject of the symposium was the culture and history of a later Plains people, the Kiowas. Archaeologist Robert Campbell presented a paper dealing with possible Kiowa origins; in it he proposed a link to the prehistoric Jornada culture of the South Plains; he also indicated a Jornada connection for the little-known, and long extinct, Jumanos and Sumas.[1] Although I am not professionally involved in archaeology, I found Campbell's ideas interesting, since my own paper, on linguistics, also pointed to a southwestern connection for Kiowa. The Jumanos, located in the South Plains, looked like a possible missing link between the Kiowas and the Jornada culture. However, this idea got little support from the other symposium participants. The identity of the Jumanos' language appeared to be crucial. Kiowa is a Tanoan language, and the Tanoan family is well represented in the eastern Pueblos, bordering the Rio Grande. It seemed likely that the language of the prehistoric Jornada people could also have been Tanoan. But Jumano was deemed to have been part of another family, the Uto-Aztecan; if this were the case, it could not be directly related to Kiowa.

My reaction to this impasse was to begin a fresh investigation of Jumano linguistic affiliation. I was surprised to find that the problem had a long history. Over more than a century, half a dozen different suggestions had been made by as many different scholars. The earliest of these, Mexican linguist Francisco Pimentel, published maps which indicated that Suma was linked to Piro, the extinct language of the southern Pueblos.[2] Since Pimentel's time, Piro has been recognized as part of the Tanoan family; the implication is, therefore, that Suma and Jumano are included in that grouping. Although Pimentel's opinion was accepted by J. P. Harrington,[3] an

expert on North American Indian languages, it was evidently ignored by later researchers, whose suggestions reflect a variety of
theories about regional cultural dynamics.

When I began to read firsthand accounts of Spanish encounters
with the Jumanos, dating from the sixteenth and seventeenth centuries, I found myself in agreement with Pimentel and Harrington.
Even though the hard data of texts and word lists in the Jumanos'
language were lacking, there were statements about intelligibility
and other indications of communication between groups which led
me to believe that the Jumanos and the closely related Sumas were
Tanoan-speakers. I concluded that in the early historical period the
geographical distribution of this group of languages was greater
than in recent times. It extended east of the Rio Grande into the
South Plains, and south of New Mexico as far as La Junta de los
Rios. The Jumanos were part of this Tanoan bloc.[4]

While I was preoccupied with the rather convoluted problem of
Jumano linguistic identity, I gradually became aware that it is just
one part of a larger mystery. Who were the Jumanos? What was
their cultural situation? What had become of them? Early in the
twentieth century, certain historical researchers had attempted to
answer these questions. However, it appeared that virtually no
progress had been made since 1940 when the convention was
adopted that *Jumano,* as used in the Spanish colonial documents,
was a general term and did not refer to any specific ethnic group or
tribe. This convention virtually terminated inquiry into the so-
called Jumano problem.[5] I was convinced, however, that it was an
oversimplification, and that the problem was still unresolved. (The
history of modern Jumano research is briefly recapitulated in the
first section of this work.)

About five years ago, I put other interests aside and became committed to a full-scale ethnohistorical study. I no longer cared
whether the Jumanos had anything to do with the Kiowas. My pre-
liminary studies had already convinced me that they were a unique
and fascinating people in their own right. They were mentioned
prominently and frequently at the time of Spanish entry into the
greater Southwest. Later, they appeared less and less frequently and
eventually disappeared from the historical record. I determined to
collect as much information as possible, hoping to put together
a coherent picture of the Jumanos and, if possible, to answer the
nagging questions about their place in history and their decline.

In the course of this study, I have been excited to discover a
people who were not only real, in every sense of the word, but also
important. I am convinced that a new recognition of the Jumanos,

as a significant presence in western North America, will eventually lead to other reassessments of Native American history. This book can be read simply as a chronological account of the Jumanos' decline and fall—their loss of territory, the breakdown of a regional economic and political system in which they played a vital part, and their eventual displacement from the South Plains. Beyond this, however, I hope to convey something of a Jumano perspective on several major cultural changes or transitions which this people witnessed. Among these are the Spanish conquest of the western borderlands, the Apachean invasion of the South Plains, the introduction of horses and the evolution of a Native American equestrian culture, and the intrusion of European power rivalries into North America. The impact of these events on the Jumanos reflects a period of cultural revolution of continental proportions.

I have followed the Jumanos' story through the seventeenth century, the point at which they disappear from Spanish colonial accounts. The questions which still remain are, directly or indirectly, germane to my original interest in Kiowa ethnogenesis, which I now see as exemplifying a later stage in the transformation of Native American society. I hope that I will eventually be able to trace specific ties linking these two peoples, and to document the steps through which remnant Jumano bands formed a new identity as the nucleus of the Kiowa nation.[6] However, that is beyond the scope of this study; it is the prospectus for a sequel, with much of the work remaining to be done.

My Jumano research began in earnest during a developmental leave granted by Texas Tech University in the spring of 1987, and was completed during a second leave in 1993. I am grateful for short-term grants and fellowships from the Newberry Library, the National Endowment for the Humanities, and the American Philosophical Society. I appreciate the interest and encouragement of a number of my colleagues, including Bob Campbell, Dan Flores, Eileen Johnson, Helen Tanner, John Moore, and Carroll Riley. I thank Andrew Hall for the illustrations. My son, Daniel Hickerson, assisted me with the notes, references, and index; and my daughter, Megan Hickerson, has read and critiqued my writing. I thank both for their amiability and unflagging encouragement.

INTRODUCTION

The Mysterious Jumanos

Anyone who peruses the firsthand accounts of Spanish exploration and colonization of New Mexico, Texas, and adjacent regions of northern Mexico soon becomes aware of the presence throughout this large area of people called *Jumanos*. In the late sixteenth century, this name was applied to some of the first Native Americans encountered by explorers who ascended the Rio del Norte (the upper Rio Grande) to enter the lands north of Mexico. It appears that Alvar Nuñez Cabeza de Vaca and his three companions—the first Europeans to travel into the interior of North America—also sojourned with the Jumanos even earlier as they made their way toward the Rio Grande and proceeded north along its course.

There are many references to encounters with Jumanos over the next two centuries, in the records of the Spanish colonies in Nuevo Mexico, Nueva Vizcaya, Coahuila, and Texas. The Spaniards in New Mexico knew the Jumanos as a Pueblo people with villages in the eastern provinces of the colony. In the regions of eastern New Mexico, they also had dealings with Jumanos who were nomads. These Indians were plainsmen par excellence—buffalo-hunters who migrated seasonally between their scattered camps and Indian farming communities along the major rivers, both east and west.

Spanish exploration of the Plains was facilitated by contacts with the Jumanos, who were quick to offer their services as guides. Spanish settlers in New Mexico and Nueva Vizcaya (later Chihuahua) traded with the Jumanos, who soon began operating as middlemen between the Spanish colonies and distant Indian groups. Among these were the large Caddoan-speaking tribes and confederacies located far to the east of New Mexico, which the Spaniards originally named *Quivira* and which they later called collectively the *Nations of the North*.

Figure 1. A Jumano trader, circa 1580 (illustration by Andrew Hall)

It would appear that the known sphere of Jumano provenance expanded as the Spanish conquerors extended their sphere of influence, as the Spaniards recorded encounters with Jumanos in virtually every region they entered after the founding of New Mexico. As exploring and missionizing extended east of the Pecos, Jumano camps, or *rancherias*, were found located in the High Plains of western Texas and on eastward-flowing rivers such as the Rio de las Nueces (a stream which is generally identified today with the Rio Colorado of Texas).

Around 1670 missionary and military parties from another border region of New Spain, Coahuila, crossed the Rio Bravo (the lower Rio Grande) and reached the vicinity of San Antonio. These explorers, as they made their way through southern Texas, also encountered Jumanos. A decade later, expeditions out of New Mexico and Nueva Vizcaya dealt with the Jumanos as leaders of a growing pan-tribal movement in Texas. At about the same time, members of the French colony founded by the Marquis de La Salle at Espiritu Santo (Matagorda) Bay on the Gulf Coast of Texas had dealings with the Jumanos in the territory of the Ceni (Hasinai), a Caddoan confederacy. Both Spanish and French accounts indicate that in the last decades of the seventeenth century the Jumanos were extremely active, both as traders and as political leaders. At this time they were evidently conducting a busy long-distance traffic between Spanish settlements along the Rio del Norte and the Indians of eastern and southern Texas (of whom the Caddoans were the most numerous and politically important).

It is not known whether the Jumano presence was aboriginal through all parts of their vast area of distribution. It is tempting to believe that they may have advanced eastward as the Spanish sphere of influence expanded. It seems certain that they had a role in native trade dating from aboriginal times; however, it also seems likely that some of their movements were the result of an expansion of this role, vis-à-vis the Spanish colonies.

By or shortly after 1700, the Jumanos lost territory and were no longer a substantial or influential presence in the Southwest and South Plains. At some time during a brief period of Spanish withdrawal from Texas, between 1693 and 1716, they apparently ceased their frontier trading activities and were thereafter rarely seen. After this, there are only a few scattered references to the Jumanos. Some remnant populations remained clustered around La Junta de los Rios. The name was still applied to individuals and groups who became gradually incorporated during the next century into the Apache bands which were dominant in that region. As a distinct people, the Jumanos were soon virtually extinct throughout their earlier heartland.

Modern ethnographic maps of native North America rarely indicate the presence of the Jumanos, although in the past, to judge by the contemporary accounts, they could be encountered almost anywhere in the Southwest or South Plains. Historians, anthropologists, and linguists have disagreed, and continue to disagree, about the identity of the Jumanos and the nature of their culture. Their place on the map, the language they spoke, and their role in history have remained a mystery, despite their obvious importance to their Native American and European neighbors and trade partners.

Efforts to piece together the outlines of Jumano history encounter difficulties which stem, directly or indirectly, from the scattered, mobile, and ephemeral nature of their presence in the greater Southwest and in historical records. For early historic times the only written records were produced by European observers. Sedentary or localized tribes—the Pueblo peoples, for example—sometimes had enduring relationships with resident missionaries or traders, many of whom kept journals and continual records of events. In such cases, a search of the official records of a particular mission or colonial district may prove a prolific source of cultural and historical information, a running account of events in the life of a single village or tribe.

By contrast, the Jumanos were widely dispersed; as their leader Juan Sabeata put it, they were an "extended" nation. Individuals and groups moved frequently. Their record is, of necessity, a pastiche of scattered information drawn from several different political units (New Mexico, Nueva Vizcaya, Texas, Coahuila), brief glimpses drawn from Spanish, French, and American sources, with little or no continuity. Catholic priests from time to time worked among Jumano groups, and Spanish settlers dealt with them—often illegally—for many years, but none of these left large bodies of documentation. There was apparently no observer of the Jumanos who provided more than passing comment on the life and times of these people.

Any attempt to write a comprehensive account of the Jumanos must therefore rely on a bare skeleton of chronological events, a few recorded cultural details, and a large amount of inference. These are the circumstances which render the Jumanos mysterious, and which have permitted specialists in regional studies of the Southwest to overlook or ignore the very existence of this fascinating and important people. They are circumstances which have led scholars to develop widely differing interpretations of the nature of

Jumano culture and of the place of the Jumanos in history. Each of these interpretations has its theoretical bias—as, admittedly, does this interpretation. Each relies on certain assumptions and an interpretive framework, and each must, of necessity, make creative use of cultural analogy in interpreting the available facts about the Jumanos.

A Century of Jumano Studies

Anthropologists and historians often refer to the Jumanos as a "mystery," or a "problem." A part of the mystery is the evident cultural variety subsumed under this name. The term *Jumano*[1] has been applied, at various times, to people living both in fertile river valleys and in arid desert lands; to some residing in substantial masonry houses and others in skin tents; to people described as "clothed" and others called "naked"; to farmers and hunters; to pedestrian nomads and men on horseback. The mystery also rests on the wide geographical distribution of Jumanos in time and space.

Between the first recorded use of the designation in 1581 and the last, an oral history recorded in 1888,[2] Jumano groups were found at locales from northern New Mexico to Coahuila; and from the vicinity of Flagstaff, Arizona, at the northwestern extreme, to Parral, Chihuahua, at the southwest, to the Trinity River of Texas, at the eastern extreme. The total area could encompass at least 500,000 square miles; in no part of it, however, is there a tract of land which can be defined with certainty as a territory of permanent and exclusive Jumano occupancy.

There has been a long history of scholarly efforts to solve the "Jumano problem"—to find a rationale in the scattered appearances of this name in the historical record, and to identify the group (or groups) in terms of known ethnic and linguistic classifications. These efforts began roughly a century ago with the awakening of a scholarly interest in the native peoples of North America and with the beginning of archival research into the relations of these peoples with the European colonial powers.

Adolph Bandelier

Modern awareness of the Jumanos begins with the work of Adolph Bandelier, a late nineteenth-century Swiss scholar who made North America his home and the subject of his research. Bandelier's studies of prehistoric sites and his research in colonial-period archives in Spain and Mexico mark the beginnings of serious scholarship on the cultures and the prehistory of the southwestern United States. He collected and made available for study many of the basic documentary sources on Spanish colonial history.

Apparently intrigued by references to the Jumanos, Bandelier noted the wide geographical range over which they were encountered, and remarked on their apparent involvement in trade. His published reports include comments on the Jumanos in Mexico and New Mexico and speculations about their history and their relations with other groups such as the Julimes of La Junta de los Rios. He remarked that the Jumanos were not as prominent in Chihuahua as they were in New Mexico, and suggested that they may have "lost . . . their individuality" in the "whirlpool" of Apache warfare.[3]

Bandelier also observed that, while the Jumanos at La Junta de los Rios were a farming people, those further to the north "subsisted on the buffalo almost exclusively." In nineteenth-century anthropology, farming was considered a more highly evolved way of life than hunting; therefore, Bandelier believed that the buffalo hunters had taken a backward step. They had become "accustomed to the life which the following of the buffalo required, [and] discarded permanence of abode, exchanging it for vagrancy with its consequences."[4] He seems to suggest that this "vagrancy"—the lack of a permanent place of residence—could account for the virtual disappearance of the Jumanos from the historical record after 1700. His writings give no suggestion that he had any doubt about the existence of the Jumanos as a distinctive people—indeed, he apparently considered them to be an exciting and interesting people, although something of a mystery. Certainly they were for him an integral part of the complex fabric of southwestern history.

Frederick W. Hodge

F. W. Hodge was the editor of the monumental *Handbook of American Indians North of Mexico*, published in 1910 by the Bureau of American Ethnology. He himself wrote several of the entries on southwestern peoples, including one on the Jumanos. Because of the influence of the *Handbook*, Hodge can be credited with establishing *Jumano* as the standard form of the name for twentieth-century scholars. However, the real baseline for subsequent Jumano research may be Hodge's longer historical essay, published in 1911.[5]

Pursuing issues raised by Bandelier, Hodge attempted to piece together a more coherent Jumano history. For him, the most intriguing part of the mystery concerned their "ultimate fate": why had they rapidly and completely disappeared? His attempt to answer this question was inspired in part by entries which the historian Herbert Bolton submitted for inclusion in the *Handbook*. From Bolton, Hodge learned that the Taovayas (or Tawehash), a division of the Wichita tribe, had been known to the French in the mid-eighteenth century as "Panipiquets . . . alias Jumanes . . ."[6] On the basis of the similarity in names, Hodge attempted to apply a technique which ethnohistorians call "upstreaming." He projected the later identification back in time to the La Junta Jumanos of the sixteenth century. With the link which he assumed existed between the two, Hodge believed he had found a solution to the mystery of Jumano disappearance from the lower Rio Grande—migration. He suggested that the Jumanos encountered at La Junta by the Espejo *entrada* of 1581 (see Chapter 3) had migrated to New Mexico by 1598, where they were found living in the southeastern Pueblos. When missionaries visited a Jumano encampment in the High Plains, some 250 miles to the east of New Mexico, Hodge reasoned that the Jumanos had moved again.

Thus, Hodge interpreted a few scattered references to the Jumanos as evidence of the constant, erratic migrations of a single group, who then followed the priests back to New Mexico to live, once more, in or near the pueblos. There, he reasoned, the Jumanos would not have been found in any "village other than their own." Therefore he speculated that the "great pueblo of the Xumanas," mentioned by early writers in New Mexico, must have been "an aggregation of dwellings of . . . [a] more or less temporary kind . . ." From this location, they would have shifted again to where they were found a few years later in the plains east of New Mexico. Missionary visits were once more made, "apparently for the purpose of bringing them back."[7]

Hodge made rather free interpretation of the locales and distances given in his sources, suggesting that the settlements in the plains were located in the vicinity of El Cuartelejo, an area in western Kansas, even though the original sources indicate locations east or southeast of New Mexico. His interpretation was evidently influenced by his efforts to establish a link between the early Jumanos and the later Wichita tribes of Kansas and Oklahoma. After 1650, he believed that the Jumano tribe divided, some of them locating in Texas and others remaining in the north to become allies of the Pawnees and French. He related these movements to changes in nomenclature: the term "Jumano . . . originated in Chihuahua and New Mexico, passed into Texas, but seems to have been gradually replaced by the name 'Tawahash,' which in turn was superseded by 'Wichita.'" Thus, according to Hodge, the Jumanos did not actually disappear from history—it was simply a matter of changing nomenclature.[8]

It is with Hodge's work that the issue of language identity became part of the "Jumano problem." Wichita, to which he linked the Jumanos, is part of the Caddoan family of languages. This grouping is associated with the Plains rather than the Southwest, and may be distantly related to the Siouan and Iroquoian families. Thus, Hodge's interpretation suggests historical connections for the Jumanos which are prevailingly eastern.

Herbert Bolton

Bolton was a renowned historian whose field of interest was the Spanish borderlands region, including northern Mexico and the southwestern United States. As noted, it was Bolton's contribution to the *Handbook of American Indians North of Mexico* which fueled Hodge's interpretations of Jumano history. However, Bolton disagreed with Hodge's conclusions. In 1911, after further researches in the archives of Mexico, he responded to Hodge with an article in which he, too, focused his attention on the mystery of Jumano identity and on their whereabouts at and after the end of the seventeenth century.[9]

Bolton disputed Hodge's identification of the Rio de las Nueces, where the Jumano were situated in 1632 and 1650, with the Arkansas River. He carefully analyzed the itineraries of several Spanish expeditions to this river and identified it as the Concho, a tributary of the Colorado of Texas. Bolton also contradicted Hodge's assertion that the Jumanos had vanished from the southern part of their range by the beginning of the eighteenth century. He cited manuscript sources which indicated the presence, decades later, of Jumanos together with Tobosos near La Junta, and allied with Apaches near San Antonio, Texas.

For Bolton, an important part of the Jumano mystery was an evident shift in loyalties. Until Spanish missionaries left Texas in 1693, the Jumanos were allies of Spain and enemies of the Apaches; however, when Spain reclaimed the territory in 1716, the former enemies had become reconciled. After this date, Spanish sources began to refer to "Apaches Jumanes," indicating that some observers considered the Jumanos a division of the Apaches. As a result, when the Wichita and Apaches were at war in 1771, according to Bolton, there could have been "people called Jumano" on both sides of the conflict.[10] This observation led him to conclude that, at least in those later years, the name did not apply to a unitary group of bands or tribes.

Bolton expressed no opinion about linguistic affiliation; however, his exposition would render Hodge's position untenable. It appeared very unlikely that the Rio Grande Jumanos of 1581 were direct ancestors of the nineteenth-century Wichita.

Carl Sauer

Sauer, perhaps the most famous of American geographers, mentioned the Jumanos in a 1934 survey of the aboriginal tribes and languages of northwestern Mexico.[11] The area includes the southern fringes of Jumano distribution, along the Rio del Norte near La Junta. Sauer presented evidence which indicated a cultural and linguistic continuity between Jumano and Suma, a people with wide distribution through northern Chihuahua and Sonora. The Sumas were almost as widely dispersed as the Jumanos, ranging west into Sonora and as far north as Casas Grandes.

On the basis of life-style and location, Sauer tentatively assigned the Suma-Jumanos and their neighbors the Julimes to different divisions of the great Uto-Aztecan language stock. The Julimes were aligned with the western Pima and Opata, while the Suma-Jumano were set apart as "the northeasternmost lot of the North Mexican Uto-Aztecan peoples."[12] Over the years Sauer's suggestion has been the most generally accepted of several conflicting opinions on the linguistic identification of Jumano.

France V. Scholes and the "Jumano Problem"

In 1940 historian France V. Scholes and archaeologist H. P. Mera combined their perspectives in an important publication on the "Jumano problem."[13] Scholes' contribution falls into three sections. In the first, he reviewed the discussion of the problem of Jumano identity up to that date, and proposed a unique solution. Observing that in certain early seventeenth-century documents, the name *Jumano* was applied to people who were also described as *rayados*, Scholes suggested that "in the early colonial period the name Jumano was used . . . to designate all *indios rayados*."[14]

As Scholes himself indicated, use of the term in this sense would have made it indiscriminately applicable to a large number of tribes, since decoration of the face and/or body with *rayas* (stripes or lines) was a widespread practice. If this were the case, a question would still remain regarding the origin of the name; Scholes left open the possibility that a specific group of "true" Jumanos could be identified, whose name had come to be used more widely. His suggestion was well received, and has been the point of departure for most subsequent discussion.

In retrospect, the wide acceptance given to Scholes' position is remarkable. It appears to have been based on very limited evidence, and the argument from that evidence is not strong. In historical sources, *Jumano* was not broadly applied to any and all painted or tattooed peoples, as Scholes appears to indicate. For example, it is not known to have been applied to the Conchos, who were known as *rayados*; or to the Tejas or other Caddo groups; or to the Apaches (only some of whom were painted). The use of the term *Jumano* was actually much more selective than is suggested by Scholes' remarks; and the possibility remained that some or all of the groups so called were linked by other historical connections.

A longer and more informative section of Scholes' essay deals with the Jumano pueblos in the Tompiro region of New Mexico, between the first Spanish *entradas* and the abandonment of the region circa 1672. Scholes made use of his own research in New Mexican church history and was able to fill in some of the gaps in Hodge's characterization of the Tompiros. Hodge had earlier argued that the Jumanos were only present in eastern New Mexico as temporary, nomadic visitors. Scholes demonstrated that they formed a substantial element in the population of southeastern New Mexico; they were distinguished, as *rayados*, from the large Tompiro group (*gente sin rayas*—people without stripes). The Jumanos were the dominant element in three or four pueblos; at least one of these (the Great Pueblo) was a town of several thousand people.[15]

Although Scholes did not attempt to resolve the question of Jumano linguistic affiliation, the final section of his paper makes a contribution toward that end. He cited sources to confirm Sauer's linkage of Jumano with Suma, but was wary of including Suma-Jumano in the Uto-Aztecan family. For the Tompiro region, he presented accounts which indicated mutual intelligibility between Piro (or Tompiro) and Jumano elements in the population. Since Piro was part of the Tanoan family of languages, this could be evidence for a Tanoan affiliation of Jumano as well. Indeed, Scholes suggested that "the linguistic phase of the problem should . . . be carefully explored, especially with reference to current speculation about the wider connections of Tanoan."[16]

H. P. Mera and Jumano Archaeology

Presented in the same publication with Scholes', H. P. Mera's paper dealt with the prehistory of the Tompiro province, with special reference to the identification of archaeological sites with historical communities. Mera confirmed the large complex of ruins now called "Gran Quivira" to be the community known, in the colonial period, as the "Great Pueblo of the Humanas."[17] He also noted very slight local variations in the archaeological materials and suggested that these could help distinguish between Jumano and Piro sites.

Archaeologists have continued to study and classify, and have partially restored, the sites in the eastern Tompiro Pueblos, which now are included in the Gran Quivira National Monument.[18] Both archaeological and historical researchers are interested in the position of these villages, situated in the Salinas, a region of arid salt flats on the eastern margin of the agricultural Southwest, and are curious about their relations with the South Plains and regions farther to the east.

Like Mera, archaeologist Stuart Baldwin divides the Tompiro province into two regions: eastern (the Salinas) and western (the Abo valley).[19] One point of interest is the attribution of distinctive pottery types to the pueblos of the Salinas region. These are, most importantly, Chupadero Black-on-White, Salinas Red-ware, and related pottery types which frequently occur as trade wares, far from their point of origin; this pottery is often found at sites in the South Plains. Pottery is an especially useful marker for the intensity and direction of trade relations between the eastern pueblos of New Mexico and the South Plains, in late prehistoric as well as early historic times.

J. Charles Kelley

Kelley did archaeological work at La Junta de los Rios in the 1940's. At that important crossroads, he located and described a series of sites, some of them identifiable with the historical communities of colonial times. Within these sites, Kelley distinguished house patterns and cultural remains which he attributed to two different population groups; he calls these groups *Jumano* and *Patarabueye*.[20] Kelley identifies the Jumanos as a hunting tribe, based in the Pecos River–Toyah Creek region of western Texas. He believes that the hunters who ranged from the Rio Grande to the Gulf of Mexico were also involved in trade. The other group, sedentary villagers, were the Patarabueyes.[21] They were closely associated with, and perhaps related to, the nomadic Jumanos; however, the nature of the relationship is left undefined.

Kelley tentatively accepts Sauer's linguistic identification of the sedentary La Junta population, the Patarabueyes, as Uto-Aztecan. For the nomadic Jumanos, he is inclined to a more eastern or northern affiliation, making a shotgun suggestion of a link to Caddoan, Tonkawan, Athabascan, or Coahuiltecan, as well as the generally accepted Uto-Aztecan. He explicitly denies any connection between the Pueblo Jumanos and those who wintered at La Junta de los Rios.

In 1955 Kelley wrote a historical study which traces the movements of the Jumanos of the 1680's and focuses attention on their leader, Juan Sabeata.[22] Here, he describes a pattern of regular travel or migration between La Junta and eastern Texas. Kelley's definition of the pre-contact Jumanos as a nomadic, buffalo-hunting, Plains tribe may be in part a projection of their late seventeenth-century culture; this was later much influenced by their acquisition of horses.

W. W. Newcomb, Jr.

Newcomb included a chapter on the Jumanos in a regional survey of the Indians of Texas, published in 1961. He relies on Kelley in discussing the remains of early historic village sites at La Junta; however, he applies the name *Jumano* to the sedentary village population (Kelley's *Patarabueyes*). Newcomb suggests that the nomadic bison-hunting people who roamed the South Plains were a derivative and, perhaps, mainly seasonal, offshoot of these "barbaric gardener" folk.[23]

The timeline for Newcomb's cultural description is the initial period of Spanish exploration; he has little to say about the culture of mounted nomadic Jumanos of a century later. He follows Sauer in assigning both the villagers and their nomadic kinsmen to the Uto-Aztecan language group.

Jack Forbes

Forbes, a specialist in Athabascan history, is one of the most recent anthropologists to offer a solution to the problem of Jumano identity and linguistic affiliation. Forbes carries the position stated by Scholes to an extreme, and in effect denies the very existence of the Jumanos as a separate ethnic or linguistic entity. Forbes' Jumanos, like Kelley's, are the nomadic Plains people; however, Forbes identifies this group as early Apaches, and thus as part of the Athabascan language stock. The La Junta village people (Newcomb's *Jumanos*) are considered by Forbes to be *Julimes*; the sedentary Jumanos of the Tompiro pueblos are simply called *Tompiros*, and the Arkansas River Jumanos of Hodge and Bolton are *Wichitas*.[24]

Forbes also focuses on the issue of language. He attempts to establish the Athabascan affiliation of the Plains Jumanos (his Jumano-Apaches) and a number of others in "a belt of tribes extending from the area of southeastern Arizona to eastern Texas."[25] Several of the sources which Forbes cites do indicate a linguistic connection among the Jumanos and Sumas, Cholomes, Cibolos, and Mansos; these tribes were also closely allied in a political sense. By demonstrating that there was an apparent absence of intelligibility with their Uto-Aztecan neighbors, Forbes makes a convincing case to counter Sauer's classification of this Jumano bloc as Uto-Aztecan. However, he seems to go beyond the limits of his data in linking the Jumanos with Athabascan; here his case rests more on cultural considerations and political alliances than on information about language.

Who Were the Jumanos?

The Jumanos disappeared from the historical record more than two centuries ago. What kind of people were they? They seem never to have been extremely numerous, but they were given a remarkable degree of respect and diplomatic attention by the government of Spanish New Mexico. Were they a scattered tribe of nomadic hunters? A sedentary tribe of horticulturalists with a penchant for seasonal wandering? Was *Jumano* the name of a single tribe, or was it a broader term applied to Indians of a certain cultural type? Was it a linguistic grouping which incorporated both sedentary and nomadic groupings? Was it, as some have contended, a term applied to all Indians who practiced a certain type of facial painting or tattooing? All of these alternative hypotheses have been suggested; however, none of them is completely satisfactory.

My own belief, which I will attempt to demonstrate in the following pages, is that Jumano was first an ethnic designation applied, in early historic times, to Tanoan-speaking Indians with a long-established territorial range in the South Plains. However, it was also applied in a narrower and more specialized sense to Indians of this ethnic type who played a traditional role as traders. In conjunction with their trade, Jumanos frequently traveled and sojourned far beyond geographical limits of their tribal territory. Throughout their history they were part of a regional system and played a key role in the exchange of staple commodities and distribution of localized resources.

In later times—and especially toward the end of the seventeenth century—the Jumanos appeared almost exclusively in the role of traders, as they were increasingly displaced from their previous territorial range by southward and eastward advances of the Apaches. The Apache occupancy of the South Plains also marked a major transition in economic and political alignments. It will be seen in the following chapters that the effects of this transition can be clearly followed in the historical record.

It is possible that a few of the primary references to *Jumanos* may represent, as Scholes and others have suggested, extensions of the term—perhaps in the specific sense of "traders." In general, however, I would argue that *Jumano*, as found in the historical sources, was the designation given to a unique, recognizable, cultural and linguistic entity. I hope to demonstrate that there is a rationale to the distribution of these people in time and space, and that most or all of the scattered individual groups were segments of this same entity.

The World of the Jumanos

Within the known territorial range of the Jumanos between the sixteenth and eighteenth centuries a focal or heartland region can be roughly defined. It encompassed the South Plains of western Texas and eastern New Mexico, and may have extended to adjacent regions of Oklahoma, Colorado, and northern Chihuahua. The South Plains are characterized overall by a semi-arid continental climate, level and open terrain, and the absence of significant natural barriers to travel. The movements of the Jumanos within and beyond their heartland region were shaped and constrained by features of the natural environment, which influenced or limited their numbers, distribution, and lines of communication.

The Great Plains of North America are a product of the same tectonic uplift which formed the Rocky Mountains some 10 million years ago and of the subsequent activity of water and wind. The entire area is prevailingly flat, and decreases in altitude from west to east. Humidity varies from semi-arid (ten to fifteen inches of rain per year) at the west, to sub-humid (fifteen to twenty-five inches of rain per year) at the east. This gradient is continued in adjoining regions; the Gulf Plain is a zone of high humidity (up to sixty inches of rain per year), while in the south and southwest the South Plains border on almost waterless deserts in northern Chihuahua.

The South Plains are edged on the west and south by the drainage system of the Rio Grande. The upper Rio Grande (Rio del Norte) flows south out of the southern Rockies, turns southeast at Big Bend, and debouches into the Gulf of Mexico. The valley of the upper Rio Grande was a focal area of Native American agriculture and the site of numerous permanent villages. Two densely populated areas within this valley are the Pueblo provinces of New Mexico, where some sixty-five villages were located along the main channel of the Rio del Norte and several tributaries; and La Junta de los Rios, where a half-dozen large villages and a number of rancherias were clustered at the confluence of the Rio del Norte and the Rio Conchos, a tributary which flows northeastward out of Mexico. Irrigation agriculture was practiced in New Mexico, as well as dry farming. At La Junta, the extensive floodplains along both rivers were cultivated, the agricultural cycle being adapted to the predictable seasonal variation in water flow. In both areas the staple crops of maize, beans, and squashes were grown; many European cultigens were adopted in the years following the Spanish conquest.

Below La Junta the Rio Grande has cut a series of deep rocky canyons as it passes through the mountainous Big Bend region. A tributary, the Rio Pecos, has its source in the mountains of southeastern Colorado, and flows across the South Plains and Edwards Plateau, to join the Rio Grande below Big Bend. The lower course of the Pecos also has deeply eroded canyons. The canyons of the Rio Grande system mark a natural limit to the South Plains as an aboriginal culture area, since they would have discouraged travel, especially in the years prior to the introduction of horses.

Besides the Rio Grande and the Pecos, a number of other rivers have sources in the South Plains and adjacent southern ranges of the Rocky Mountains. All of these rivers flow toward the east or southeast, and empty into the lower Mississippi or the Gulf of Mexico. Among them are the Arkansas River and its major tributaries, the Canadian and Cimarron; the Red River; the Brazos; and the Colorado River of Texas. Further to the south, the Guadalupe and Nueces systems rise in the Edwards Plateau (a rugged extension of the South Plains) and flow across the Coastal Plain into the Gulf. Many of the rivers of the South Plains originate as or are fed by natural springs. Although the surface flow of these streams may be low or even absent in dry seasons, their deep valleys appear as oases, often containing the only concentrated growth of trees in a given area. The valleys, or canyons, often a mile or more in width, may be unnoticed until approached at close range, due to the general absence of surface elevation.

Temperatures in the South Plains often rise to 100°F. or more in the summer months. Winters are not severe, though brief subfreezing cold spells are common; *blue northers*, with high winds and blowing snow, occasionally sweep through the region. High winds are characteristic at all times of year; in the summer months, tornadoes and thunderstorms occur in the region. Although annual average rainfall is low, the amount in any given year is variable and unpredictable. Rainfall follows a seasonal pattern occurring mostly between April and November, with peak amounts in late spring and in early autumn.

The Llano Estacado, or High Plains of western Texas and eastern New Mexico, is one of the flattest regions in the world. This interested early European travellers; for example, Coronado noted the "limitless plains" with "no more landmarks than as if we had been swallowed up in the sea"; there was "not a stone, nor a bit of rising ground, nor a tree, nor a shrub, nor anything to go by." [26]

Another well-known feature of the Llano Estacado is the concentration of *playas*, small lakes which fill during rainy periods and hold water for weeks or months until drying up during the dry season. The *playas* are a function of the underlying Ogalala aquifer, and reflect a network of buried stream valleys. As a seasonal environmental resource, they make the region attractive to migrating animals and waterfowl, and have also influenced the movements of nomadic human populations for many centuries.

High surface relief features are, for the most part, marginal to the South Plains. At the west, the Plains rise in altitude to meet the foothills of the Rockies. South of the Rockies, a series of small mountain ranges—including the Sangre de Cristos, Manzanos, Guadalupes, Sacramentos, Chizos, and Davis Mountains—lie both east and west of the Rio Grande Valley. These ranges are not massive and are interspersed with a number of ground-level passes. Both river courses and mountain passes have helped to shape interregional routes of travel and communication throughout human history.

Beyond the South Plains, the Jumanos' historical occupancy extends into neighboring regions to the west and east. In the west, they were a familiar presence in the village provinces of New Mexico and at La Junta de los Rios. In New Mexico, the Pecos and Tompiro provinces were centers for interregional trade. These gateway communities were strategically located in relation to important trails;

for example, Pecos Pueblo overlooks Galisteo Pass, a major point of entry for the Plains trade. The villages at La Junta de los Rios and El Paso were also situated at natural crossroads, where the river met east-west highways. La Junta de los Rios was perhaps the most important such communications center south of New Mexico. This was the point of intersection of routes linking Mexico, New Mexico, the South Plains, and the Gulf Plains. Trails which followed the Rio Conchos and Rio del Norte to La Junta made connection, by way of the Davis Mountains, with the Pecos, the Colorado, and other rivers of Texas. This linkage of riverine routes with overland trails took optimum advantage of springs and other water sources and exemplifies a type of communication network adapted to the arid South Plains environment. Such water routes were especially important prior to the introduction of horses and more advanced means of communication.

The variety of food resources available in the South Plains made this an attractive area for hunting and gathering. However, the seasonality of certain key resources conditioned a pattern of nomadism for the aboriginal population. Large and small game included deer, antelope, and elk; rabbit, armadillo, beaver, porcupine, and many rodents; and snakes, turtles, and fish. Bison may have been present in some number year-round, but the largest herds were found between mid-summer and late autumn; autumn was the preferred hunting season. Migrating birds would also have been found in largest numbers in spring and fall; the *playas* are still a favorite sanctuary for migratory Canadian geese and other waterfowl.

The concentration of rainfall between spring and fall, and the natural reservoirs which retained a plentiful supply of standing water throughout this period, are environmental features which dictated that a pattern of seasonal transhumance was adaptive to the South Plains environment. The protohistoric Jumanos probably did maintain and regularly occupy permanent bases in propitious locations on permanent watercourses (e.g., in Yellowhouse Canyon, on the Double Mountain Fork of the Brazos). However, all or most of the Jumano bands probably wintered in or camped near the villages of their trading partners along the Rio Grande; they set out for the Plains in the spring, and turned westward in the fall.

Both staple foods and other trade goods (such as bow-wood, mineral pigments, pottery, and gemstones) were transported between the farming villages along the Rio del Norte and hunter-gatherers whose territories lay in the South Plains. These societies were linked in a pan-regional exchange system, some features of which can be traced far back in the archaeological record. The Jumanos played an important role in the exchange between Pueblos and Plains and also served as middlemen in a more distant trade, which brought them into contact with both agricultural and non-agricultural peoples whose territories lay far east of the Plains.

The Jumanos' bases in the Plains must have had something of the character of trading posts. They shared the use of their hunting grounds with a number of other tribes; out of these intertribal contacts, they developed a special role as traders and middlemen. However, the seasonal buffalo hunt was only a part of a complex pattern of shared utilization of regional and localized resources. The seasonal harvests of such wild foods as tunas (prickly pears), pecans, piñon nuts, and shellfish were the occasions for multi-band and multi-tribal gatherings. These gatherings had social and political, as well as economic, functions. It is likely that the fairs to which the Jumanos traveled as traders coincided with an annual calendrical round of gatherings of this type.

In the seventeenth century, the Jumanos made annual trips as far as the Hasinai region of eastern Texas. They traded horses and goods of European manufacture to the Texas Indians; it would seem that fur and pelts were an important part of the goods which they received in exchange. It is unclear whether trading expeditions of this magnitude were aboriginal; in any case, they increased in scope after the supply of horses became plentiful in the South Plains.

The Indians originally obtained horses from the Spanish colonies. The Jumanos sometimes raided the horse herds of their enemies, the Apaches (as the Apaches also raided the Jumanos). However, the Jumanos were especially well known as horse traders. The size of their herds, with a surplus supply available for trade, can be explained by the availability of natural pasturage and a permanent water supply within the Jumanos' heartland. In the 1680's, large Jumano horse herds were located along the upper Rio Colorado, a convenient location for their trade to the Hasinai, Wichita, and other eastern tribes.

PART ONE

JUMANO CHRONOLOGY, 1535–1610

FIRST ENCOUNTERS: INDIANS AND CONQUISTADORES

1.

THE TRAVELS OF
CABEZA DE VACA

Alvar Nuñez Cabeza de Vaca,[1] Alonso del Castillo, Andres Dorantes, and Estevan, Dorantes' Moorish slave, were shipwrecked on the Gulf Coast of Texas in the winter of 1528. These four—the only known survivors of an original company of more than six hundred—eventually made their way overland to Mexico, where they arrived roughly eight years later. The story of this incredible odyssey is known principally through the *Relation* of Cabeza de Vaca, which was published after his return to Spain in 1537. Other details are supplied by the *Joint Report*, a summary of a debriefing conducted soon after their arrival.[2] For more than five centuries, Cabeza de Vaca's account of his travels has been popular reading, simply as a story of adventure and survival. However, it is also of great anthropological and historical value. It may be of special importance to anthropologists because of the information about native peoples in the earliest historic period in North America, even though many of the groups named in the account can not be specifically identified with the tribes later found in the area.

Some interesting aspects of Cabeza de Vaca's narrative are the locations, routes, and trade relations which were of importance to the Indian tribes, and which became crucial to the Spaniards as well. It appears that the leadership role played by Cabeza de Vaca in the Spaniards' successful journey across the continent derived in large part from his own active participation in the native trade system. Cabeza de Vaca and his companions may have encountered the people later known as the Jumanos, while traveling from the Texas coast to the valley of the Rio del Norte, en route to Mexico. Over much of the itinerary, the four Spaniards followed the same network of trails and visited the same locales where the presence of the Jumanos is well documented a century later.

The Gulf Coast, 1528

The Narvaez expedition set out from Cuba in 1527 to explore the coast of *La Florida*—a term which Spain applied in the sixteenth century to the entire area of North America lying between the peninsula of present-day Florida and Panuco, the northernmost Spanish settlement on the western Gulf Coast. The right to explore and colonize this vast expanse of territory had been granted to Panfilo de Narvaez, the leader of the expedition. Cabeza de Vaca was one of the officers, the second in command to Narvaez.

Due primarily to ineptitude and poor judgement on the part of Narvaez, most of the men were put ashore in the general vicinity of Apalachicola, on the Gulf Coast of Florida, while the ships were sent on ahead to survey the coast. From the beginning, the Spanish officers seem to have had no realistic idea of the continental land areas and the distances involved in travel toward Mexico. When the ships did not return on schedule, the stranded army attempted to advance on foot. Narvaez evidently believed that the remaining distance to their destination was a matter of a hundred leagues or so, roughly one-tenth of the actual distance to Panuco.

After struggling through virtually impassable swamps and fighting several battles with Indians, the men finally built barges covered with the hides of their slaughtered horses and set out by water, attempting to follow the coast westward toward Panuco. Many of the men were drowned when their barges were swamped or swept out to sea, but a group of around ninety survivors, on two barges, finally made landfall in an area which they called *Malhado* (*Doom*). This was on or near Galveston Island, on the northeast coast of Texas.

Some of the better swimmers decided to continue southward, seeking Panuco and help for the rest; their fate is unknown. The others were taken in and given shelter by native Indians, apparently of the coastal Karankawa tribe. Many of them died at Malhado during the winter of 1528–1529. Gradually, the dozen or so remaining became separated, living with different native bands. Most of them eventually died of disease or were killed by their hosts, who were hard-pressed economically and held the Spaniards responsible for the epidemics which followed their arrival.

Cabeza de Vaca himself remained at Malhado, recovering from illness. He lived for a year or so with the Capoques, a Karankawa band whose subsistence depended on seasonal alternation between winter gathering of shellfish and summer harvesting of berries, nuts, and plants on the neighboring mainland. His friends Dorantes and Castillo, along with several others, spent this time among the Han, a neighbor group. These and other bands congregated on the mainland during the summer, the time of the most abundant food supply, for a month of ceremonies and social activities. Contacts made during these summer gatherings gave Cabeza de Vaca the first opportunities to expand his knowledge of people and places and to begin planning the journey to Mexico.

Life as a Texas Trader, 1530

The islanders wanted to make physicians of us without examination or a review of diplomas. Their method of cure is to blow on the sick, the breath and the laying-on of hands supposedly casting out the infirmity. They insisted we should do this too, and be of some use to them. . . . Our method, however, was to bless the sick, breathe upon them, recite a Pater noster and Ave Maria, and pray earnestly to God our Lord for their recovery. When we concluded with the sign of the cross, He willed that our patients would directly spread the news that they had been restored to health.[3]

After thus being briefly pressed into service as a shamanistic curer by the Capoques, Cabeza de Vaca discovered a means for achieving more independence and greater freedom of movement. Early in 1530, he began operations as a trader. In this capacity, he was able to travel far from Malhado Island, both along the coast for a distance which he estimated at forty or fifty leagues, and a considerable distance into the interior.[4]

At about this time, he and others—including Castillo, Dorantes, and Estevan—had moved down the coast to take up residence on a large bay, which Cabeza de Vaca was able to identify from prior acquaintance with maps of the Gulf Coast as the Bay of Espiritu Santo (the Spanish designation of Matagorda Bay). There, his base of operations was with the Mariames, probably another Karankawa band.

Cabeza de Vaca's description of his life as a trader is of great value for insight into the workings of aboriginal exchange systems in North America.

The various Indians would beg me to go from one quarter to another for things they needed; their incessant hostilities made it impossible for them to travel cross-country or make many exchanges. But as a neutral merchant I went into the interior as far as I pleased . . . and along the coast forty or fifty leagues . . . My principal wares were cones and other

pieces of seasnail, conches used for cutting, sea-beads, and a fruit like a
bean which the natives value highly, using it as a medicine and for a ritual beverage in their dances and festivities. This is the sort of thing I
carried inland. By barter I got and brought back to the coast skins, red
ochre which they rub on their faces, hard canes for arrows, flint for arrowheads, with sinews and cement to attach them, and tassels of deer
hair which they dye red.

   This occupation suited me; I could travel where I wished . . . Wher-
ever I went, the Indians treated me honorably and gave me food . . .
They were glad to see me when I came and delighted to be brought
what they wanted . . . I avoided the pursuit of my business in winter, a
season when . . . the natives retire inside their huts . . .[5]

Although Cabeza de Vaca showed great initiative in taking this
step, it should not be thought that his specialization in trade represented a cultural innovation of his own devising. Clearly, he was
part of a larger system. He had a place in a network of exchanges
which extended from coast to interior. Certain goods, such as the
ochre and arrowheads, may have originated hundreds of miles in
the interior and possibly passed through several other hands before
reaching his. Similarly, the goods which he collected along the
coast—shell beads, shell knives, etc.—could have been traded to
distant regions. Such materials have been found in archaeological
sites in the Great Plains and Southwest, hundreds of miles from
their point of origin.

   The "fruit like a bean" which Cabeza de Vaca carried in trade is
of considerable interest. It may have been the mescal bean, a powerful hallucinogen native to southern Texas, which was widely
used for ceremonial purposes before being displaced by peyote, from
Mexico.[6]

   The narrative makes it clear that an important attribute of the
trader was his neutrality; he had freedom of passage among warring
tribes. As a tribeless individual, Cabeza de Vaca must have been ad-
mirably suited for this role, which the Indians evidently encouraged
him to pursue. As a European, his distinctive appearance would
have been an asset, making him quickly and easily recognized by
his clientele.

   Cabeza de Vaca could come and go freely, and was widely sought
after. He adapted to his role by learning routes, making contacts,
and acquiring languages. He mastered a vocabulary of words and
phrases sufficient for conducting transactions in (as he indicated toward the end of his narrative) six Indian languages. Some of these
languages were acquired from everyday use over long periods of

time; others must have been deliberately learned because of their importance as trade languages, in use over wide areas. Knowledge of such linguae francae would have become especially valuable in the trek which he and three others would eventually make westward across the continent. This knowledge may serve to explain the apparent success of the Spaniards in communicating with the members of numerous tribes and bands with which they came in contact.

Sign language was another mode of communication which was also of use in their dealings with unfamiliar tribes. Use of sign language may be another skill which Cabeza de Vaca acquired during his years as a trader. In more recent years, such an intertribal system of signs was found throughout the Great Plains of North America. It has been suggested that this system may have originated in Texas, where there was a multitude of aboriginal languages and dialects.[7]

It is important to note the seasonal patterning of native trade. Among the coastal and southern Texas tribes, most trade took place during the spring or summer, usually in the context of the large gatherings which assembled for seasonal harvest of berries, nuts, tuna (prickly pear), etc. Further west, the late summer or autumnal buffalo hunt set the occasion for such intertribal gatherings. These were also the times of year when a surplus of abundant foods and other resources—nuts, fruits, meat, etc.—could be processed, stored, and packaged for use in barter with the traders, who would direct the commodities into areas where they were scarce, and therefore valuable in trade. Cabeza de Vaca's activities followed a seasonal rhythm which will later be recognized in the annual cycle of the Jumano traders. There is every reason to believe that he was a cog in the same broad transregional system in which the Jumano were also participants.

Passage to the Hill Country, 1533

We found mosquitoes of three sorts, all abundant in every part of the region . . . for protection, we encircled ourselves with smudge fires of rotten and wet wood . . . Inland are many deer, fowl, and beasts other than those I have spoken of. Cattle come as far as here. Three times I have seen and eaten them. I think they are about the size of those in Spain. They have small horns like the cows of Morocco; their hair is very long and flocky like merinos. Some are tawny, others black . . .[8]

Cabeza de Vaca asserts that his decision to become a trader was made to provide the basis for an eventual transit to Mexico.

"Trade," he indicated, "served my main purpose, which all the while was to determine an eventual road out."[9] He was involved in trade, along the coast and into the interior, for at least two and perhaps as many as five of the six years which were spent in eastern and southern Texas.[10] This involvement in the extensive network of routes and peoples may have given him knowledge which would later be used for his and his comrades' long-range purpose. Toward the end of their stay on the coast, the four men who would eventually strike out for Mexico contrived to locate themselves in neighboring bands and to make a variety of preparations for their departure.

There have been several attempts to reconstruct the four Spaniards' itinerary, in whole and in part.[11] Although none of these efforts has been universally accepted, most agree in tracing a route which crosses some part of Texas and which reaches the Rio Grande at or near La Junta de Los Rios (the confluence of the Rio Grande and its tributary, the Rio Conchos). Of the several possible itineraries, the one proposed by Hallenbeck, and extended by Sauer with minor modifications to its termination in Mexico, seems reasonable and has been accepted by many. This is a road which follows the Colorado of Texas, its tributary the Concho, a portion of the lower Pecos, and joins the Rio Grande at or near its confluence with the Rio Conchos, an important crossroads which the Spaniards later called La Junta de los Rios. One of the points in favor of this route is that it closely corresponds to an important native highway which was in use in the following century, and which continued to serve white settlers as well as Indians for many years thereafter (Map 1).

> These Indians are so used to running that, without rest, they follow a deer from morning to night. In this way they kill many . . . They are a merry people, considering the hunger they suffer. They never skip their fiestas and *areitos*. To them the happiest time of year is the season of eating prickly pears. They go in no want then and pass the whole time dancing and eating, day and night. . . .[12]

Still living with the Mariames, the Spaniards traveled to the Texas Hill Country, for the prickly pear harvest.[13] Here, many bands of foraging Indians gathered, whose lives centered around hunting small game and gathering seasonal crops of nuts, such as pecans, and wild fruits, the most abundant of which was the tuna or prickly pear. The Spaniards undoubtedly encountered some of the many small Coahuiltecan-speaking bands which inhabited much of southern Texas and northeastern Mexico.

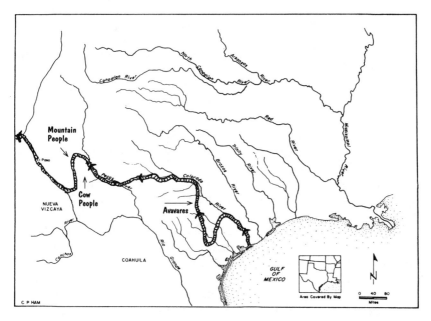

Map 1. Route of Cabeza de Vaca (1533–1535)

At one of the large tuna thickets, perhaps in the general vicinity of San Antonio, they affiliated themselves with certain of these bands. Their stay in the interior of Texas covered most of 1533 and 1534, during which time the men gradually shifted from one group to another, attempting to progress westward.

The Journey toward the Sunset

Like most pioneers, Cabeza de Vaca and his companions did not make their way through "untracked wilderness." Rather they followed roads which were already established and usually had the advice and assistance of native guides. Hallenbeck's reconstruction of the Spaniards' westward route indicates a general skirting of the Colorado River, with periodic deviations in areas where wild crops such as tuna, pecans, and mesquite were plentiful. In particular, the tuna thickets south of the Colorado of Texas were important centers for intertribal gatherings and for trade fairs. Eventually, the Spaniards arranged to rendezvous at one of these, planning to depart in the company of the Avavares, Indians who came from the west to trade in arrows.

It may have been at this point that the Spaniards made contact with people whose network of contacts extended as far as northern

Mexico; the Avavares, according to the *Joint Report*, "had some knowledge of Christians, though little."[14] At least at second hand, then, the Avavares must have known who the Spaniards were. In the course of a decade, rumors of the conquest of Mexico and of the awesome power of Spanish arms must have traveled at least that far. From this point on, as Cabeza de Vaca and his companions made their way westward—and especially when they were on the main highways of native trade—the Indians they encountered were increasingly knowledgeable about recent events in the lands which Spain had conquered.

Sojourning for several months with the Avavares in the winter of 1534, the Spaniards participated in several more intertribal gatherings and spent brief periods with two other bands, the Maliacones and Arbadaos, while remaining in the general region of the Texas Hill Country. Cabeza de Vaca again became involved in trade. He made combs and mats of a type used as house coverings and dealt in these products, as well as in bows, arrows, and nets which came from the west. This work helped him to survive in an area of general scarcity; it would also have enabled him to further extend his geographical and demographic knowledge of this inland area.

A century and a half later, in the 1680's, Jumano traders carried bows, arrows, and arrowheads eastward from the vicinity of La Junta and conducted trade over routes which followed the course of the Colorado and its tributaries. They visited the same areas where Cabeza de Vaca had sojourned. The Jumano traders, like the Avavares, traveled over a regular itinerary to visit with other tribes, and conducted fairs during intertribal gatherings such as the tuna harvests. Still, it must be a moot point whether or not the Avavares were actually a Jumano sub-group. In the 1530's, the small Hill Country bands such as the Avavares and Maliacones appear to have operated at a subsistence level of hunting and gathering while conducting some seasonal trade. The Avavares may have been only indirectly in contact with the primary suppliers of the trade goods, such as bows and mineral pigments, which came into the area from the west. It may well be that the range of the Jumano traders in the later period was greater, facilitated by the use of horses, and perhaps also stimulated by an increased market for certain goods, such as pelts and furs.

In any case, it can be seen that in the sixteenth century the Avavares were part of a network of exchanges. They may simply have received goods which originated further to the west—the arrows and other valuable items—from agents higher on the Colorado, and relayed them to bands living downstream and away from the river.

Reciprocally, they would have transmitted the shell beads and knives obtained from eastern groups to those further west. On the other hand the Avavares were, by Cabeza de Vaca's testimony, widely known as a trading group. Their arrival at the tuna thickets for trade was a scheduled event, eagerly awaited by bands and tribes gathered there. They must have had a wider range of movement than the more sedentary, localized bands; this was, after all, the reason for the Spaniards' decision to become associated with the Avavares.

The Colorado-Concho Highway

After passing from the Avavares to the Arbadaos and Maliacones (simply separate clans or bands, as Hallenbeck concludes), the Spaniards struck out overland on their own. They eventually made contact with men, with whom they were able to converse, who guided them to a village. The Spaniards were evidently back on one of the tributaries of the Colorado River of Texas. After pausing briefly at the village they departed with a party of traders who were also traveling west. By this time, it is clear that the arrival of the Spaniards was anticipated and awaited in the settlements through which they passed. During this period, their reputations as healers continued to grow. All four were, to some degree, involved in this practice, and they were repeatedly sought out to pray over and bless the ill.

Cabeza de Vaca was probably in contact with ancestors of the seventeenth-century Jumanos at the point when the four men reached a river "as wide as the one in Seville" (i.e., the Guadalquivir), and arrived at a "village of a hundred huts."[15] Hallenbeck has suggested that this village was located in the vicinity of Big Spring, Texas, a spot which is high on the main course of the Colorado. Sauer believed a location in the vicinity of San Angelo on the Concho, a major tributary of the Colorado, to be more likely.[16] Sauer's interpretation is preferred, because it makes it possible to identify the site as a historically important crossroads, which was the location of a Jumano base in the seventeenth century. Cabeza de Vaca's narrative suggests that the situation in the mid-sixteenth century was much the same.

From the time they reached this Rio Concho village, the Spaniards were treated with remarkable respect, almost reverence. This has been attributed variously to native fear of the unfamiliar (the Spaniards were believed to be supernatural beings or gods), to divine intervention (manifested in the apparently miraculous cures they seem to have performed), or even to chicanery on the part of the four travellers (the Spaniards putting on a convincing show as shamans or curers). It seems more realistic to believe that respectful treatment of the Spaniards increased as they came into contact with people who had knowledge—though still, perhaps, not at first hand—of Spain's power and of the Spanish conquest of Mexico. Thereafter, the men were recognized as representatives, or as an advance guard, of that seemingly omnipotent power. They were lionized, showered with gifts, and escorted by excited crowds of people from one community to the next.

A growing band of travellers—the Spaniards and increasingly large numbers of Indian escorts—proceeded westward through the Concho Valley, probably taking the middle fork, and continued overland via a route which led them toward the Rio Pecos. This is also a segment of the trail followed by the Jumanos on trading expeditions between the Rio del Norte and the Texas tribes to the east, a trail which Hallenbeck described as "a well-known road . . . used from prehistoric times by the Indians . . . [and] afterward used for a century by the white pioneers."[17] In later years, this was a segment of the Chihuahua Trail, linking Texas and the Mexican state of Chihuahua.

Along this leg of the journey the Davis and Guadalupe ranges of mountains began to come into view, in the west and northwest respectively. These were the first mountains the Spaniards had seen since leaving the coast. As they approached the Pecos, ". . . we headed toward these mountains, with our newest hosts, who were willing to guide us by way of a related settlement but by no means to risk letting their enemies get in on this great good which they thought we represented."[18]

There is a clear statement that the people living along the trail—from the Concho to the Pecos and beyond—were related. The goods which were brought out as presentations, as they entered new communities—beads, ochre, and small bags of mica—were all highly valued trade goods, most of which would have reached the area from regions further west. The goods were passed along by the Spaniards, distributed to their native escorts "who thereupon resumed their dances and festivities and sent to a nearby village so their relatives could come and see us."[19]

> . . . we decided to continue our course on the same trail toward the mountains . . . Having found the people of the interior better off and milder to us, we preferred to bear inland. We also felt sure of finding the

interior more populous and more amply provisioned. We further chose this course to find out more about the country so that, should God our Lord please to lead any of us to the land of Christians, we might carry information of it with us.[20]

After the Spaniards had reached and crossed the Rio Pecos, the Indians tried to persuade them to continue westward on the same trail, "by way of the mountains." However, the men insisted on traveling northward, taking a path which followed the Pecos upstream; they rejected their guides' warnings that people would be few and food scarce. This is an extremely important point in the itinerary: there is a reference to a route which was much used in later years, a link between the large native population at La Junta de los Rios, the lower Pecos, and the Concho-Colorado river system. The fact that the Indians urged the Spaniards to follow this route through the mountains indicates that it was the established thoroughfare to the west.

> When the Indians saw our determination to keep to this course, they warned us that we would find nobody, nor prickly pears or anything else to eat, and begged us to delay at least that day; so we did. They promptly sent two of their number to seek people along the trail ahead. We left next morning, taking several Indians with us. The women carried water . . .
> Two leagues out, we met those who had scouted ahead. They said they had found no one; which news seemed to hearten our escort, who again pleaded with us to go by way of the mountains. When they saw we would not be swayed, they regretfully left us and returned down the river to their huts, while we ascended alongside it.[21]

At this point, the Spaniards apparently insisted on proceeding upstream along the Pecos because they did not understand the overall configuration of the continent and feared that the trail through the mountains might lead them back toward the coast. The *Joint Report* indicates that "[the] Christians did not want to go in any direction but inland to higher ground. This was because they had earlier experienced painful mistreatment at the hands of those people of the coast."[22] The mountain trail did lead to the valley of the Rio del Norte. Perhaps they had learned this from their Indian companions and realized that this river flowed into the Gulf of Mexico. However, if they had taken the trail, they would have arrived at La Junta de los Rios, and from there could have traveled south by way of the

Rio Conchos, directly toward Mexico. This was a much more direct route of entry to Mexico than the one they eventually completed; it was, as Hallenbeck commented, the route they *should* have taken.[23]

There had been a continuity of population and indications of kinship between communities from the Concho to the Pecos. At the Pecos, the Indians expressed a predilection for the westward trail through the mountains to La Junta while attempting to discourage travel northward along the Pecos. All of this can be taken as evidence that the situation in this area resembled that which existed a century later, when Jumano communities on the Concho and Pecos conducted trade westward with their relatives at La Junta and eastward via the Colorado with various Texas tribes.

A Detour to the Rio del Norte

It can be surmised that it was while making their way along a deeply entrenched and saline portion of the Pecos, beginning a few miles upstream from the westward path, that the Spaniards were met by "a throng who had come a long way to give us a reception on the trail comparable to the one we had been receiving in the villages and *rancherias* lately."[24] This was apparently a new population, different from the residents of *rancherias* further down the Pecos. The depopulated stretch, through which they had just passed, must have been a transitional area or intertribal buffer zone.

These were people "of another nation and tongue."[25] They could have been the enemy group previously mentioned by the Jumanos on the Pecos. They led the Spaniards to their homes, some fifty leagues into the mountains. By Hallenbeck's calculation, the Spaniards must have left the Pecos around Carlsbad, New Mexico, and followed the Rio Peñasco and Elk Creek into the mountains. The Spaniards had passed through a no-man's land between hostile nations. The mountain people whom they now encountered were very likely Apaches.

> . . . we went over a mountain seven leagues in magnitude. At night we came to many dwellings on the banks of a very beautiful stream. The residents came halfway out on the trail to greet us, bringing their children on their backs.[26]

The Guadalupe-Sacramento Mountain region has long been an Apache homeland and is today the location of the Mescalero Apache reservation. Cabeza de Vaca's account can be taken as evidence that Apaches were present there in earliest historic times. If so, it would seem that the first Apache footholds this far south may have been in those mountains. This would have been the end point of an early Athabascan migration southward along the eastern ranges of the Rockies. Eastward movements of the Apaches extending their hunting territories and the ensuing struggle to gain control of the South Plains represent a later stage of Apache expansion. The process would soon be accelerated by the use of horses, which were acquired in early years of the Spanish presence.

> We told our new hosts that we wished to go where the sun sets; but they said people in that direction were remote. We commanded them to go and make known our coming anyway. They stalled and made excuses, because the people to the west were their enemies, whom they wanted to avoid. Not daring to disobey, however, they sent two women—one of their own and the other a captive from the "remote" enemy people—for women can deal as neutrals anywhere, even during war.[27]

It is clearly indicated that the mountain people—evidently Apaches—were at odds with the population living to the west, along the Rio Grande. The river valley population from La Junta de los Rios to the vicinity of El Paso was identified as solidly Jumano by the Espejo and Rodriguez expeditions, which explored the region four decades later.

After a few days in the mountains, the Spaniards again insisted on traveling west and eventually arrived near the confluence of rivers at La Junta, to which the other trail would have led them. Their change was stimulated in part by the reports their Apache hosts gave them concerning the Pueblo villages, and the shawls, blankets, and other goods from that region which they had in their possession.

While accommodating the Spaniards' desire to travel westward toward the Rio del Norte, the mountain people went to great pains to avoid direct contact with the Jumanos living along the river. As a first approach, the two women were sent out to reconnoiter. They were gone for several days, then returned "saying that they had met very few people, nearly all having gone after the cows, as it was the season."[28] Most of the escorting group then remained behind— many of them were ill—and a small party accompanied the Spaniards for a three days' journey. Contact was finally made with a village near the Rio del Norte through the agency of one of the women, the captive who was originally from that village. She guided them over a series of trails to her father's house.

The People of the Cows

It is not clear at what point, and by what route, the Spaniards reached the Rio del Norte. If the approach was through the Tularosa Basin, as Hallenbeck argues, the trail would have approached from the north. He traces a route which reaches the river at El Paso. However, this seems too far north, considering later evidence that the Spaniards were present near La Junta. Another main trail was the one which they had earlier refused, which crossed the mountains and reached the river at La Junta. Whatever the route, they probably stayed clear of the main Jumano thoroughfares. Hallenbeck's northern trail could have been taken, with the approach to the river village made by way of a secondary trail—perhaps the one which, on Hallenbeck's map, follows the Diablo Mountains and reaches the Rio del Norte midway between La Junta and El Paso. Such a little-used trail would have been the preferred choice if, as seems to be indicated, the guides wished to avoid meeting Jumanos who were in transit between the villages and the buffalo range. The village may have been situated on a path branching off from this trail.[29]

> They are the best looking people we saw, the strongest and most energetic, and who most readily understood us and answered our questions. We called them the "Cow People" [or "People of the Cows"] because more cattle are killed in their vicinity than anywhere. For more than fifty leagues up that river they prey on the cows.[30]

This was clearly not La Junta. There, the Rio del Norte would not have appeared hemmed in by mountains as Cabeza de Vaca's description suggests. Further, the Rio Conchos, at that confluence, is broader than the Rio del Norte itself. Since the primary sources make no mention of the Conchos or of the joining of the rivers, it seems unlikely that the Spaniards visited there.

In the later reminiscences of Indian witnesses, however, there is considerable evidence that Cabeza de Vaca's party did make contact with the Jumanos near La Junta, though perhaps a little distance upriver from that point. If Cabeza de Vaca's figure of fifty leagues (roughly 130 miles) approximates the distance between the village which the party first approached and the end of the Jumano country as they proceeded north along the Rio Grande, then that village should have been located near the half-way point between La Junta and El Paso. This would have been in the territory of the people whom Luxan later called Caguate, located upstream from the Otomoaca (or Patarabueye) villages clustered around La Junta. The

Caguates—Cabeza de Vaca's "People of the Cows"—are probably also to be identified with those later called *Cibola* (literally *buffalo* or *cows*), a division of the Jumano.

When the party had approached to a distance of six leagues from the Rio del Norte, the women were sent, along with two of the Spaniards, Castillo and Estevan, into the village. A welcoming delegation came out with gifts, which the Spaniards turned over to their escorts as was their usual practice. The escorting group departed, avoiding a confrontation with their enemies. The Spaniards were then free to enter the village, where they were received with festivities. As they proceeded from one settlement to the next they received gifts, including many buffalo-skin robes.

These people had a good supply of beans, squashes, and corn, but evidently farmed little or not at all. It is likely that they, like the nomadic Jumanos of later times, received farm produce through trade, and in return supplied meat and hides to those who grew crops in abundance. The country of the People of the Cows, according to Cabeza de Vaca, was incredibly populous.

> We asked how it happened they did not plant corn. So they would not lose what they planted, was the answer; moles got the seed; must have plenty rain before planting again . . . Where, we asked them, did they get the corn they had? From where the sun goes down; in that country it grew all over; the quickest way there was the path . . . along the river northward . . . [31]

To the "Land of the Christians"

After tarrying a few days, Cabeza de Vaca and his companions continued their journey west. They made their usual inquiries about the location of clothed people who lived in settled communities and grew maize, and they were urged by their Jumano hosts to travel northward to the Pueblo villages on the Rio del Norte. This maize-growing area "was the closer one, and all the people on the way to it were friends and of the same language." [32] However, they insisted on going west, and so were given directions for that route: they were to walk northward for nine days (it took them fifteen), to cross the river at a designated ford, and then to turn toward the west. Hallenbeck locates the ford near Rincon, New Mexico; from there, the westward trail would have followed the course of the Gila River for some days, and then crossed overland through the Chiricahua Mountains. After reaching Pima country, they were guided by Indian escorts through a series of trails to the western

highway which paralleled the Pacific coast, crossing the drainage
systems of the Sonora, Yaqui, and several other rivers in western
Mexico.

> At this time, Castillo happened to see an Indian wearing around his
> neck a little sword-belt buckle with a horseshoe nail stitched to it. He
> took the amulet, and we asked the Indian what it was. He said it came
> from Heaven. But who had brought it? He . . . said that some bearded
> men like us had come to that river from Heaven, with horses, lances,
> and swords, and had lanced two natives . . .
> We gave many thanks to God our Lord. Having almost despaired of
> finding Christians again, we could hardly restrain our excitement . . .
> We told the natives we were going after those men to order them to
> stop killing, enslaving, and dispossessing the Indians; which made our
> friends very glad.[33]

The *Relation* of Cabeza de Vaca, together with other reports of
the Spaniards' adventures—both written and by word of mouth—
created tremendous interest and anticipation regarding the lands
north of Mexico. The impact was perhaps the most intense among
the Spaniards already in New Spain. Many of these were settlers
and entrepreneurs who were eager for an opportunity to go north to
explore the new lands and make their fortunes. The most exciting
details were found in the reports about the *cibolos*, the bison or
"cattle"; the rumors of mines, precious stones, and other riches
waiting to be discovered; and the stories of cities, inhabited by
people who tilled fields, wove textiles, and practiced other arts and
crafts. Besides wealth *per se,* there was a growing need for raw materials and for laborers in the mining and agricultural industries already established in northern Mexico.

The Church, also, was interested in exploring the virgin territories. The Franciscan fathers were particularly glad to have the news
which indicated that there were sedentary people living in permanent communities. Such people, they believed, would be docile and
amenable to missionary teachings. Almost all of the *entradas* north
during the next five decades were influenced in one way or another
by the odyssey of Cabeza de Vaca, Dorantes, Estevan, and Castillo.

2.

EXPLORATIONS BY WAY OF THE WESTERN CORRIDOR

The arrival in Mexico of Cabeza de Vaca and his companions precipitated a wave of exploration of lands to the north. The information which the four men provided was a stimulus to prospectors, missionaries, and adventurers, many of whom were already eager to extend Cortez' conquest toward the interior of North America. The three hidalgos of the group—Cabeza de Vaca, Dorantes, and Castillo—made an official report in Mexico which was dispatched to the Spanish *Audiencia* in Santo Domingo. Less formally, the adventurers would surely have passed along both factual news and rumors gleaned in their travels concerning people, places, animals, mineral wealth, and other resources. Cabeza de Vaca may thus have enlarged on the favorable assessment which is conveyed in his *Relation*, indicating the potential of the lands and peoples for future development.

Soon after the four travellers made their presence known in Mexico, plans were under way for an organized *entrada* which was, at least in the planning stages, intended as a follow-up to the Narvaez expedition. Viceroy Mendoza acted quickly to make use of the valuable intelligence which had fallen into his lap. In fact, efforts were made to recruit the services of both Dorantes and Cabeza de Vaca for the projected expedition. Dorantes did accept a commission, apparently intending to share the command with Cabeza de Vaca. When the latter determined instead to return to Spain, Dorantes also demurred, but settled his contract with Mendoza by selling him the slave, Estevan.

The command of the *entrada* was then given to the newly appointed governor of Nueva Galicia, Francisco Vasquez de Coronado. While the lengthy process of recruiting and outfitting the expedition was under way, an advance party was sent out. This was headed by a Franciscan friar, Marcos de Niza, who had come to Mexico after service in Peru.

The Journey of Fray Marcos de Niza

Fray Marcos' scouting trip was under way in the spring of 1538, approximately three years after Cabeza de Vaca's arrival in Culiacan. His companion and scout for the journey was to be Estevan, who thus provides one direct link between the earlier and later *entradas.* It is safe to assume, however, that there were others. Many of the same Indians—of what tribes or languages cannot be known—who had traveled from the north with Estevan, had remained as his companions and were recruited for the new expedition. The nameless Indian auxiliaries who were part of this and other Spanish *entradas* provided a reservoir of experience and information on which the leaders must have relied heavily.

Fray Marcos was charged to make observations on terrain, flora, fauna, and people, and to look for likely sites for future missions in the new lands. While he postponed his departure to await the arrival of a second cleric who had been delayed by illness, he sent Estevan on ahead. The slave far outdistanced the friar, traveling days in advance and sending back messengers with crosses to symbolize his progress.

Some aspects of the friar's account are specially valuable in relation to communication and economic ties linking the provinces in western Mexico, the Pueblos, and elsewhere. Traveling north from the Opata farming town of Vacapa, in Sonora, Marcos was able to get reliable information from coastal Indians, probably from the Seri tribe, who had been to Zuni as seasonal farm workers. They were asked "for what they went so far from their homes, and they told me that they went for turquoises, cowhides, and other things . . . I asked what they exchanged for such articles, and they told me the sweat of their brows and the services of their persons, that they went to the first city, which is called Cibola, where they served in digging the ground and doing other work, for which work they are given oxhides, of the kind produced in that country, and turquoise . . ."[1]

Another interesting group of companions along this stretch of the highway were "three of those Indians known as Pintados, with their faces, cheeks and arms all decorated . . ." who ". . . told me that, having had news of me, they had come to see me . . ." The Pintados were a second source of reliable information about the Zuni and other provinces, and the location of the Zuni villages. They had prior knowledge of the Cabeza de Vaca party, and—as they indicated—may have heard via native networks of the renewed Spanish exploration project. It is tempting to think that the Pintados may have been Jumanos, although there is no definite precedent for a Jumano presence this far to the west. The Jumanos were often referred to as *rayados* or *pintados:* they did travel over great distances and on other occasions were known to give aid to Spanish expeditions. The added information that ". . . they live over toward the east and their territory borders on those near the seven cities . . . ,"[2] while vague, is consistent with the general picture of Jumano and other tribal locations.

Historians have disagreed as to whether, and under what circumstance, Fray Marcos reached the province of Zuni. It is known that Estevan was killed, together with some of the Indians, at Hawikuh, the first of the Zuni villages. Marcos evidently received a report of Estevan's death, and retreated south. However, he later indicated that he had surveyed the "city" of Hawikuh from a distance; he gave a glowing account of its size and wealth to Coronado and Mendoza. His veracity is suspect, however; the accepted interpretation is that he turned back short of Hawikuh, and simply based his report on the Indians' descriptions.[3]

The Coronado Expedition

Coronado's army left Culiacan early in 1540, as soon as possible after receipt of royal approval of his command. Like Fray Marcos, Coronado took a route west of the Sierras, the western corridor which roughly retraced the path which Cabeza de Vaca and his companions had taken on the last leg of their journey. This was, evidently, a major native highway which linked provinces such as the Cahita and Opata of western Mexico with others farther to the north, including the Zuni.[4] After leaving Culiacan, Coronado proceeded to Chichilticalli, near the Gila River in Pima country, where a base was established. Part of the army remained there, while Coronado proceeded eastward with a large contingent of men, pack horses, and Indian auxiliaries.

Zuni was a populous province made up of several separate towns and villages. Spanish imagination, influenced by a long tradition of legendary promised lands, had made this native province a "kingdom"; it became famous as the "Seven Cities of Cibola." It was an important exchange point in native intercourse between the western Pueblo area and northwestern Mexico, as well as an agricultural center. This was the first goal of Coronado's expedition, and the early center of his operations in the Southwest.

The Spaniards had anticipated that Zuni, or Cibola, would be a wealthy nation and that its pueblos, whose names they had already learned from Mexican informants, would be populous cities. Farther to the north were other nations and kingdoms, including one believed to be the richest prize of all—the kingdom of Gran Quivira. After securing the surrender of Cibola, the commander sent a portion of the army north to the neighboring province of Tusayan (the Hopi villages), which threatened resistance but quickly capitulated.

In the summer of 1540, a group of visitors arrived at the Zuni villages—evidently a trading party, but also seeking contact with the Spaniards. These men had come from Pecos, or Cicuye, a large community which was situated at the eastern edge of the Pueblo area, on the upper Pecos River. A party of soldiers was dispatched, under the leadership of Hernando de Alvarado, to accompany the Pecos Indians on their return. Alvarado was instructed to explore the country and in particular to investigate the plains east of Cicuye and the "cattle" of that area, which had excited such enthusiastic reports by Cabeza de Vaca.

At Cicuye, the Spaniards were welcomed enthusiastically and given "many presents of cloth and turquoises, of which there are quantities in that region." Soon after their arrival, they became acquainted with a captive, whom they called "Turk," a native of the "country toward Florida"—i.e., lands to the east; he may have been a Caddo or Wichita. This man was taken as a guide by Alvarado in an initial exploration of the plains, but "he told them so many and such great things in his country that they did not care about looking for cows, but returned after they had seen some few, to report the rich news to the General."[5] Alvarado awaited Coronado's arrival to prepare for a major expedition.

Eventually, the main body of the army followed, marching east before the onset of winter. Tiguex, the province of the Rio Grande Tewas, became the center of Coronado's operations in New Mexico. During the winter, the billeting of troops in their pueblos and the commandeering of their food reserves led the natives of the Tewa province to revolt. Punitive measures were taken by the Spaniards, and two of the villages were sacked and burned. The winter ended in a rather sullen standoff between the Rio Grande villagers and the Spanish invaders.

In the spring of 1541, Coronado followed up on Alvarado's scouting trip by setting out in search of Gran Quivira himself, with a large part of the army. After assembling near Cicuye, the company of Spaniards marched into the plains of eastern New Mexico accompanied by both Mexican and Pueblo Indians and guided by the Turk. Most of the points of interest in relation to the Jumanos

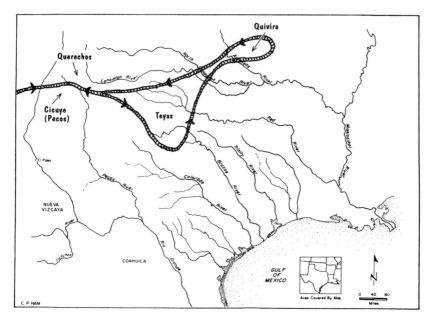

Map 2. Route of Coronado (1541)

derive from the firsthand accounts of participants in the Alvarado and Coronado explorations of the plains (Map 2).

The Exploration of the Plains[6]

Coronado's army was on the move for four days out of Pecos Pueblo before pausing to build a bridge to cross a river. This was probably the Pecos River, though some interpretations have taken the Canadian River as the point of departure; the choice between these two possibilities makes a great deal of difference in tracing the rest of the itinerary. Ten days after crossing the river, they began to encounter Querechos, nomadic hunting people "who lived like Arabs" in tents, following the "cows" and killing them for food.[7] Querecho bands were seen repeatedly during the trek through the plains. The identification of the Querechos as Apaches seems certain; they are culturally recognizable as Plains Indians, and the name *Querecho* is consistently used in other early historic sources to refer to Apaches.

Another people, the Teyas, were found some distance to the east. Distances and directions cannot be reckoned with much confidence, in part because the army moved slowly, encumbered by those on foot and by herds of livestock, and in part because the native guides were evidently leading the Spaniards by a circuitous route, attempting to confuse or discourage them. The Teyas were found established in several canyons or *barrancas*, the most northerly of which—with the largest population—may have been Palo Duro Canyon. The series of canyons, in any case, must have been those along the eastern edge of the Llano Estacado, the High Plains of western Texas. Castañeda's description of the surrounding landscape includes the mention of numerous "lakes . . . found at intervals . . . as round as plates, a stone's throw or more across . . ." This seems a clear reference to the *playa* lakes which dot the Llano Estacado after the seasonal summer rains.[8]

The Querechos (Apaches) and Teyas (who are here considered to be Jumanos) were enemies. The most obvious connecting link between the Coronado accounts and others, both earlier and later, is found in the recurrent theme of the enmity and warfare between two contending native peoples in the plains east of New Mexico. However, in scholarly discussion of the Coronado accounts, there has been much disagreement about the identity of the warring groups, particularly the Teyas. Some historical scholars interpret the evidence to indicate that the Querechos and Teyas were simply two different bands of Apaches, competing for possession of the Plains.[9] Others have asserted that the Teyas were Caddoans, outliers of farming tribes living in river valleys further to the east.[10] One basis for arguing this position is the resemblance of the name *Teya* to the Caddo word *texia*. This is the source of *Tejas*, a name rather loosely associated with the Hasinai, or Caddo, of eastern Texas, and their neighbors. However, in the seventeenth century, this term (literally *friend* or *ally*), was evidently applied to a number of allied tribes, whether Caddoan-speaking or not.[11] The Apaches were never a part of this alliance; in fact, they seem to have been regarded generally as a common enemy by the allied tribes.

It is certain that in the seventeenth century the Jumanos were allies as well as trading partners of the Hasinai and a large number of other Texas tribes. Earlier, they evidently had a similar relationship with the tribes of Quivira (the Wichita and their neighbors). It was primarily through the Jumanos, as intermediaries, that these Caddoan tribes were linked by trading ties with the Pueblo provinces of New Mexico. On this basis, it can be suggested that *Teyas* was a general term—the *Allies*—which could be used to refer to members of this trade network and alliance. It could as easily have applied to the Jumanos, who were central to the alliance, as to the more distant Caddoans. Castañeda recorded that *Teyas* was used by

Coronado's guides, who were Tanoan Indians from the eastern Pueblos, to identify the camps of Indians who were their trading partners and allies.

The Teyas encountered by Coronado may have been a branch of the Jumanos. Support for this identification is found in the geographical location of the Teyas' *rancherias,* in cultural similarities to later Jumano groups, and in indications of enmity between this group and the Querechos, who are firmly identified as Apaches. The site of the largest of the Teyas' *rancherias,* by scholarly consensus identified as Palo Duro Canyon, is in the same general location in which Juan de Salas would find Jumanos living in 1629. With this as a point of reference, the relative position of the site in relation to the villages of Quivira also seems appropriate; in this and later sources, Quivira is said to be several days' travel, or about fifty leagues distant, to the east or northeast.

> The general sent Don Rodrigo Maldonado, with his company, forward . . . He traveled four days and reached a large *barranca* (ravine or canyon) like those of Colima (in western Mexico), in the bottom of which he found a large settlement of people . . . They found an Indian girl here who was as white as a Castilian lady, except that she had her chin painted like a Moorish woman. In general they all paint themselves in this way here, and they decorate their eyes . . .
>
> From here, the general sent out to explore the country, and they found another settlement four days from there . . . The country was well inhabited, and they had plenty of beans (*frijoles*) and plums like those of Castille, and tall vineyards. These village settlements extended for three days. This was called Cona. Some Teyas, as these people are called, went with the army from here and traveled as far as the end of the other settlements with their packs of dogs and women and children, and then they gave them guides. . . . These said that Quivira was toward the north, and that we would not find any good road thither.
>
> The ravine which the army had now reached was a league wide from one side to the other, with a little bit of a river at the bottom, and there were many groves of mulberry trees near it, and rosebushes . . . There were walnuts, and the same kind of fowls as in New Spain, and large quantities of plums like those of Castille. During this journey a Teya was seen to shoot a bull right through both shoulders with an arrow, which would be a good shot for a musket.
>
> These people are very intelligent; the women are well made and modest. They cover their whole body. They wear shoes and buskins made of tanned skin. The women wear cloaks over their small under-petticoats,

with sleeves gathered up at the shoulders, all of skin, and some wore something like little *sanbenitos* (kilts or aprons) with a fringe, which reached half-way down the thigh over the petticoat . . .

[T]hese people are always roaming over this country . . . and so know it thoroughly. They keep their road in this way: in the morning they notice where the sun rises and observe the direction they are going to take, and then shoot an arrow in this direction. Before reaching this they shoot another over it, and in this way they go all day toward the water where they are going to end the day. . . .[12]

[The people of the settlements] . . . usually call these people *Teyas* or brave men, just as the Mexicans say *chichimecas* or braves, for the Teyas whom the army saw were brave. These knew the people in the settlements, and were friendly with them. And they [the Teyas] went there to spend the winter under the wings of the settlements. The inhabitants do not dare to let them come inside . . . Although they are received as friends, and trade with them, they do not stay in the villages over night.[13]

Thus Castañeda, the chief chronicler of the Coronado expedition, describes the first contacts with the Teyas, who rescued the Spaniards from their confused wanderings over the plains and showed them the correct route for their travels to Quivira. The way of life of the Plains dwellers, both Querechos and Teyas, was of great interest to the Spaniards. Castañeda describes the use of the dog travois, methods of drying meat, preparing pemmican, working with skins, and flint-knapping, and other aspects of material culture, much of which seems to apply to both Querechos and Teyas. Since his account was written from memory, after the passage of several years, it is likely that some points of distinction between the two groups may not have been accurately recalled. Nevertheless, there are certain cultural features which are consistent with the identification of the Teyas as Jumanos. Most obviously, perhaps, are the descriptions of Teya facial painting and of clothing styles, which may be compared with descriptions from the Espejo expedition, forty years later.

The brief references to Teya trading practices also suggest later accounts of the Jumanos. The Teyas were, at the time, trading at Cicuye (Pecos), and apparently at other northern pueblos.

Cabeza de Vaca and Dorantes had passed through this place, so that they presented Don Rodrigo [Maldonado] with a pile of tanned skins and other things, and a tent as big as a house, which he directed them to keep until the army came up. . . . When the general came up with the army and saw the great quantity of skins, he thought he would divide them among the men, and placed guards so that they could look at them. But when the men arrived and saw that the general was sending some of his companions with orders for the guards to give them some of his skins, and that these were going to select the best, they were angry because they were not going to be divided evenly, and made a rush, and in less than a quarter of an hour nothing was left but the empty ground. The natives who happened to see this also took a hand in it. The women and some others were left crying, because they thought that the strangers were not going to take anything, but would bless them as Cabeza de Vaca and Dorantes had done when they passed through here.[14]

The Teyas, it is noted, had large stockpiles of buffalo skins on hand. According to Castañeda they were anticipating the more humane treatment exhibited by Cabeza de Vaca and his companions, who had conformed to native patterns of behavior. Their initial eagerness to trade and to deal in a straightforward way with the Spaniards, however, is reminiscent of later Jumano encounters with Europeans. The Teyas supplied reliable information to Coronado about the route to Quivira, correcting the misinformation given him by the Turk. They provided guides both to lead the main body of the army back to Pecos, and also to deliver Coronado's scouting party to Quivira by a direct route. Their attitude is evocative of the continuing relationship between the Jumano and Spanish colonists throughout most of the following century.

It remains to point out what may be the most convincing evidence for the identification of the Teyas as Jumano: the attested links with the Jumanos of La Junta and, through them, with Cabeza de Vaca's party. The accounts of both Castañeda and Jaramillo indicate that the Teyas had witnessed the earlier visit of the four Spaniards. Jaramillo specifies a source of this information: ". . . we found another settlement of Indians of the same sort and way of living as those behind [i.e., Teyas], among whom there was an old man with a beard, who gave us to understand . . . that he had seen four others like us many days before, whom he had seen near there and rather more toward New Spain, and we so understood him, and presumed that it was Dorantes and Cabeza de Vaca and those whom I have mentioned."[15] The fact that this encounter is said to have taken place further to the south, toward New Spain (Mexico), is important. It strongly suggests the location of the Jumano population near La Junta, on the lower Rio del Norte. It thus also suggests that there was at this time, as in the next century, a mobility of population between widely separated Jumano locales.

The actual route of Coronado's expedition and the location of Quivira have been the subject of almost as many variations in interpretation as was the itinerary of Cabeza de Vaca. In this case, the route was circuitous, but finally—with Teya guidance—proceeded due north, arriving at a location which was evidently in central Kansas, at or near the great bend of the Arkansas River. This locale is supported by archaeological evidence, which includes finds of chain mail and other Spanish artifacts in the area.[16] After crossing the Arkansas, the Spaniards spent roughly a month visiting more than a dozen separate villages, probably representing a number of different tribes. These communities were, from the Spaniards' viewpoint, disappointingly small and lacking in wealth. Presumably, some or all of the villages were inhabited by the Caddoan groups later known collectively as the Wichitas.

Return to Mexico

Still guided by the Teyas, Coronado's party returned to Cicuye by a direct route, arriving there at the beginning of October 1541. The expedition had found no riches in Quivira. Once more, the reports which were made to authorities praised the potential of the region for agriculture and stock raising, but saw no promise of immediate profit. This junket effectively put an end to Coronado's explorations. His party returned to the Rio Grande to find the Tewa Indians rebellious, and the army impatient and discontented. At this point, Coronado himself was injured in a fall from a horse. News arrived of a revolt which had broken out at Chichilticalli, where the rear guard was stationed. At this, the army departed en masse, marching to the west to consolidate their forces.

However significant Coronado's accomplishments as an explorer, there was general disappointment in New Spain at the results of the expedition, which had been extremely expensive to mount and support. Even though a second trip was immediately proposed, it was given no priority. No official initiative was taken in that quarter for several decades, until the colonizing expedition led by Juan de Oñate, just before the turn of the seventeenth century.

One aspect of this and other Spanish *entradas* which excites curiosity, but on which there is very little information, is the matter of communication. Cabeza de Vaca had lived among the Indians for such a long time that he gained at least a rudimentary grasp of several languages; so, presumably, did his companions. Beyond this, they must also have been able to deal with certain tribes through bilingual translators. Finally, when necessary, they were able to use sign language.

For Fray Marcos and for Coronado, the abilities of Estevan Dorantes, and of various Indians of different nationalities must have been of great value. Some of the Indians who accompanied Coronado undoubtedly had fluency in Nahuatl as well as in the northern languages. Along the main trade routes, such as that between Sonora and the Zuni pueblos, Nahuatl would have been widely known. Other languages employed in trade, such as Pima and the Tanoan dialect of the Jumanos, could also have been useful in communicating with bilinguals. Even in fairly remote regions the Spaniards may have been able to obtain information through the use of two or more translators—translating, for example, from Spanish to "Mexican" (Nahuatl), from Mexican to Pima, Pima to Zuni, etc.

Sauer has commented on the apparent ease of communication experienced by the Coronado expedition throughout their travels: "There appears to have been no difficulty of communication anywhere . . . Coronado and his men obtained specific data repeatedly from people of different languages. Whether by sign language or linkage of interpreters, the news service worked and did so over large distances."[17] In the light of Sauer's observation, it should be added that only among the Querechos (Apaches) did the narrators explicitly state that signs were used; this may have been the only point at which that expedient was necessary. The Teyas (Jumanos), on the other hand, apparently communicated easily with Coronado's Tanoan guides, and there would no doubt have been some among them who also spoke the Caddoan language(s) of Quivira. The army, of course, had brought along the Quiviran captives, who may have been able to serve as translators. Unfortunately, we do not know how many different tribes and languages were actually encountered in Quivira. It was, however, specifically in reference to this part of the expedition that Coronado himself remarked, in a letter to the king, that "the diversity of languages . . . because they speak their own language in each village, has hindered me."[18]

3.

OPENING THE CENTRAL CORRIDOR

Late in the sixteenth century, Spanish exploration north of Mexico began to follow an alternative route. This was the central corridor, across the interior desert plateau, flanked by the eastern and western cordilleras. The impetus for these expeditions was the rapid development of mining operations in northern New Spain. From central Mexico, the search for precious metals led prospectors north past the mines of Zacatecas and Inde and into the new colonial province of Nueva Vizcaya (present-day Chihuahua). In the 1560's, rich strikes of silver and other minerals resulted in rapid development of the region around San Bartolome and Santa Barbara (now Allende); agricultural and livestock enterprises soon followed. These new centers were situated close to the headwaters of the Rio Conchos, which flows on a northeastern course to join the Rio del Norte at La Junta de los Rios, near the modern towns of Ojinaga, Chihuahua, and of Presidio, Texas.

The Indians who lived along the Rio Conchos drainage area—the Conchos, Tobosos, and Julimes—were eventually drawn, willingly or unwillingly, into the labor force needed for the mines and plantations of Santa Barbara. Within a few years, Spanish slavehunters had followed this route at least as far as La Junta de los Rios. The populous cluster of native towns and villages at La Junta did not constitute a powerful nation or confederacy. They were not politically unified, and had few defenses against Spanish inroads. Situated along the floodplains of the two large rivers, this was the best pocket of agricultural land for many miles around. Since river systems were also highways, La Junta was a crossroads of travel and trade. From this point, also, the trail through the Davis Mountains provided the shortest route to the Colorado and other river systems of Texas.

The burgeoning economic developments around Santa Barbara, and the centrality of the river systems as arteries in Spanish trade, missionization, and military movements, meant that these Indian villages would be quickly despoiled and depopulated, and their residents conscripted, dispersed, or overwhelmed. However, at the time of first Spanish exploration through the area, La Junta had a large native population. There were at least eight towns, totaling perhaps twenty thousand people, concentrated near the junction of the Conchos and Rio del Norte.[1]

Two expeditions departed from Santa Barbara within little more than a year, both of them following the river route north via La Junta. Accounts of the Rodriguez and Espejo *entradas* in 1581 and 1582 give the first look at this region, situated at the other end of the mountain trail earlier rejected by Cabeza de Vaca and his companions. Each of the parties included both religious and military personnel; in accordance with the royal decree of 1573, Spain undertook to further the interest of two authorities—the royal Crown and the Church of Rome. However, unlike Coronado's huge army of exploration and conquest, these expeditions were small enterprises, and the initiative for undertaking them was private (though with the necessary official sanctions).

The Rodriguez-Chamuscado Expedition [2]

The first *entrada* to depart from Santa Barbara was jointly organized by Fray Agustín Rodriguez and Captain Francisco Sanchez Chamuscado. Rodriguez was eager to begin preaching the gospel among the settled village tribes of the north, of which he had news through the report of Cabeza de Vaca and other travellers. Although the project appears to have been jointly planned, the petition to the viceroy was presented by the friar. He was granted permission to enroll two additional religious members and no more than twenty military personnel.

The main interest of Captain Chamuscado and the other secular members of the party lay in mining; Santa Barbara was, above all, a mining town. The junket to the north was a prospecting trip in search of new deposits of silver and other minerals. These men, like most others in this frontier province, were members of the militia. However, their first concern was mining, not soldiering.

The expedition left Santa Barbara in June of 1581. The party consisted of Fray Agustín Rodriguez and two additional priests, Captain Chamuscado and eight soldiers, and several Indian servants, including translators recruited from natives of the La Junta region who had been working in the mines of Santa Barbara. The itinerary followed the Rio Florida and the Rio Conchos to La Junta. Here, the members of the party sojourned for several days, relaxing and visiting the towns located along both sides of the river, and collecting whatever information they could discover about the country upstream. Then they went on their way, following the trail along the Rio del Norte toward the Pueblo villages of New Mexico.

The Rodriguez-Chamuscado party spent fifteen days traveling to the southernmost Pueblos (the Piros), instead of seven as expected. After proceeding upriver, they spent the summer exploring the Pueblo provinces along the upper Rio del Norte, and then visited the buffalo plains, where they seem to have wandered rather aimlessly. In late autumn, they traveled west to the villages of the Zunis. Along the way, the men concentrated on searching for ore deposits, and took samples for assay.

At the Rio del Norte, with the onset of winter, the friars determined to remain with several Mexican Indian servants at the Tewa village of Puala. Captain Chamuscado was so opposed to this plan that he had a notarized statement of protest drawn up. However, in the end he acceded, and the priests were left behind as the rest of the party retraced their route southward. On the return trip, Chamuscado became ill; he died on the Rio Conchos a few days out of Santa Barbara. Because of this and other irregularities, Hernan Gallegos and several of the other participants proceeded directly to Mexico to make an official report.

Among the Tewas, Fray Agustín Rodriguez was almost immediately martyred, as were his companions. Rumors of their deaths soon reached Santa Barbara. The official mission of the Espejo expedition, which departed a year later, was to investigate the fate of Rodriguez.

As was the usual practice, both of the expeditions made use of natives—most of them either captives or slaves—as guides and translators. The journal of Hernan Gallegos, one of Chamuscado's officers, reveals that he himself had participated in several previous forays through the Conchos valley, out of Santa Barbara. One purpose of such raids was to capture Indians, preferably children or young adults, who could be trained as translators for future use. Gallegos had already traveled toward the north, and was quite familiar with the country and its people as far as La Junta; he evidently had participated in slave raiding in that area. In addition, by interrogating Indian captives he had acquired a considerable amount of information about the lands further to the north.

One native of La Junta who accompanied this expedition was called Juan Cantor. An interpreter, Juan Cantor was possibly a slave; in any case, he surely had worked for some years in or near Santa Barbara. The form of his name suggests that he had been baptized, and that he had received some training in Church ritual. It is noted that, besides his own language, he was fluent in Mexican (Nahuatl).

The Espejo Expedition[3]

The Espejo party set out from San Gregorio, just northeast of Santa Barbara, on November 10, 1582. This group included two clerics and thirteen soldiers, and a number of native servants and translators. There are two accounts of the Espejo *entrada*, one written by Espejo himself and the other, longer and more informative, by Diego Perez de Luxan, the second in command. One native servant who accompanied this party, a boy of thirteen, has a special prominence throughout Luxan's narrative. This boy, Pedro, was the nephew of Juan Cantor, the Patarabuey translator of the Rodriguez expedition. Pedro had been captured six years earlier by a slaving party and raised in Luxan's household, where he was trained as a translator.

The initial leg of the Espejo itinerary parallels that of Rodriguez and Chamuscado. Both parties traveled along the Conchos to La Junta, and then took a path along the west bank of the Rio del Norte, crossing to the east bank at the ford just south of modern El Paso, Texas (a much-used crossing which gave that city its name). They then followed a trail up the river as far as the Pueblos of New Mexico, where their paths diverged.

After visiting the Pueblo provinces, and after making a westward prospecting trip to survey mineral deposits in Arizona, Espejo and his men undertook more extensive travels in the plains east of New Mexico than did Chamuscado. Then Espejo routed the return trip to La Junta along the Rio Pecos, rather than the Rio del Norte. They reached Santa Barbara in September of 1583 (Map 3).

Traveling the Rio Conchos

As the expeditions set out via the upper Rio Conchos they encountered Concho and Toboso Indians. These tribes—actually dialect clusters or congeries of many little-known bands—had been in contact with the Spaniards for several years, around Santa Barbara. Luxan's journal indicates that three weeks were spent passing through the lands of the Concho Indians, "naked people who cover

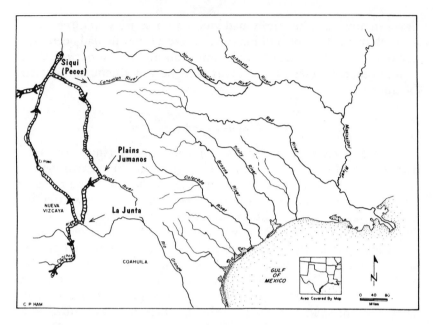

Map 3. Route of Espejo (1582–1583)

themselves with skins of rabbit and deer."[4] On December 5, the party finally came to the end of Concho territory and encountered the "warlike Pasaguates."

According to Luxan, the Pasaguates communities were similar in house styles and food to those of the Conchos. The Pasaguates were a small tribe, situated between the Conchos and the Patarabueyes of La Junta. They were intermediaries, who "speak all three languages."[5] It is not completely clear what these three languages may have been. Patarabuey (or Pataraguey), according to Luxan, was evidently a pejorative term which the slavehunting Spanish soldiers applied generally to the people living around La Junta. It thus seems to cover a mixture of languages and peoples, and cannot be equated definitely with any specific tribal group.

Gallegos referred to two different groups at La Junta, distinguished by language; he called them Cabris and Amotomancos. The same distinction is made by Luxan, who called the two groups Abriaches and Otomoacas. It is the second group—the Amotomancos, or Otomoacas—to which Espejo first applied the name *Jumanos*.

> Marching down the river [Conchos], we met the messengers we had sent to notify the natives of our coming, and as soon as they reached us

we halted on the bank of the river in order to learn at once what they had to say. A short time later many Indians came to meet us, very handsome men and beautiful women. We asked them the name of their language, because it seemed different from the one we had just heard [Cabri], although the two peoples understand one another. They answered that it was "Amotomanco."[6]

According to Gallegos, the Amotomancos—first encountered while the Rodriguez party were still on the lower Rio Conchos—indicated that "their nation extended for one hundred leagues" and that "many more were to be found beyond this land."[7] This is the first recorded encounter with one of the groups later called *Jumano*; it might be noted that the remark here quoted by Gallegos is in line with the wide distribution later attributed to this people.

The Cabris, or Abriaches, who can be identified as the people later called *Julimes*, were probably of the Uto-Aztecan language family as were the neighboring Conchos and Tobosos. They were situated primarily on the lower Rio Conchos, while the Amotomancos, or Otomoacas, had most of their territory along the Rio del Norte. Both groups, however, had villages situated at or near La Junta, the confluence of the two rivers.

La Junta de los Rios

When Espejo's party approached their villages, the Otomoacas attacked, killed several of the horses, and then fled into some hills above their village. It is likely that they already knew some of these Spaniards, from previous contacts with them as slavehunters. However, Pedro, the young Patarabuey interpreter, interceded, "telling the natives not to fear but to come down and be friends with the Christians, who did not wish to harm them. The chieftains of the Otomoacas then asked the interpreter to identify himself; and the boy told who he was and whose son, exchanging many other questions and answers."[8]

After peaceful relations were established, Espejo's party spent more than a week visiting the villages around La Junta de los Rios, resting, gathering information, and preparing for the trek up the Rio del Norte.

These people (Otomoacos or Jumanos) go practically naked, with their privy parts exposed. They cover themselves with well-tanned skins of the *cibola* (bison). The hides they tan and beat with stones until they are soft. They fight with bows and arrows. The bows are Turkish, all reinforced and very strong, and the strings are made from the sinews of the buffalo. For these people ordinarily go after meat and skins where the buffalo range, which is about thirty leagues from this province.

The women wear tanned deerskin bodices of some sort, resembling scapularies, for covering their breasts, and other tanned deerskins as skirts, using as cloaks tanned hides of the cattle. These Indians wear [part of] their hair long and tied up on their heads. The men have their hair cut very short, up to the middle of their heads, and from there up they leave it two fingers long and curl it with minium paint in such a way that it resembles a small cap. They leave on the crown a long lock of hair to which they fasten feathers of white and dark birds such as geese, cranes, and sparrow-hawks. They cultivate corn, beans, and cala-bashes, although very little in this *rancheria*. There are large numbers of this people all along the Conchos river; they farm together.[9]

Some of the villages above and below La Junta were those of the Otomoacas, while others belong to the Abriaches (Cabris). These were a ". . . people different from the Otomoacas, where a different language is spoken, although they are friends and understand one another."[10] Among the Abriaches young Pedro was able to make himself understood, and pacified the villagers as he had those in the first Otomoaca village.

On December 9, at an Otomoaca *rancheria*, the party came face to face with Juan Cantor, Pedro's uncle. He had been left in his home community the previous year, by the returning Rodriguez expedition. Juan Cantor evidently accompanied Espejo's party to the next large Otomoaca town which the Spaniards named San Bernardino. There he helped to persuade the people, who had fled, to return to their homes. In San Bernardino, also, Espejo's men repaired a cross which Fray Augustin Rodriguez had erected. They remained for eight days, resting their horses, and made this village their base while they visited neighboring communities, both Cabri and Otomoaca.

The Spaniards went to another pueblo [Santiago], the largest of all, whose cacique . . . was respected by the rest of the caciques . . . In this pueblo, as in all of them, they told us of how Cabeza de Vaca and his two companions and a Negro had been there. All of the Indians of this community are farmers, the river being very appropriate for agriculture, because it forms many damp islands and bays; and even though they live in the pueblos they have flat-roofed houses in their fields where they reside during harvest time . . .[11]

As Espejo's party continued upriver, they—like Cabeza de Vaca and his companions—were always escorted by people from one village or *rancheria* as they went on to the next. On December 23, they reached a place they called La Hoya; there also they found "peaceful people of the language and dress of the Otomoacas."[12] They paused for several days to spend Christmas and departed on December 27. On December 31, they met another large group of Otomoacas.

> Upon our arrival, there came to us, in procession and singing, more than two hundred Indians, men and women, from the same Otomoacos nation. They presented us with shawls, tanned deerskins, mescal, and ornaments like colored feather bonnets which they said they obtained from the direction of the sea. On this night the natives staged great dances and festivities. They make music by beating their hands while sitting around a big fire. They sing, and in time with the singing they dance, a few rising from one side and others from the opposite, with two, four, or eight persons performing the movements to the rhythm of the song . . .[13]

When the two expeditions visited the villages and *rancherias* near La Junta, information was repeatedly solicited, and usually obtained, concerning the location of "clothed" people. Captain Chamuscado had previously carried samples of woven textiles to use in eliciting such information. Cabeza de Vaca had asked the same questions fifty years earlier; once again, the responses to the inquiries indicated that such people were well known, and that they were located in two directions—upriver to the north, and more distantly, to the west.

The leaders of the expeditions of the 1580's may, as Hammond suggests,[14] have been unaware of Coronado's explorations in the north—though this really seems quite unlikely. Be that as it may, comments by both Gallegos and Luxan make it quite clear that they had read and were much influenced by the *Relation* of Cabeza de Vaca. His story was, as Joseph Sanchez comments, the standard "primer for those who would . . . go north."[15]

> We inquired of these [Indians at La Junta] and many other Indians whether they knew from observation or hearsay what there was in the interior, whether it contained cotton (textiles), corn, and many inhabitants. They told us that thirteen days from the Concepcion river [the Rio del Norte, or Rio Grande], upstream there were many clothed

people who cultivated and gathered much corn, calabashes, and beans, as well as much cotton, which they spun, wove, and made into blankets for covering and clothing themselves. This pleased us very much. We asked them whether they had been there, to which they answered no, but that they had heard about it long ago from the men who hunted the buffalo and that they considered the report very reliable.[16]

Ascending the Rio del Norte

Espejo's account used *Jumano* as a general term for the population on the Rio del Norte as far as El Paso, as did the seventeenth-century historian Obregon in recounting the exploits of these expeditions.[17] Luxan's more detailed account, doubtless assisted by the Patarabuey translator Pedro, distinguished three regional subgroupings between La Junta and El Paso: the Otomoacas, closest to La Junta; the Caguates, further upstream; and the Tanpachoas, living in marshy areas near the crossing. The last of these groups has been identified with the Mansos, whom Oñate encountered near this same point, two decades later; their territory extended as far north as Las Cruces, New Mexico.

The information about faraway peoples which Rodriguez and Chamuscado obtained at La Junta appeared to be secondhand, since the explorers were told that the news came "from the men who hunted the buffalo," who had visited those places. The meaning of this statement is not immediately clear, but the answer lay in the report written some nine days later among an upriver hunting and trading group which Luxan called *Caguates*. From their location, these people can be identified with Cabeza de Vaca's "People of the Cows," and thus with the later Cibolo (literally, *buffalo*). When the Rodriguez expedition reached Caguate territory, about midway between La Junta and El Paso, the Spaniards learned about these distant places firsthand, from those who claimed to have been there.

> After two days we [the Espejo party] came to another nation of friendly people [the Caguates or Cibolos], fine men who received us well and offered us of what they had . . . Among the things they gave us were two bonnets made of numerous macaw feathers . . .[18]

According to the Caguates, the "clothed people" located on the river farther to the north (the Pueblo people of New Mexico) could be reached in seven days' travel. Rodriguez and Chamuscado were also specifically warned about another people who might be encountered along the way, who "were numerous, very brave, and warlike" and who had caused a great deal of trouble, "being members of a different nation."[19] This may be a reference to Apaches, located in approximately the same location—the Guadalupe-Sacramento Mountain region—in which Cabeza de Vaca found them some years earlier. From this base, they evidently were raiding Caguate villages or waylaying trade parties as they passed alongside the river or on trails through mountain passes.

Espejo's passage through Caguate territory was probably facilitated by the presence of the interpreter Pedro. Once again, the boy was among his kinsmen.

> We . . . went four leagues to a place we called La Guardia del Caballo. An old cacique from the Caguates nation named Guaxi came to us here. He was a grandfather of Pedro, the interpreter, servant of Diego Perez de Luxan. The natives are friendly. They are intermarried with the Otomoacos and have almost the same language. This cacique had a sorrel horse, for it seems that Francisco Sanchez Chamuscado had left it there, exhausted, when he returned . . . We were met here by more than three hundred people, men and women. They performed impressive dances after their fashion and offered us gifts from what they had. From here the natives led us to some mines which were of little value. We erected crosses for these people.[20]

High on the Rio del Norte, while still in Jumano country, Espejo told of an encounter with travellers going north on the same trail. These were evidently not natives of the region; there were "numerous Indian men, women, and children who wore clothes, some of chamois skin." By pointing out that these travellers were clothed, Espejo explicitly contrasted them with the local Jumanos, whom he had repeatedly characterized as "naked" Indians. These people could not be identified by nationality because there were no interpreters for their language. It would appear likely that they derived from one or another of the Pueblos, perhaps from the Hopi province, a center for weaving. They presented the Spaniards with goods which included "cotton shawls, striped blue and white, resembling some that are imported from China." The Spaniards asked their usual questions, pointing to samples of metals and of minerals which were on hand; the Indians seem to indicate, through their signs in response, that they had trade contacts with an area "five days' march" to the west of their own villages, where silver ores (which the Spaniards were eager to discover) were to be found.[21] It is clear that the Rio del Norte trail was an important thoroughfare; evidently these Indians were traveling northward, since they accompanied Espejo's men for four days as they proceeded along the river trail.

Just before arriving at the crossing place, El Paso del Rio del Norte, the Espejo party encountered the Tanpachoas. Because of their location, it is usually assumed that these were the same people that Oñate later called the *Mansos*.

> . . . We named this site [below El Paso] Los Charcos de Canutillo, because there were numerous reeds and large marshes and pools with quantities of fish close by the river. A large number of Indian men and women from another nation, called Tanpachoas, came to this place. During the six or seven days we rested there . . . they brought us a large quantity of mesquite, corn, and fish for they fish much in the pools with small dragnets. They are people of the same blood and type as the Otomoacos, and of the same dress, except that the men tie their privy parts with a small ribbon.
>
> Their mode of fighting is with Turkish bows and arrows, and bludgeons as much as half a yard in length, made of tornilla wood, which is very strong and flexible. We all made stocks for our harquebuses from this tornillo wood because it was very suitable for the purpose. . . .[22]

Among the Tanpachoas, the Spaniards were once more told about "clothed people" who lived "on a very large lake" fifteen days' travel to the west.[23] The accounts of both expeditions are full of such allusions, which indicate a wealth of trade and intergroup contacts among Indian peoples over a wide geographical range.

Beyond the crossing at El Paso, both Spanish expeditions had to make their way through the Jornada del Muerte, a barren stretch of about eighty miles, where the path is turned away from the river by the rugged Fray Cristobal Mountains. However, they continued northward to explore the densely populated village provinces which later became known as New Mexico. The Espejo party reached the first of the Piro villages on February 1, and spent the next six months exploring the Pueblo provinces and prospecting for mineral deposits. They identified a community called Puala, in the province of Tiguex (the Tiwas), as the place of Father Rodriguez' martyrdom.

Through many of the Pueblo villages, the expeditions of the 1580's had been preceded by the Coronado *entrada*, four decades earlier. Over the following years, there would be an increasing number of both official and unofficial exploring parties, probably including several illegal junkets which were not historically documented.

At La Junta, Espejo and his men had heard about mines which were located far to the west, and they had been told that Jumano people would be found in those locations. Weeks later, after exploring the Pueblo villages, Espejo led a party to investigate mineral deposits west of the Hopi pueblos, following a trail which was retraced and described in more detail by members of the Oñate expedition. At the time of the later visit, there were Jumanos at the site.

Both Chamuscado and Espejo devoted some time to exploring the buffalo plains, reached by way of Pecos Pueblo. There are several recorded encounters with nomadic natives in that area; descriptions include references to typical Plains Indian culture traits such as skin tents, the dog travois, bow and arrow, etc. However, identification of specific ethnic groups is generally impossible. The Rodriguez-Chamuscado exploration of the plains was brief; the party was not able to obtain native guides and wandered for some time apparently in the vicinity of the Rio Pecos. Their attention was preoccupied by the buffalo, which they unsuccessfully attempted to corral. Their return route took them south of Pecos Pueblo, probably through the region east of the Manzano Mountains (an area in which the Jumano pueblos, first documented two decades later, were located).

The accounts of the return trip by the Espejo expedition deserve special attention because of their extensive travel through the plains, following the course of the Rio Pecos, and their encounters with natives who can be definitely identified as Jumanos.

Following the Rio de las Vacas

In July, Espejo and his men arrived at the easternmost Pueblos, which they called Siqui (Pecos Pueblo, Coronado's Cicuye). Here, a brief skirmish was precipitated by the refusal of the Pecos Indians to provide food for the Spaniards. From Siqui, Espejo began a trek south by way of the Rio Pecos, apparently intending to continue along that stream until it joined the Rio del Norte some miles downstream from La Junta.

> We . . . stopped at the pueblo of Siqui. . . . This pueblo is very large, similar to the one before [San Cristobal, a Tano village]. It must have contained about two thousand men armed with bows and arrows. When asked to give us some pinole, the Indians replied that they had none. . . . Thereupon six armed men entered the pueblo, determined to burn it, and the people were so frightened that they gave us the food against their will.
> We left this place on the fifth of the month of July and took two Indians by force to direct us to the buffalo. . . .[24]

The party encountered Indians, on the Pecos and in the mountainous country between that river and the Rio del Norte. Their first contacts came after they had spent almost a month following the Pecos—120 leagues (more than 250 miles), according to Espejo's calculations. They then came upon three Indians whom they recognized as Jumanos.

> [July 25] . . . We continued and went six leagues, halting by the said river [Rio de las Vacas, or Pecos] close to a marsh. We called the place El Mosquitero, because of the many mosquitoes. In all this trip we did not find any buffalo, nothing but many tracks. Hence we came to a stop, greatly troubled by lack of food . . .
>
> [July 31] . . . After traveling two leagues, (we) halted by the same river, where a large stream, bordered by many walnut trees, empties into it. We named this place El Dudoso, because we noticed the sierra of the Pataragueyes and wondered whether it was the stream which the native Pataragueyes had told us emptied into this Rio de las Bacas. Although the whole region is full of dung and bones, God willed that we should not see any buffalo . . .
>
> [August 6] . . . We met three Jumana Indians, who were out hunting, and we were able to understand them through Pedro . . . They said that the Rio de las Bacas came out very far below the Conchos river; that they would take us by good trails to the junction of the Rio del Norte with the Conchos, which is among the Pataragueyes. This brought us no little joy, as men who had eaten nothing but pinole. We halted for the night at a large marsh where there were many water holes . . . we called the site La Cienega Salada.[25]

It is significant that the Spaniards were able to communicate with these Indians by relying on the Patarabuey translator Pedro, as this indicates a close linguistic relationship to the population at La Junta de los Rios. After informing the soldiers that the route they were following was long and difficult, the Jumanos directed them to a shortcut to La Junta, through the Davis Mountains. Since the Indians were first encountered on the Pecos, at a point which must have been in the approximate vicinity of Pecos, Texas, it appears likely that the trail was the same one in use in the next century as the main route between La Junta and the East. The Jumanos led the party, by good trails, an estimated forty leagues, to the east bank of the Rio del Norte.

Before their departure on this trail, the Spanish party rested and were entertained at the Jumanos' *rancheria*, probably located on Toyah Creek.

We left La Cienega Salada on the eighth and went five leagues, three
of them up a stream [Toyah Creek]. We found many Jumana Indians
from the *rancheria* of the people who were guiding us. They were on
their way to the river, to the mesquite trees. We stopped by this stream,
where the *rancheria* was situated. The Indians, men and women, received us with music and rejoicing. As an additional sign of peace and
happiness, a dance was held amid the tents of the Indian men and
women. We rested for a day because we had an opportunity to catch
some catfish . . . some were half a yard in length, a difficult thing to
believe. The food was delicious.[26]

They passed other small Jumano camps before arriving at the
river. All along the way, they were received hospitably by Jumanos
who, according to Luxan, "in their clothing, appearance, and habitat
are similar to the Pataragueyes."[27] (The similarity, as already noted,
also extended to language.) On August 16, Luxan indicated that the
Spanish party reached the Rio del Norte nine leagues from San
Bernardino, the town which they had earlier visited in the company
of Juan Cantor. Proceeding along the river toward San Bernardino
they passed through a number of smaller settlements or *rancherias*.

All the *rancherias* . . . gave us a great reception, according to their custom and presented us with quantities of ears of green corn, cooked and
raw calabashes, and catfish. They put on great dances and other festivities
as a sign of peace. The same was done at the pueblo of San Bernardino,
where all the caciques of the pueblos came to welcome us. Our feeling of
security was so great that we went about almost in shirt sleeves . . .[28]

As they prepared to return, via the Rio Conchos, to Santa Barbara,
the party was forced to halt at the village of Santo Tomas for three
days by high water which prevented their crossing.

Not being able to cross the [Conchos] river because it was too high,
we rested here for three days. The companions all traded in blankets, of
which the natives had many, buffalo skins, and Turkish bows reinforced
with sinews. These are the best and strongest there are in the land that
has been discovered. The inhabitants gave us calabashes, beans, and
ears of green corn. They are fine, bright people who would readily accept the holy faith.[29]

Finally, the Spaniards traveled rapidly up the Conchos, through
the lands of the Toboso and Conchos Indians, and reached San Bartolome on the tenth of September.

These accounts of the Espejo expedition, especially that by Diego Perez de Luxan, provide the best evidence that in the early contact period of the late sixteenth century Jumanos hunted in the valley of the Pecos, far downstream from Pecos Pueblo, and that they inhabited the country between that river and the Rio Grande in the neighborhood of La Junta. From the linguistic evidence provided by the interpreter Pedro, the identification of the Indians along this route as Jumano is unimpeachable, as is the indication that their speech and that of the La Junta population was mutually intelligible.

The Espejo party made its way intact to Santa Barbara with confirmation of the details of the death of Fray Agustín Rodriguez. They also brought information about the location of a number of mineral deposits—some of them, including those in Arizona, already mined by natives of the area, and they carried with them a collection of samples to be assayed. Luxan's day-by-day account of the itinerary amounts to an excellent record of the conditions, distances, and communities and peoples encountered. Despite the incident at Pecos Pueblo, the overall success of this party in dealing with the native population was remarkable, especially after the precedent of hostile relations established by Coronado and the high-handedness of Chamuscado, both of whom had preceded them in most of the provinces. There was no immediate follow-up to these two expeditions, however, although much of the information gathered by Espejo and his predecessors was eventually of use to the subsequent expedition of conquest headed by Juan de Oñate.

4.

THE ILLEGAL *ENTRADA* OF CASTAÑO DE SOSA

Before the end of the sixteenth century, there was another point of access for entry into the interior, or *tierra adentro*. This was the newly settled northeastern frontier of New Spain. Spreading inland from coastal Nuevo Leon, mining interests began to open up the region which would become the province of Coahuila. Before 1590, prospectors and slavehunters had crossed the Rio Bravo (the lower Rio Grande) and penetrated some distance into the interior, perhaps even as far as the Pueblos of New Mexico. Gaspar Castaño de Sosa, the lieutenant governor of Nuevo Leon, had already gained some acquaintance with these regions, although perhaps secondhand, before he himself set out on a colonizing adventure in the autumn of 1590.

There were doubtless a number of such illegal exploring parties, some of them completely unreported, others known but essentially undocumented. The *entrada* of Castaño de Sosa is one for which there is substantial documentation, in the account written by the leader himself. This *entrada* has some significance in relation to the Jumanos, since Castaño traveled the length of the Rio Pecos, which lies within the total area occupied by the Jumanos in the South Plains.

At the time, Gaspar Castaño de Sosa was the acting governor of Nuevo Leon in the absence of his superior, Luis de Carbajal, who had been imprisoned by the Inquisition. Rumors of Castaño's filibustering plans had reached the viceroy, the Marques de Villamanique, in Mexico City. The viceroy dispatched Captain Juan Morlete to Nuevo Almaden, with orders to contact Castaño de Sosa, to caution him about his past involvement in slavetaking and to forbid explicitly an expedition into New Mexico. Nevertheless, Castaño proceeded to organize a colonizing party which included the entire Spanish contingent at Nuevo Almaden and a number of the

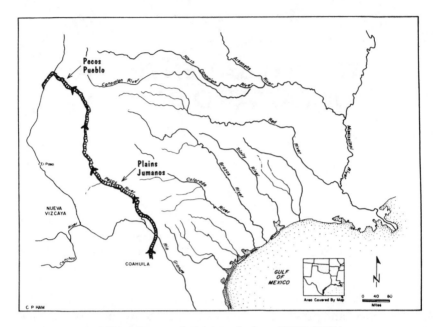

Map 4. Route of Castaño de Sosa (1590–1591)

regional Indians. He may have gambled on being able to justify his
efforts later, once a colony was successfully established.

There were about two hundred prospective settlers with their
household goods and supplies loaded in a train of oxcarts and herds
of cattle, sheep, and other livestock trailing behind. After leaving
Nuevo Almaden at the end of July, they moved slowly toward a
crossing of the Rio Bravo, somewhere near the present site of Del
Rio, Texas. Here, they waited for several days for the tardy arrival of
a party of men who had been dispatched with a last-minute petition
to the viceroy. In the meantime, scouts were sent ahead to prospect
for mines and to determine the route to be followed. The plan was
to find and follow the Rio Salado (the Pecos), which Castaño was
confident—either from Espejo's account, or from the findings of
slavers out of Nuevo Almaden—would lead him to Pecos Pueblo
and eventually to the other provinces of New Mexico (Map 4).

Traveling beyond the Rio Bravo, the expedition made a difficult
crossing of the Rio de Laxas (Devil's River). They spent most of October wandering northward over the waterless and almost impassable terrain of the Edwards Plateau, searching for the Rio Salado.
On October 26 they found the river flowing through a deep, steep-
sided canyon.

Throughout the early stages of the passage northward, Castaño's journal makes no mention of any contact with natives, although his scouting parties may have found some. Periodically, throughout the *entrada*, contingents of captives were evidently sent back to Nuevo Leon for sale, a fact that is not noted in Castaño's journal. The first report of an encounter with Indians was around October 26 from a scouting party which had been sent out to follow "certain human tracks"—i.e., evidence of a trail, running alongside the river.

> The following day [Oct. 27], while we were at the river, Alonso Jaimez arrived with the men he had taken along, saying . . . that he had followed the trail specified by the lieutenant governor [Castaño], and that after three days of travel he had come upon a large number of people of the Tepelguan [or Depesguan] nation, who received him cordially. When he explained to them through the interpreter the purpose of the trip, the natives were highly pleased and gave him many buffalo and chamois skins, fine shoes of the type they themselves wore, and a quantity of meat. They also indicated that we might travel through their region and that they would lead us to places where there were settlements and an abundance of corn. So Alonso Jaimez turned back, very satisfied with the friendship shown him by the Indians.[1]

The Indians were camped beside a stream which emptied into the Pecos, apparently at a permanent *rancheria*. They were almost certainly Jumanos. The name—*Tepelguan* in one edition, *Depesguan* in another—can be interpreted as *Tepehuan*, the name of a large Indian population of Chihuahua.[2] The use of this term may indicate simply that the appearance of the Indians—their costume, hair style, etc.—suggested association with that region, perhaps by contrast to the Coahuiltecan Indians native to Coahuila and Nuevo Leon. The Jumanos of the lower Pecos had trading contacts via La Junta and the Rio Conchos which extended into Chihuahua. Captain Alonso Jaimez, Castaño's second in command, was able to communicate with them through an interpreter; it is likely that the language used was Mexican (Nahuatl). It should be noted that these Indians had a large supply of deer and antelope skins on hand, and were ready to trade with the Spaniards. As in other Jumano encounters with Spanish explorers, they offered goods and services; they volunteered to guide the party, probably assuming that the Spaniards were seeking the same settlements, i.e., the towns of New Mexico, as Espejo and other previous parties.

A few days later, when the main body of the expedition advanced along the river trail, they found only abandoned *rancherias*. They pursued some Indians who attempted to flee from them. Among these was a party of traders or returning hunters, traveling with packdogs laden with hides. In all later encounters with Indians in this same general region, the Indians were much less forthcoming than in the first, and the Spaniards usually found only abandoned camps. It would seem that, despite the apparent friendliness of the initial encounter, the Indians had passed on a warning of the Spaniards' arrival—slavehunters from the south had, after all, previously penetrated the region. There appear to have been numerous *rancherias* along the lower Pecos, one of the largest situated near an impressive saline. The expedition went to some pains to capture Indians to train as interpreters, which suggests that the Jumanos' own language was unknown to the party from Coahuila. Thus it would seem that the Jumanos had not yet developed contacts with the northeastern province.

There were more encounters, usually hostile. Indians were caught trying to steal some of the oxen; one was hanged, and the other three held captive, for future use as interpreters. However, the captives soon escaped, successfully making off with an ox in the process.

Castaño de Sosa's account is sketchy, and locales are only vaguely indicated. It was already late October when the first group of Indians was encountered. The company spent the first half of November following the Pecos valley from around Sheffield, Texas, up to the vicinity of the Texas–New Mexico border. In the weeks after this, there is no mention of Indians or of deserted *rancherias*. Columns of smoke—perhaps signal fires—were spotted as the expedition skirted the Guadalupe Mountains. In this same vicinity, they examined a "very large corral used by the Indians for enclosing cattle"—a hunting technique commonly practiced by Apaches and other buffalo hunters.[3] It is likely that the Indians living in these mountains were Apaches, just as may have been the case earlier, when Cabeza de Vaca passed this way.

Continuing north, beyond the mountains, there were very few signs of human occupancy. Tracts of grassland had been burned, however, probably as a hunting tactic. There is no mention of settlements until the sighting of some small *rancherias*, which can be identified as outliers of Pecos Pueblo.

Castaño de Sosa reached Pecos Pueblo around Christmas of 1590. An advance party entered the pueblo, where they were welcomed and given some corn. When they returned the next day and demanded more, however, the Indians disarmed them, confiscated most of their weapons and their saddles, and sent them packing. Castaño then came up with cannon and laid siege to the pueblo,

which was taken after a protracted battle; it was subsequently abandoned by the Indians, leaving the Spaniards in possession.

Eventually, however, Castaño's company left Pecos, and moved
on toward the Rio del Norte, where they next occupied the Pueblo
of Santo Domingo. There, in the spring of 1591, Castaño de Sosa
was finally overtaken by a company of men, marching north via the
Rio del Norte, and led by Captain Morlete. Castaño was immediately arrested, shackled, and was returned under guard to Mexico,
along with the rest of the colony.

5.

JUAN DE OÑATE AND THE CONQUEST OF NEW MEXICO[1]

Following the *entradas* commanded by Chamuscado and Espejo, almost two decades elapsed before any new activity signaled the interest of the Spanish crown in the lands north of Mexico. The explanation for the delay lies in the slow workings of the official bureaucracy, which was in the process of reviewing candidates and selecting the leader for a full-scale expedition of conquest and colonization. Juan de Oñate was the candidate finally selected to receive a royal commission as leader of the conquest, and to be designated as the first governor of the colony of New Mexico. Oñate, the scion of a wealthy family involved in the mining industries of Zacatecas, assembled his army at Santa Barbara in the winter of 1595. However, a series of delays and repeated inspections postponed the departure north until January of 1598.

To make up for some of the lost time, and to bypass native rebellions which had sprung up around La Junta, Oñate dispatched his nephew, Vicente de Zaldivar, to open a more direct overland route between the upper Conchos and the crossing at El Paso del Norte (Map 5). This new trail became the main highway, and continued to be used by the regular supply trains between Santa Fe and Mexico after the colony was established.[2] Once this route was adopted, there is a period of almost a century in which there seems to have been very little Spanish traffic through the valley of the Rio del Norte below El Paso. Almost nothing is known about conditions during this period. It is clear, however, that the native population of La Junta de los Rios continued to be drawn toward the upper Conchos valley and the economic and population centers located there.

From El Paso, Oñate led an advance party up the Rio del Norte, demanding and receiving the submission of the villages along the river. The rest of the colonists and the supply train followed. He established his temporary headquarters at the Tewa pueblo of Kaypa,

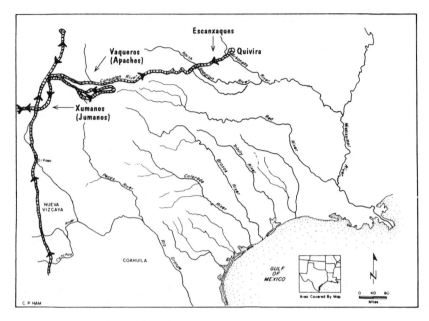

Map 5. Explorations during the Oñate period (1598–1601)

which was renamed San Juan. This was the capital of New Mexico for the next two years. Oñate then relocated the capital in a neighboring village, which he dubbed San Gabriel. San Gabriel served as the administrative center until Oñate's successor as governor, Peralta, ordered the construction of the permanent capital of Santa Fe, in 1611.

Like those invaders who preceded him, Oñate had plans for exploration and conquest extending well beyond the villages of New Mexico. Since the time of Coronado, hopes of finding riches in New Mexico had faded, to a degree. Oñate funded the colonization project largely out of his own and his family's resources. In exchange, by the terms of his royal charter, he had almost absolute power. Unfortunately, in searching for an immediate return on his personal investment, Oñate neglected to provide an adequate economic base for the colony, in terms of agricultural or industrial development. He did not grant *encomiendas* to his settlers, or develop plans for community holdings. Instead the colonists were temporarily supported in large part by levies on the native population, whose reserve supplies were quickly depleted. This was quite ruinous in a marginal ecological area such as New Mexico, where the native population had sustained an agricultural economy through judicious rationing of a limited water supply. One result of Oñate's policies, quite obviously, was economic distress for natives and colonists alike. Another was the continuing, impatient search for new sources of wealth.

When the territories immediately around the Pueblo provinces had been explored, and the relative poverty of resources revealed, the lands beyond—Gran Quivira—were seen as the next best possibility for conquest. Oñate lost little time in launching explorations in that direction.

Initial Exploration of the Plains

In September of 1598, a party of soldiers, led by Vicente de Zaldivar, set out from New Mexico to explore the plains east of the Pecos. The Spaniards began to encounter Indians in hilly country only a few miles beyond their crossing of the river, in the general vicinity of Las Vegas, New Mexico. Two days further along, the party visited an Indian camp, where Zaldivar, speaking through an interpreter, "gave them some presents and told them . . . that Governor Don Juan de Oñate had sent him that they might know that he could protect those who were loyal to his Majesty and punish those who were not." The Indians, called *Vaqueros*—obviously the Plains Apaches earlier known as *Querechos*—took the officer at his word. They appeared to be delighted, and immediately "asked him for aid against the Xumanas, as they call a tribe of Indians who are painted after the manner of the Chichimecos." Zaldivar declined, simply giving diplomatic assurances that he would "endeavor to insure peace . . . since he had come to this land for that purpose." [3] The closest Jumano community to these Apaches could, at this date, have been located only a short distance to the south, just east of the Manzano Mountains; others could have been found further to the east.

After another three days of travel, the expedition began to encounter bison. The Spaniards wandered for several days, exploring the country and pursuing the herds, before beginning to construct a corral, with the intention of capturing some of the animals. They were, again, near low mountains and near a river, probably the Canadian. The "cattle," however, were soon dispersed by the arrival of large numbers of people. The Spaniards watched while parties of the Vaqueros crossed the river, "coming from trading with the Picuries and Taos, populous pueblos of New Mexico, where they sell meats, hides, tallow, suet, and salt in exchange for cotton blankets, pottery, maize, and some small green stones (turquoise) which they use."[4] The account of Zaldivar's expedition thus indicates that there were ongoing hostilities between Apaches and Jumanos, as there were at the time of Coronado's exploration. The Apaches were now dominant in the vicinity of the northernmost Pueblos, where they evidently came and went freely for purposes of trade. At the same time, they were still warring with the Jumanos, and effectively preventing Jumano access to those communities.

The Spaniards visited an Apache camp near the river. Zaldivar greatly admired the light weight and fine workmanship of the Indians' tents, and bartered for one, which was carried back to base at San Juan. Eventually, Zaldivar's party traveled around fifty leagues beyond the Rio Pecos, while remaining south of the Canadian. Once more, the men built a corral and spent several days attempting to drive the animals into it, but again had no success. The land thereabouts is described as "very level mesas" broken, at some points, by "glens or valleys" containing cedars and springs. No further specific encounters with Apaches are described, but Zaldivar indicated that the Vaqueros Indians "are numerous in all that land," following and living off the cattle.[5]

The last point reached by Zaldivar's expedition, by Bolton's estimate, must have been near the Texas–New Mexico border. It would have been distant by a hundred miles or more from the canyons at the eastern edge of the High Plains, where Teya (Jumano) *rancherias* were earlier discovered by Coronado, and where, three decades later, the Jumanos were visited by Fray Juan de Salas. Other accounts of explorations under Oñate's orders, however, do provide additional information about areas of reported Jumano provenance, one of them within and two outside of the limits of New Mexico. These accounts are essential to an overall picture of Jumano demography, although, in each case, the identities of the groups have been debated.

The Tompiro Jumanos

After designating San Juan as the colonial capital in August of 1598, Oñate had ordered the construction of several public buildings, including a church. On September 6, when these projects were completed, a ceremony was held which formalized the dominion of Spain over the indigenous population. It is in the proceedings of this ceremony that we find the first mention, by name, of the "Xumana" villages in New Mexico.

At San Juan, Oñate received formal indications of "obedience and vassalage" from the designated Indian captains of several provinces, and presented them with staffs of office. At the same time, he assigned religious responsibility for the "provinces and pueblos thus far discovered" to the eight Franciscan friars who had come from Mexico. The apostolic commissary, Fray Alonso Martinez, then made missionary assignments, dividing the colony into seven separate geographical districts. The Jumano villages were part of the large territory assigned to Fray Francisco de San Miguel.

> To Father Fray Francisco de San Miguel, the province of the Pecos with the seven pueblos of the *cienega* (salt marsh) which lies to the east, and all of the Vaquero (Apache) Indians of the cordillera as far as the Sierra Nevada: and the pueblos of the great saline which lies across the sierra of Pueray; and, in addition, the pueblos of Quanquiz and Hohota, Yonalu, Xotre, Xaimela, Aggei, Cutzalitzontegi, Acoli, Abbo, Apena, Axauti, Amexa, Cohuna, Chiu Alle, Atuya, Machein; and, also the three great Pueblos of the Xumanas or Rayados called, in their Atzigui language, Gennobey, Quellotezei, Pataotzei, together with their subjects.[6]

Scholes, reviewing the colonial documents relative to this group of pueblos, stated that "it is clear that the pueblos of the Jumanos-Rayados were on the eastern frontier of pueblo settlement, not far from the salt marshes and the Tompiro village of Abo."[7] *Atzigui* is a term sometimes applied to the Piro pueblos; here, it is used as a language name, which Scholes takes as evidence that the Piros and Jumanos spoke the same language. This is an important issue in determining the identity of Jumano.

Following the installation ceremony in San Juan, and at about the same time that Vicente de Zaldivar was exploring the plains to the east, Oñate made a tour of inspection which took him, first, southeastward to the area of the Salinas, and then westward. His official account refers once more to the Jumano pueblos.

> On the sixth of October in the year 1598 the governor set out from this pueblo of San Juan, province of the Teguas. On the first day we traveled four leagues, to the first pueblo of the Canada de los Teguas; on the next day, six leagues to San Marcos; on the following day six leagues to the Pueblo del Tuerto [a small tributary of the Rio del Norte]. On the next day, two leagues to the first pueblo over the mountains [the Manzano range], the last pueblo of Puara; next day five leagues to the first pueblo of the Salines; next day four leagues to the last pueblo of the

Salines [or Salinas]. We remained there three days and visited the salt
deposits which lie to the east five or six leagues from there. They consist
of white salt; there are many very large and good ones, and they are
seven or eight leagues in circumference. Next day we went three
leagues to the pueblo of Abo, and the next day four leagues to the Xumanas. There are three [Jumano] pueblos, one of them large like Sia and
two small ones. The said pueblos of the Salines and the Xumanas all
rendered obedience to his Majesty.[8]

During this tour the governor received oaths of allegiance at the
Pueblo of Acolocu on October 12 from the Indian captains (or
caciques) of the villages of Paaco, Cuzaya, Junctre, and Acolocu.
And on October 17, in Cueloce, "which they call 'of the Rayados,'"
he met with four captains, whose names are indicated: "Yolha . . .
captain of the pueblo and people of this same pueblo of Cueloce:
Pocaetaqui, captain of the pueblo of Xenopue; Haye, captain of the
pueblo of Pataoce; and Chili, captain of the Pueblo of Abo."[9] Scholes
suggests that the two groupings of the Pueblos may reflect linguistic divisions; four Tiwa towns were represented by the captains
who gathered at Acolocu, while Abo, considered to be a Tompiro
pueblo, and the three Jumano towns, were represented at Cueloce.[10]
Colonial accounts are inadequate to completely clarify the identify of all the communities mentioned in inventories such as this
one, not to mention their geographical locations. The Salinas, east
of the Manzano Mountains, were a frontier area of New Mexico,
somewhat off the beaten track. Some accounts suggest that there
were not three, but four, Jumano communities in the area. The status of Abo is unclear; it may, by some, have been counted as a Jumano pueblo.
There are early indications of unrest—rebellious actions, and
Spanish reprisals—in the Salinas area. Discontent was perhaps intensified by the fact that this was a marginal zone with a sparse and
insecure water supply, chronic agricultural failures, and food shortages. The Spanish levies of foodstuffs and textiles, which quickly
drained all of the Pueblo provinces, must have been especially op-
pressive in the Salinas. One incident occurred in July of 1599, when
Vicente de Zaldivar, at the head of a group of twenty-five soldiers,
asked for food supplies in an unspecified Jumano community, perhaps the "great pueblo" of Cueloce. In reply, Zaldivar was offered
stones instead of bread—an unmistakable symbolic comment on
the poverty of the people and the injustice of the demand. Soon
after this incident, a punitive expedition was led by Oñate himself,
perhaps because Zaldivar was at the time absent in the west.

. . . when the governor had arrived at the pueblo of the Jumanos, he asked them for mantas [blankets, a standard item of tribute], and the Indians collected about twelve or fourteen and gave them to the governor, giving them to understand that they had no more to give. And herewith the governor went about half a league away from there to certain water holes . . . and on the following day he returned to the pueblo, taking with him as interpreter an Indian who understood the language of the Jumanos, and through him told them that he wanted to punish them because they had been unwilling to give supplies to the sargento mayor [Zaldivar]; and that he would treat with love and good will those who did what he wanted with a good grace. And when they had been informed of this, he set fire to certain groups (*cuarteles*) of houses of the said Indians. When they saw this, they withdrew to their houses and *azoteas* [flat house-tops] and the governor ordered that a fusillade of arquebuses be fired at them, as a result of which five or six Indians fell dead, not counting those who must have been wounded. And the governor ordered that two, who appeared to him to be the most bellicose, should be hanged, and it was done. And having told the interpreter to tell the said Indians certain things . . . it was the opinion of a certain soldier that what the said interpreter told them was to the contrary and so he told the governor, who ordered him [the interpreter] to be hanged.[11]

This action, as one might expect, led to new incidents. It was reported that five soldiers, on their way to Mexico, were waylaid in the Salinas area, and two of them killed. This took place near the pueblo of Abo, and was attributed to the Jumanos. It led to new Spanish demands for vengeance: ". . . the Father Commissary Fray Juan Escalona, together with all the friars who were in this kingdom, asked the governor to punish the Jumanas Indians for having killed Juan de Castañeda and Bernabe de Santillan, and also all the captains and soldiers of this army and even the women made the same plea."[12] Vicente de Zaldivar was once more in command, as an Indian village was laid waste.

. . . after . . . many *requerimientos* [official demands] that they should submit peacefully . . . the Indians only desired war and to fight. It was declared and siege was laid to the pueblo, and they fought them for six days, by night and by day without resting. . . . A large force of the Indians, who were in a plaza and of whom there were probably more than two hundred, were desirous of fleeing the blockade, and in order to do so they made an attack in a street. The *maese de campo* [Zaldivar] was near there and with his arms and horses he . . . forced them to retreat. . . .

He returned the greater part of the Indians to the pueblo, and he and those who accompanied him overtook those who got out . . .[13]

On this occasion, Zaldivar's punitive measures seem relatively mild, at least by contrast to those at Acoma, where he took bloody reprisals. When the battle was over, most of the Jumano population was released, but the "most guilty," over the age of twenty-five, were distributed in servitude to Zaldivar's soldiers. The chain of events seems clearly to have begun with the Jumanos; however, the attack on the Spanish troops was said to have occurred near Abo, and the community attacked by Zaldivar may have been the pueblo of Acolocu.[14] In any case, it would appear that the trouble between the natives and their Spanish rulers was a regional problem, and not confined to specific villages or language groups. Through the years of Oñate's rule, it is doubtful that any real progress was made toward the missionization of the Salinas area, or even that there was a permanent cadre of Spanish administrative staff in the Tompiro province.

The Expedition to the Mines

Later in the fall of 1598, after the several days which he spent in the Salinas, Oñate turned his itinerary toward the west, leading the army on a tour which included a visit to Acoma, the province of Zuni, and in the second week of November, the province of Mohoqui (Hopi). While some of the men rested and toured this province, Oñate delegated Captain Marcos Farfan de los Godos and eight men, to explore and evaluate a mining area some distance to the west.

Chamuscado had known of these mines, at or near a site later famed as a semi-legendary *Sierra Azul*. Espejo had visited them and drawn maps of the route; these maps were probably in Oñate's possession.[15] The Espejo accounts are brief, and include little information about the Indians encountered in the area. The narrative of Captain Farfan, on the other hand, contains considerable detail and makes reference to at least two separate native groups; the first of these was specifically indicated to be "Jumano Indians." These Indians were contacted, according to the account, sixteen leagues southwest of the "province of Mohoqui" at a camp in or near the San Francisco Mountains, some distance southeast of modern Flagstaff, Arizona.[16] The Jumano *rancherias* were located and identified by Indians, probably Hopis, who were serving as guides for the

Spanish party. They were, at the time, under the command of Captain Alonzo de Quesada.

> He [Quesada] took the Indians ahead of him, and after traveling about
> three arquebus shots from where we [Captain Farfan and other soldiers]
> were lodged the Indians saw lights and dwellings . . . and signaled to the
> captain that there were the Jumano Indians. The captain, finding him-
> self so near, told them to go over there, and having arrived there he
> found many Indian men and women in four or five *rancherias,* who sur-
> rounded them with their bows and arrows. The captain told them that
> he had a message for them; that he was not coming to do them harm,
> but instead, to give them of what he had. Thereupon they were reas-
> sured, and two Indian chiefs of the said *rancheria* came on with the cap-
> tain and friendly Indians to where the witness [Farfan] and his compan-
> ions were. The witness treated them very well, showing them marks of
> friendship, caressing them, giving them beads and other presents. He
> then sent them back to their own *rancherias,* telling them that they
> should reassure the rest of the people, because they were not going to
> injure them but to be their friends, and to find out where they secured
> the ore which the witness showed them.[17]

From this *rancheria,* the following day, one of the Jumano men
was persuaded to guide the Spaniards to the mines which they
sought. The description of the route, from the Hopi villages to the
Jumano *rancherias,* and from that point on to the mines, gives some
details of terrain and indications of distances. However, as is so
often the case, there is disagreement about the exact locations. The
journey from the *rancheria* occupied a full day and part of the next.
At the end, they found ". . . a petty Indian chief with about thirty
Indians, stained with ores of different colors, and as many as eight
or ten dwellings in which were women and children."[18] These
were, it seems, members of a different tribe; based on the region,
they may have been Yumans, perhaps Yavapais.[19] These Indians
worked the mines, extracting the ores which were, as pigments,
valuable and widely used. The Jumanos were probably in the region
for that reason, in order to obtain an important trade commodity.
    The Spanish captain had brought beads and other trinkets which
he distributed. In return, he received ". . . powdered ores of different
colors and apparently rich." These Indians were "dressed in the
skins of deer, otter, and other animals."[20] At this point, the Jumano
guide chose to remain behind. It may have been the case that the
location of the mines was privileged information, not ordinarily
revealed to outsiders. The chief of the *rancheria* then led the

Spaniards through broken pine forest and across rivers, until they finally reached and explored the mines. Captain Farfan's account gives an enthusiastic account of the mineral vein and its outcroppings, to which he and his companions immediately laid claim, staking "from twenty-eight to thirty claims for themselves and for the companions who remained at the camp as a guide to the Señor governor."[21]

At the end of the day, Farfan assembled the Indians and interrogated them about the country and the course of the rivers they had crossed.

> They said and indicated by signs, joining them on the ground with a rod, that the said three rivers and two others which joined them further on, all united and passed through a gorge [the Grand Canyon] . . . and that beyond the gorge the river was extremely wide and copious, and that on the banks on both sides there were immense settlements of people. . . . Conditions described on this river and settlements were understood to extend to the sea, which they showed to be salty by dissolving a small quantity of salt in water . . .[22]

There follows more description of the setting of the mines, the richness of the land, the maize and other crops, and the beaver and other pelts seen in the *rancherias*. The return trip is not described.

Oñate's plans to go on from the Hopi villages, to explore the west as far as the sea, were interrupted by the arrival of news that Juan de Zaldivar, his elder nephew and second in command, had been killed in a battle at Acoma village. Acoma was subsequently subjected to a bloody punitive attack, led by Vicente de Zaldivar. Vicente then assumed the position of *maestre de campo*, the role in which he conducted the punitive expedition to the Jumano villages in the Salinas and later participated in Oñate's exploration of the Great Plains.

The Expedition to Quivira

The second and longer expedition into the Plains, led by Oñate, departed from San Gabriel in the third week of June, 1601. Between eighty and one hundred Spanish soldiers made up the exploration party, with five hundred or six hundred horses, mule-drawn provision wagons, and a number of Mexican and New Mexican Indian servants. Most of the Indians were evidently drawn from San Gabriel, and perhaps from neighboring villages in the Tewa province as well. An advance party waited at the pueblo of Galisteo until joined by the others; the whole group then proceeded through Galisteo Pass and marched eastward to cross the river which they called the San Buenaventura (the Salado, or Pecos). Three days later they reached the Rio Magdalena (Canadian), and followed it toward the east.

Such an expedition, to retrace Coronado's journey to Quivira, had been projected from the beginning. However, Oñate's curiosity about the north was also stimulated by the arrival in New Mexico of a Mexican Indian, Jusephe, who had been part of an illegal junket led by Captains Francisco Leyva de Bonilla and Antonio Gutierrez de Humaña. Little is known of this *entrada* aside from the accounts given by Jusephe, which indicated that, after exploring the Pueblos, the party had traveled north through the plains and reached the banks of a very large river—probably the Arkansas, but perhaps the Mississippi. On the way, the leaders quarreled, and Leyva was murdered. The fate of the other Spaniards is unknown. Several of the Indians fled toward Mexico. Jusephe, possibly the only survivor, lived among Apaches for a year or more, until he learned of the presence of the Spaniards in New Mexico, and went to seek them out. Jusephe's stories, perhaps fanciful, created a renewed anticipation of the discovery of new kingdoms and riches in Quivira. He accompanied Oñate's expedition, as a guide and translator.

While following the eastward course of the Canadian River, the Spaniards met and traded with several groups of Indians whom Oñate identified as Vaquero Apaches. These, he stated in his report, were "the ones who possess these plains."[23] They were first encountered about forty leagues from San Gabriel, and were seen over the next sixty leagues (roughly, between 100 and 250 miles east of New Mexico). Through Jusephe, they were able to communicate with the Apaches, who received them peacefully and gave them information about the country ahead.

> Along the way we met some Apache Indians, who follow the buffalo and kill them for their fat and tallow, which they sell and trade to the pueblo Indians for corn, blankets, and tobacco . . . These Indians live in *rancherias*, which they move from place to place. They pack their huts, which are made of hides, on some small dogs. They go about naked, and when it is cold they wrap themselves in the hides. . . . These natives do not grow anything, depending entirely for their food on the meat of the cattle they kill. They carry bows and arrows; they always met us peacefully, and we gave them presents, both coming and going.[24]

The expedition followed this river to the vicinity of the Antelope Hills, roughly four hundred miles from their point of departure.

They then turned to the northeast, crossing the North Canadian and Cimarron; they reached, but evidently did not cross, the Arkansas. Before that point, a second large group of Indians was encountered, near the Cimarron in a region now known as the Great Salt Plain. These were the people who are referred to in several accounts as Escanxaque (or Escansaque).

> . . . the *maese de campo* (Zaldivar) went ahead to explore with twelve
> soldiers, including this witness (Rodriguez). We discovered a very large
> *rancheria* that seemed to have five or six thousand Indian warriors,
> whom we named Escanxaques, because when we met them they raised
> their hands to the sun and then placed them on the breast as a sign of
> peace, saying "escanxaque." This same sign of peace was made by the
> Apaches. . . . The huts in which these Indians lived were round and
> made of branches and straw, most of them covered with buffalo hides.
> These people do not grow anything, as they live on fruit and meat.
> Their weapons are bows and arrows, small war clubs, and large leather
> shields which protect most of the body. Both men and women are
> painted with stripes. . . . They are tall and well proportioned, but dirty
> and naked. They wear buckskin and buffalo hides like the Apaches;
> some of the latter live among them and furnished us with this infor-
> mation, since the Mexican Indian Jusephe understood them.[25]

Here, the Spaniards learned of another large settlement, two days' travel farther on; these people, Zaldivar was told, were those who had killed the Spaniards (Humaña and his men). Many of the Escanxaques accompanied the party as they traveled on toward the Arkansas; they urged the Spaniards to attack this *"gran poblacion,"* who were their enemies.

The Spaniards were peacefully received, however. Oñate and his party were welcomed "in the Mexican language" by these Indians, who were identified, by those from San Gabriel, as *Jumanos*.[26] Influenced by the Escanxaques' accusations, Oñate eventually had several of the men of the settlement seized and held in chains, in an effort to secure the release of any surviving members of the Humaña party. Although these hostages were subsequently released, the rest of the villagers had fled. The Escanxaques then began to loot and burn the houses, and were finally driven away by the Spaniards.

> . . . the witness (Rodriguez) said that he entered the pueblo and many
> of its houses; that they were all built of poles stuck in the ground and
> covered with straw. They were wide at the base and narrow at the top
> like pavilions. Inside they had beds on the one side, built on poles; near

the top of the houses they had some terraces, to which they climbed on the outside by means of ladders that could be moved about. In these houses there was some corn, but not much, and some beans and a few calabashes. Near their houses but apart from them they had silos for their corn. We saw also ollas and jugs of clay and some primitive grinding stones, different from the metates and stones used . . . in New Spain . . .

. . . The people who were seen at this settlement, about four or five hundred men, were all well built, with stripes painted on their cheeks. All were stark naked, although in the houses we saw some skins ready for tanning. No women were seen. The men all carried bows and very short arrows, with good flint heads . . . The Indians around San Gabriel called these people from the settlement Jumanos; in fact, they gave this name to all of the Rayados.[27]

From the Escanxaques, the Spaniards had learned that there were many, much larger, settlements further to the north, located on many rivers. In the Jumano settlement itself, more than a thousand houses were counted, interspersed with small cornfields. The settled area continued toward the east, along the river. The Escanxaques warned Oñate not to proceed, since "the people who had withdrawn from this settlement had done so in order . . . to assemble their friends, who were so numerous that in the course of a whole day they would not be able to pass by their houses . . ."[28]

At this point, Oñate's army began to retrace their path toward the south. The soldiers had presented a petition demanding to return, while at the same time the officers became aware that the Escanxaques were preparing to attack. A five-hour battle was fought as the Spaniards forced their way through Escanxaque country: in the process, they captured several men, women, and children. Eventually, the women and girls were released; the men were held as guides, and released further along the way; and the boys were given over to the friars to be trained as translators. One man, called Miguel, who had been living as a captive among the Escanxaques, was subsequently taken by Zaldivar to Mexico, where he was interrogated in an official inquiry about the expedition to the north.[29]

The expedition to the north was one of the last achievements of Oñate's rule in New Mexico. He returned from this exploration to find that the colony had virtually collapsed, and that most of the Spanish colonists had fled to Santa Barbara. Because of this and other indications of the overall failure of the undertaking—which was, by this time, also apparent to the viceroy—much of the remaining period of his administration was spent in defending, justifying, and attempting to remedy the desperate straits of the colony.

Oñate finally resigned the governorship, and Pedro de Peralta assumed the position in 1609, under completely different conditions. Oñate had gone into the *tierra adentro* as an entrepreneur, investing his own wealth and working primarily for personal financial and political return. In 1609, New Mexico became a royal colony, financed by the crown and operated on a much reduced budget. The colony continued to be supported, primarily, in order to maintain a Spanish presence as a northern buffer for New Spain. There was also an obligation to minister to the fairly small number of Indian converts to Christianity. The increased degree of power given to the religious establishment in the colony is reflected, in later years, in chronic bickering, cross purposes, and sometimes outright warfare between religious and secular authorities in New Mexico.

The next news of Jumanos, in New Mexico and the South Plains, was found in church records from the 1620's, derived principally from the writings of a Franciscan priest, Alonso de Benavides.

6.

THE JUMANOS AT
THE DAWN OF HISTORY

These years prior to and just following the turn of the seventeenth century constitute the period of initial entry of explorers, colonists, and missionaries into the interior of North America north of Mexico. Firsthand accounts of the contacts between Spaniards and Indians give us our earliest view of the native peoples. However, these contacts did not necessarily give the Indians their first inklings of the approach of the Europeans. Well before the time of the Spaniards' arrival in their lands, the natives of the greater Southwest would have received early warnings of the invaders' presence. Then, inexorably, the advance parties began to arrive, following native highways; even though they withdrew, the conquest must have been anticipated.

The existence of an established network of highways, linking the Southwest with Mexico and with other regions of North America, has been inferred and can be projected far into the past. Prehistoric trade is evidenced by the wide distribution of artifacts of local and regional types, which clearly were transported great distances from their point of origin. It is in the documentary records of the sixteenth and early seventeenth centuries that some connection can be made between the archaeological evidences of extensive native trade and the actual behavior through which exchanges were carried out. A focus of attention on the Jumanos of the contact period, whose connection with trade is well documented, may contribute to understanding the dynamics of this picture, especially in its broader aspects.[1]

It is, for present purposes, fortunate that the early expeditions into the interior followed a number of different paths. This makes possible a more extensive survey than can be accomplished for the subsequent decades, when the territorial limits of the Spanish colony in New Mexico were established, routes of travel became more standardized, and activities were focused more on internal

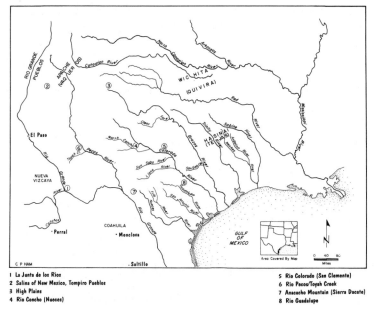

1 La Junta de los Rios
2 Salina of New Mexico, Tompiro Pueblos
3 High Plains
4 Rio Concho (Nueces)

5 Rio Colorado (San Clemente)
6 Rio Pecos/Toyah Creek
7 Anacacho Mountain (Sierra Dacate)
8 Rio Guadalupe

Map 6. Jumano locations, 1535–1700

problems than on exploration. It has been possible to obtain at least a sampling of several areas in which people identified as Jumanos, at various points in their history, are known to have been present.

La Junta to El Paso

At the time of the Rodriguez and Espejo expeditions, there were eight villages at La Junta, some of them with as many as two to three thousand people (Map 6, no. 1). This was an important farming region, the fields being located in the floodplain at the mouth of the Conchos, and along adjacent stream valleys. The term *Patarabuey* (Pataraguey, etc.) was applied early to the people living here. This term was evidently derogatory; Luxan indicated that it was coined by the slaveraiders who had, over the previous decade, already made this region a hunting ground for laborers for the fields and mines around Santa Barbara.[2] Espejo appears to have equated Patarabuey with Jumano; however he, like the other narrators, made it clear that there were two main population groups at La Junta, distinguished by language. One of these, the Abriaches (Gallegos' Cabris), predominated in certain villages on the lower Conchos and near La Junta de los Rios. The other, the Otomoacas (or

Amotomancos) also had large villages near the confluence, and were found in scattered small villages and *rancherias* extending several days' march northward, along the Rio del Norte. Espejo used the term *Jumano* for natives all the way through the river valley, between La Junta and El Paso del Norte. However, Luxan distinguished—from south to north—the Otomoacas, Caguates, and Tanpachoas. His narrative suggests that all of these were culturally similar and spoke similar dialects.

Both expeditions found many signs of trade at La Junta. There are numerous references to the people to the west (probably the Opata) and the north (the New Mexican Pueblos). Many buffalo hides from the Plains were found there, with indications that the village farming population at La Junta received these and other goods from "the men who hunted the buffalo." Modern anthropologists have disagreed in interpretation of the primary sources, some seeing the hunter-traders as part of the same population as the farmers, and others believing that these were completely separate groups. The people whom Luxan called Caguates, encountered upriver from La Junta, were less intensively agricultural and apparently more actively involved in hunting and trade than the Otomoaca and Abriaches. They can be identified as Cabeza de Vaca's "People of the Cows," the later Cibolos (or Cibolo-Jumanos); they may also be equated with the nomadic Jumanos whose comings and goings were remarked at La Junta.

These hunter-traders, who traveled north and east to the buffalo grounds in the summer, brought meat and hides, as well as other trade goods to La Junta. In exchange, they received agricultural and wild plant products, as well as crafts products and other goods. There is also an indication that they received, either directly or indirectly, goods from the Pueblos to the north. This would seem the most likely source for the blankets for which Espejo's men traded—along with buffalo hides, bows, and garden produce—before crossing the Conchos at La Junta on their return from the Plains.

Toyah Creek–Rio Pecos–Rio Concho

There are several early references to individuals and groups of people located along this route, who can be, either absolutely or inferentially, identified as Jumanos. The encounter that can be the most precisely localized—providing a point of reference for interpreting the others—is the meeting of the Espejo party with three individuals, some 120 leagues down the Rio Pecos from Pecos Pueblo. Luxan called these men *Jumanos*, and also commented on their close resemblance to the population at La Junta. There is a clear indication that the language was the same as, or very close to, that of the people on the Rio del Norte. Luxan's account indicates a series of Jumano settlements, both on Toyah Creek and on the road through the mountains, along which the Spaniards were led to La Junta (Map 6, no. 6). This is important, as explicit evidence of a demographic continuity between the Jumanos in the Plains and the cluster of villages at La Junta.

The Jumano guides were familiar with the course of the Pecos as far as its mouth, and knew the geographical relationship of the Pecos and Rio del Norte. They indicated that the terrain along the lower Pecos was difficult, and that the mountain route was shorter and easier. The road through the Davis Mountains followed by Espejo's party may well be identical with the route "by way of the mountains" which was noted—but not followed—by Cabeza de Vaca. It can therefore be assumed that the Indian occupants of the region were, at the earlier time, also Jumanos. Further, since Cabeza de Vaca indicated a relationship between the Indians at the eastern end of the mountain road and those further to the east, on the river which can be identified as the Concho or Colorado of Texas, a Jumano occupancy can be inferred for that region as well. The village on the Concho may have marked the eastern limit of Jumano occupancy in the proto-historic, pre-horse years. However, the orbit reached by Jumano trade could have been considerably broader.

Traveling north along the Rio Pecos in 1590, Castaño de Sosa recorded several contacts with Indians, and the sighting of numerous *rancherias* from which the residents had fled. The group referred to as *Tepehuan* (Depesguan or Tepelguan), who were found on the Pecos some distance below Toyah Creek, were probably Jumanos. Their *rancheria* was on a stretch of the river which forms a part of the Jumanos' route between the middle fork of the Concho and the trail through the Davis Mountains. Castaño noted other *rancherias*, mainly abandoned, and a party of Indians with loaded pack dogs, also apparently traveling along this route.

When Castaño's party passed alongside the foothills of the Guadalupe Mountains, they spotted fires on the slopes. They would, at this point, have been passing through Apache territory. In this region also, they found a pen or corral, most likely used by the Indians in hunting. Further upstream, past the mountainous country, there were no sightings of people until the environs of Pecos Pueblo were reached, though there were scattered traces of human activity, including burned grass, indicating the use of the Plains as hunting grounds. Although Castaño's account is sketchy, and the geographical locations can only be roughly inferred, it seems to mesh well with the information from earlier sources. It appears that, along the Rio Pecos, Jumano settlements were found south of the approximate site of Pecos, Texas. Beyond that point, there were indications of camps or *rancherias* in the mountains west of the river. The people living in that region, tentatively identified as Apaches, apparently chose to stay out of the sight of passing Spaniards. Neither Castaño nor any other early source reports traffic along this stretch of the Pecos.

Castaño de Sosa's route followed almost the entire length of the Pecos. For the lower river, below the point reached by Espejo, his journal is the only early source of information. It suggests that there must have been a sizeable area of Jumano occupancy there (though mainly by reference to abandoned *rancherias*).

The Salinas Region of New Mexico

The first indication of a Jumano presence within colonial New Mexico comes when three Jumano pueblos are listed in official documents of the conquest period. It would appear that most of the earlier expeditions which reached New Mexico either approached or passed through the Salinas region, and noted the existence of these outlying pueblos; however, there are no recorded visits to the communities themselves, prior to the founding of Oñate's colony. Although the Jumano pueblos are identified by name in the colonial records—Genobey (Xenopue), Quellotezei (Cueloce), and Pataotzei (Pataoce)—their exact locations, and their spatial and political relationships with one another, are never made clear. For administrative purposes, these three were grouped together with the pueblo of Abo. This grouping may be significant, since there are later indications that there was a substantial Jumano element in the population of Abo, although it is not named as a Jumano pueblo (Map 6, no. 2).

Scholes and Mera and more recently, Schroeder, have addressed the problem of the identity and affiliation of the Salinas pueblos.[3] The three Jumano Pueblos, all of which were abandoned toward the end of the seventeenth century, can be roughly matched with as many major archaeological sites in the Salinas region, east of the site identified as historic Abo. It has been established that the site now called Gran Quivira corresponds to the town which in the seventeenth century was often simply called *Las Humanas* (or Xumanas). This large community must have been one of the three named in the Oñate documents; it seems to have been the largest in the region, at least in the later years of its occupancy. This was probably Cueloce, the site at which the oaths of allegiance of the Jumano captains were taken in 1598.[4]

In the official proclamations of 1598, reference is made to the "three great pueblos of the Xumanas" (or Rayados); a few decades later, Las Humanas would be singled out by Benavides as "the great pueblo of the Xumanas." These Jumano communities were situated in the most arid of the settled regions of New Mexico, where annual rainfall averages less than ten inches, and where farming would have been precarious in the best of years. Only one major resource was abundant: salt. This was a valuable commodity, which was mined in the arid flatlands of the Estancia Valley and exported to other regions.

The region was always short of water. The town of Las Humanas, with perhaps three thousand people, had no access to permanent running water, and relied to a great extent on wells which were located a considerable distance away. The residents also built tanks, in which the meager supply of rain water was collected and stored. Obviously, the Jumano Pueblos were not well situated for farming. Their survival may have hinged on their status as trading centers, rather than on agricultural self-sufficiency. For local use and for trade, agricultural products from the fields along the Rio del Norte and its tributaries would have been imported. Las Humanas was also a collection center for the meat, hides, and other goods which were brought from the regions to the east. Thus, a substantial portion of the food supply for the resident population of communities in the Salinas region could have been drawn from sources external to the region—from the agricultural pueblos to the west, and from the plains to the east.

The drain which the Spanish colony imposed on the native economy had an immediate impact on native life throughout New Mexico. Taxes and levies absorbed any surplus production, impoverishing the standard of living of Indian households, and diverting many man-hours of labor from traditional occupations. Reserve supplies were soon depleted, and shortages were felt throughout the native villages. The occupation must have had a catastrophic effect in the Salinas region, since these communities produced no agricultural surplus, and probably were not even marginally self-sufficient. Spanish confiscation of surplus production in other regions would inevitably have meant famine in the Jumano communities, which lived—at least in part—through trade. The impact of the Spanish occupation may have been at its worst during Oñate's reign—or, at least, until the colonists became economically productive and

Spanish entrepreneurs became involved in trade. It has been noted that in the years immediately after the conquest efforts to extract tribute from the villages of the Tompiro province met with great resistance, and eventually with defiance. This defiance, in turn incurred harsh reprisals. The Jumanos of New Mexico gained a reputation for rebelliousness at this time. Eventually, however, some Spaniards would begin to deal in a practical way with native agencies, including the Jumanos of both Pueblos and Plains.

The Llano Estacado

The first explicit mention of Jumanos (Xumanas) in the plains east of New Mexico came in connection with Vicente de Zaldivar's exploring trip in 1598. Leading a company of men east from Pecos Pueblo, Zaldivar had initial encounters with Apache *Vaqueros*, some of whom requested Spanish aid in fighting their enemies, the Xumanas. It is clear that at this time the regions bordering the northern pueblos—from Taos to Pecos—were held by the Apaches, at least for the extent of the fifty leagues or so that Zaldivar traveled, along and south of the Canadian River. Later, Oñate's expedition to the north found the Apaches as much as one hundred leagues east of San Gabriel. On neither occasion did the explorers have direct contact with the Jumanos, and there is no indication of the location of their habitations in this region. However, Oñate's expedition did find a large settlement near the great bend of the Arkansas, of people who were called both *Jumanos* and *Rayados*.

The situation of 1598–1600 may be compared to that in the earlier period of exploration. As in Oñate's time, Coronado's explorations found one Indian nation, the Querechos, to be predominant in the plains east of Pecos Pueblo. It is generally conceded that the Querechos were Apaches, the same people later known as Vaqueros. Extending the parallel, it would seem that the opposing group, at the time of Coronado's expedition, the Teyas, were the precursors of the Jumanos of Oñate's era. The Teyas were already at war with the Querecho Apaches. Their identification as Jumanos draws important support from the fact that they recalled the visit of Cabeza de Vaca and his three companions, and indicated that this had occurred "further south, toward New Spain." The Teyas were evidently able to penetrate and cross Querecho territory, since they camped and wintered near some of the eastern Pueblos. Their camps or *rancherias* in the *barrancas*, or canyons, were located farther to the east than was reached by Oñate's expedition, fifty years later.

JUMANOS AT THE DAWN OF HISTORY

Quivira

Coronado's expedition passed through the territory of the Querechos (Apaches), and was guided to Quivira by the Teyas (Jumanos)
from the Llano Estacado of western Texas. *Quivira* was a name applied by the Spaniards to a region north of the Arkansas River, evidently encompassing a variety of peoples and languages. The accounts of the expedition remark on this cultural variety, though the
different groups are not distinguished by name.

Oñate's expedition passed through territory dominated by Vaquero Apaches in eastern New Mexico and Texas. Traveling beyond
the region covered by Zaldivar's earlier sortie, the Spaniards encountered Apache camps for two hundred miles or more. Comparing the locations indicated in the Coronado and Oñate documents,
it appears that by the later period the Apaches had gained ground,
having pushed further to the south and also established a wider
zone of control. The Apaches clearly dominated the trade at the
northern pueblos. This was roughly the same situation that would
be found by Salas, three decades later.

Some one hundred miles northeast of the Vaquero Apaches, Oñate
encountered the Escanxaques. The identity of this people has been
much debated. Hyde, looking both to location and, perhaps, to some
similarity in names, suggested that they could be identified with
the Cancey.[5] This is a name applied by French explorers, many
years later, to Apaches who lived near the Red and Canadian Rivers,
and who have been suggested as ancestors of the Kiowa Apaches.
However, other scholars prefer to identify the Escanxaques as Caddoans, suggesting, for example, that they may have been a Wichita
group on a seasonal hunting expedition. The latter opinion seems to
reflect a general conviction that the region north of the Arkansas
and its tributaries was occupied exclusively by Indians of the Caddoan linguistic grouping. Newcomb and Campbell, most recently,
have claimed that a close reading of the testimony given in 1602 at
an inquiry into the conduct of the Oñate expedition, makes it possible to link these Indians with a specific group, the Aguacanes.
They believe that this tribe, which was present in central Texas in
the 1680's, was Caddoan.[6] However, the same testimony, along with
Oñate's own narrative of the expedition, also contains information
which makes it seem doubtful that the Escanxaque—whether or
not they are identified with the Aquacane—were Caddoans; certainly, they were not Wichitas. They were antagonistic toward their
eastern neighbors, the Jumanos of the "large settlement," who were
allied with the tribes—presumably Wichitas—beyond the Arkansas

River. In fact, the Escanxaques indicated their hostility toward the entire alliance.

Witnesses' descriptions of the Escanxaques, their artifacts, clothing, and housing do not indicate a resemblance to the Wichitas in particular, nor Caddoans in general. All the witnesses indicated the Escanxaques to be a nomadic hunting people; they were "not a people who sowed or reaped, but they lived solely on the cattle."[7] This was not seasonal hunting, and the Escanxaques were said to be a people with no association with agriculture. They were evidently skilled nomads. Those who followed the Spaniards to the Arkansas "in a few hours quickly built a *rancheria* as well-established as the one left behind, which caused no little wonder to all."[8]

All the accounts make mention of the Escanxaque houses. Some of these "huts" were small, some were quite large; they were built of branches, and "some were covered with the tanned hides of the *cibola* cattle and shaped like the tents of the Apaches."[9] Oñate wrote that they "consisted of branches an *estado* and a half long placed in a circle . . . most of them were covered with tanned hides, which made them resemble tents."[10] These were evidently substantial but fairly crude tents, lacking the portable framework and sewn and fitted covering of the Vaquero Apaches' tipis, with which the Spaniards were already familiar.

There are several indications that the Escanxaques could have been, as Hyde suggested, a division of Apaches separate from the Vaqueros, or they may have been a group allied with the Vaqueros, perhaps a more distantly related Athabascan people. First, there are cultural resemblances. It is to the Vaquero Apaches that the witnesses repeatedly compared the Escanxaques, in their clothing, weapons, and demeanor: "They have the same characteristics as the Apaches."[11] According to one witness, the name which the Spaniards gave this people came from their greeting, which was *Escanxaque*, accompanied by raising the hands to the sun and then placing them on the breast. This, it is stated, was the same greeting used by the Apaches.[12]

Further, it is evident that the expedition found numerous Apaches living with the Escanxaques. This is stated repeatedly, along with the indication that Jusephe, since he knew the Apache language, was able to get information from this tribe. It is true that there was a difference between the Vaquero Apaches' language and that of the Escanxaques. However, this does not preclude their being Athabascan, or even Apachean. (Kiowa Apache is classified as a separate Athabascan language, not readily intelligible to the other Apache divisions.)

Oñate's expedition foundered among the Jumanos near the Arkansas. The accepted view is that these, too, were a Caddoan people, part of the Wichitas of Quivira. It was, in fact, the Spaniards' use of *Jumano* in reference to these people that led Scholes to his view that the term was applied loosely to people of different cultural identities, and was not the name of a specific ethnic group. However, it seems at least as reasonable to assume that this was simply another group of Plains Jumanos, related to those of New Mexico, La Junta, and other locations. This becomes more credible when we consider the overall pattern of Jumano culture, including their extensive nomadism, and realize that the dispersal of these groups may have been, at least in part, the result of their war with the Apaches in the South Plains. There is an obvious parallel between the location of this Jumano group on the southern edge of Quivira, and the equally marginal situation of those at La Junta and on the eastern frontier of New Mexico.

There are additional details that suggest that the Jumanos of the *gran poblacion* were a separate people with the mobility and wide geographical distribution of the Jumanos in general. First there is the fact that, according to one witness, some members of this group spoke the "Mexican" (Nahuatl) language: they "told us in the Mexican language, which was clearly understood, that we should wait because the women were grinding the corn."[13] This is consistent with other indications, in both earlier and later sources, of Jumano contacts with Mexico.

Second, it was the Tewa Indians from San Gabriel who identified the people of this settlement as Jumanos; this must indicate a close resemblance to the Jumanos (also called Rayados) in New Mexico, with whom the Tewas were familiar. Rodriguez' observation that "thus they call all the Rayados" has been read by Scholes and others as an indication that painted people, in general, could be called *Jumanos.* However, in the entire body of testimony concerning the expedition, the term was used, by this witness and others, only in reference to this specific group and to those in the Tompiro Pueblos.[14]

West of New Mexico

There are other Spanish accounts of probable or possible encounters with Jumanos in the early period. Combined with those already discussed, the evidence is sufficient to indicate that, even though the overall territorial range of their wanderings may not have been as great as in the following century, the Jumanos were a widespread and highly peripatetic people at the dawn of history. The account of

Farfan's expedition to the mines indicated that there were Jumano *rancherias*—perhaps permanent, but more likely semi-permanent or seasonal—at a location near the Verde River (south of the site of Flagstaff, Arizona) on a main trail west from Hopi mesas. The prospecting party made contact with these Jumanos, who provided a guide to lead them to the mining area and put them in touch with the Indians who worked the mines. It should be noted that the Jumanos were not, themselves, involved in mining; however, it would seem that they had important trade contacts here. They were optimally situated to obtain the powdered ores which were used as pigments for body painting, textile work, and other purposes. These mineral pigments were widely traded throughout the Southwest and Plains.

PART TWO

JUMANO CHRONOLOGY, 1610–1685

FRANCISCANS AND INDIANS IN NEW MEXICO

7.

NEW MEXICO IN THE 1620'S

At the time of the Spanish conquest, church and secular authorities had worked together in founding the colony of New Mexico. The conquerors divided the Indian villages into eight administrative provinces, each of them assigned to the spiritual care of one of the original group of Franciscan priests. However, through the first two decades of the century there was little missionary activity in the outlying pueblos, and apparently none at all in the plains to the east.

Fray Francisco de San Miguel, posted to Pecos Pueblo in September of 1598, was assigned custodianship over a huge and largely unexplored area which included Pecos Pueblo and the neighboring Galisteo basin, the Apaches beyond the Pecos River, and all of the pueblos located east of the Manzano mountains. Fray San Miguel remained in residence at Pecos for less than two months, returning to the capital, San Juan, in December of the same year. This move was part of a general consolidation and retrenchment of the Spanish colony, following the uprising and the severe reprisals taken at the pueblo of Acoma.

Aside from exploring parties and punitive military expeditions led by Oñate and his officers, the activities of the colonists remained largely confined to the Tewa and Keresan villages in the upper valley of the Rio del Norte. Within this limited arena, missions were established in several villages: San Juan and San Gabriel, the earliest centers of Spanish settlement; Santo Domingo, which became the ecclesiastical headquarters for the colony; and a few others. Fray San Miguel was relocated from Pecos to San Ildefonso, a Tewa community a few leagues downriver from Santa Fe. From there, it is very doubtful that he or any other priests journeyed as far as the remote *visitas* beyond the mountains. The colonists feared the vengeance of the Indians, and the friars, evidently, saw little hope of success in their missionary activities as long as military rule was so severe that the resentment of the natives was high.

After Oñate's resignation in 1609 and the subsequent reorganization of the colony under Pedro de Peralta, budgetary and personnel reductions were necessary in both the government and the missionary establishment. The relative position of the religious order, however, became stronger. The chief justification for maintaining the colony was now the continuation and safeguarding of the missionary enterprise. The Franciscan order was maintained in New Mexico at a great expense to the Spanish crown, and results, in the form of conversions and other evidences of devotion to the faith, were needed to justify that expense.

An upsurge in missionary activity was under way, and new contingents of religious workers began arriving—ten friars came in 1612, an additional seven in 1616, and still more in the years after 1620. New missions were built, including those at San Felipe, Galisteo, and Isleta, which became the southernmost of the missionized pueblos. In 1613, the first permanent mission was established east of the Manzano Mountains, in the village of Chilili; the priest stationed there, Fray Alonso Peiñado, may have had some contact with the Tompiros and Jumanos of the distant Salinas region. The mission at Pecos was reestablished; the construction of a new church of monumental proportions, reputed to be the largest and most beautiful in the colony, began in 1621.

An era of vigorous missionizing was ushered in with the arrival of Alonso de Benavides bearing a dual appointment as Custodian (*padre custodio*) of the Franciscan order in New Mexico and Agent of the Inquisition. Benavides was a man of tremendous energy and missionary zeal; he was to become the first active promoter and publicist for the New Mexican colony. Benavides brought a dozen new priests with him when he came from Mexico in 1626: three years later, another group of twenty-nine arrived, recruited by Fray Estevan de Perea, who was Benavides' successor as Custodian.

During the decade of the 1620's, many tendencies which were already visible in the early days of the colony became even more pronounced. The most obvious of these is perhaps the strong position of the Franciscan order, which grew even more powerful. Along with this, there was a rivalry—or downright hostility—between church and state, which appears to have increased in the reorganized colony. In one historian's estimation, "the single most notorious feature of life in colonial New Mexico was the war between the governors and the Franciscans."[1]

[The] Spaniards serve as escorts to us, as well as to the Christian Indians; were it not for this, the barbarians [Apaches] and those who have not yet been converted would have eaten us alive and also the Christian Indians. So great is the fear that God has instilled in them of these few Spaniards that they do not dare to come near where they are.[2]

Governor Peralta's first responsibility had been the planning of a new town, Santa Fe, which became not only the colonial capital, but also the single real population center for the Spanish colonists. Once Santa Fe was founded, the colonists were, for the first time, able to move out of the pueblos that had been requisitioned from the Indians, and to begin building their own homes. Fields were laid out and crops planted. The small group of settlers who remained in the colony after Oñate's departure became self-supporting, to a degree. The reduction in their numbers relieved, for a time, the pressure on the native economy. New laws protected the native, at least in theory, against unreasonable infringement on their persons and property. Tension between native and Spanish population may have been eased somewhat.

As time went on, however, many other causes of tension arose. Thirty-five colonists were granted *encomiendas*, which meant that they could levy tribute, in goods and labor, from Indians under their jurisdiction. The government continued to tax, and the missionaries required labor and sustenance from their converts—an increasing burden as the number of priests and missions grew. Church and state often had conflicting interests, and made conflicting demands on both colonists and natives who were frequently forced to take partisan positions.

The impact of this rivalry can be imagined. There was, for example, an ongoing struggle for power between Governor Peralta and the irascible and contentious Fray Diego Ordoñez. Ordoñez at one time excommunicated Peralta and hurled his pew from the church into the street, and another time had him arrested and publicly displayed in chains. Ordoñez arrogated to himself both religious and civil authority over the Indian pueblos, and conducted trials and executions. Ordoñez' actions finally brought intervention by the Crown, and new regulations were issued in an attempt to put limits on the power of the Franciscans. However, such abuse continued for decades under successive office-holders uncontrolled from abroad. None of his immediate successors, at least, was as combative as Fray Diego.

A large part of the rivalry between civil and religious authorities focused, and directly impinged, on the Indian population. The Indians, especially those who lived in the central area of Spanish settlement, were subject to taxation, work levies, conscription, and confiscation of their goods and resources.

Governors and lower officials were often corrupt. The great distance the appointed officials had to travel, from Mexico to Santa Fe, and the financial burden of undertaking the term of service in the distant colony, led many to attempt to enrich themselves in the process. It was commonplace, for example, for office-holders to deal illegally in buffalo pelts, piñon nuts, textiles, salt, and other goods; these goods were processed or produced with native labor, shipped south on the official supply trains, and sold in Mexico.[3]

In later years of the colony, wagons were also built and outfitted in New Mexico for this trip; the Indian workers recruited to accompany the trains were sometimes left stranded in Mexico, with no provision for their return home. Native labor was conscripted for these and other private enterprises. Indian children could be taken from their homes, on the pretext that they were orphans, and pressed into service in the colonists' households. There were also numerous slaves, usually captives acquired from the Apaches and other tribes outside the Pueblo area. Some of these were held in New Mexico, but most were transported south and sold in Mexico.

> This [Tewa] nation suffered great famines for lack of water for irrigating their lands, and Father Fray Andres Baptista, great minister versed in the language of this nation, industriously got water for them from the Rio del Norte, with which they irrigate their lands, and now they live in plenty. He also founded for them in the pueblo of San Ildefonso a convent and church, very spacious and beautiful. He has them well taught and trained in all the crafts and arts. Three other convents have been founded in this nation . . . The church of the pueblo of Santa Clara I [Benavides] founded myself, and, as I am the commissary of the Inquisition, these Teoas Indians prided themselves that I lived among them, and they painted the coat of arms of the Inquisition in the church of the pueblo of Santa Clara . . . since they did not wish any other church to have it.[4]

The Franciscans were, by the terms of the charter given their order, entitled to the use of native labor in building and maintaining the churches and other properties, and providing for their own needs. They also initiated agricultural projects and established workshops for training their charges in various skills and in occupations such as carpentry and cabinetmaking. In some cases, the training projects developed into flourishing enterprises, and the religious order profited at the natives' expense. However, for the most part, such works were apparently undertaken with good intentions, to benefit—as the priests saw it—the Indian people. In many cases, no doubt, they did so, giving Indian craftsmen and their families a new niche in the growing colonial society.

> . . . Once the Indians have received holy baptism, they become so do-
> mestic that they live with great propriety. Hardly do they hear the bell
> calling to mass before they hasten to the church. . . . They attend mass
> and hear the sermon with great reverence. . . . When they come to con-
> fession they bring their sins, well studied, on a knotted string . . . and,
> in all humility, they submit to the penances imposed on them. . . .
> When they fall sick, they at once hasten to confess, and they have great
> faith and confidence in the priest merely laying his hands upon their
> heads. They are very subservient to him . . .
> They all assist in a body in the building of the churches with all good
> will, as can be seen by the many we have built, all spacious and neat.
> The first of their fruits they offer to the church in all reverence and
> good will. Lastly, they are all very happy and recognize the blindness of
> idolatry from which they have emerged and the blessings they enjoy in
> being the children of the church. . . .[5]

Needless to say, the demands of government and private interests for Indian labor often outraged the missionary priests. The gover-nors and their agents, for their part, sometimes countermanded the church's authority, drafting Indian workers for their own undertak-ings. The Indians, especially in marginal regions such as the Sali-nas, were hard-pressed to eke out a living before the Spaniards ar-rived, and were now put in a very difficult position vis-à-vis these conflicting claims on their persons, labor, and lands.

The situation, however, was not understood by any of the parties involved simply in terms of man-hours or profit and loss figures; from any point of view, it had a moral dimension. Even though some individuals were able to adapt to and even prosper in the colo-nial society, most Indians must have resented the Spaniards' en-croachments, especially as time went by and the social hierarchy became rigid.

The church's position was evangelical and paternalistic; the friars considered the Indians to be childlike but sinful beings. They were to be saved from perdition through baptism and, that accomplished, their way of life was to be transformed. The implied contract be-tween priests and natives was one of protection and guidance in ex-change for belief, obedience, and proper behavior. By contrast, many colonists, whether officials or private citizens, took a more *laissez faire* attitude in relation to the Indians' spiritual lives, and were perfectly willing to tolerate their traditional cultural and religious practices as long as business could be conducted. If trade brought them profits through the sale of buffalo skins, or native captives to use as slaves, they were willing to overlook standards of dress or etiquette which were indecorous by Spanish standards, and they could tolerate religious practices which the priests denounced as *hechizeria* (sorcery). They undoubtedly resented the activities of the church which required the time and labor of the Indians.

The religious and secular branches of the colony continued to operate at cross-purposes throughout the century, until the colony itself was destroyed in the revolt of 1680.

> . . . the Apaches surround the . . . [Pueblo] nations on all sides and have continuous wars with them.[6]

Within the framework of the imposed colonial system, there remained old problems of relations between Indian villages and tribes. At times, the sedentary townsfolk of New Mexico traded and dealt peacefully with the Apache Vaqueros, but they were often at odds. The numerical strength and territorial demands of the Apaches were evidently on the rise when the Spanish conquerors came into the Southwest. With the strain which the colonists put on the food supply of the region, the Pueblo farmers had little or no surplus corn and other agricultural produce to offer the Apache hunters of the plains. The pressure on the native economy, which fueled the resentments of the Pueblos against the Spaniards, also led to an increase in tensions between villages, and an increase in Apache raids along the frontiers of New Mexico. Ironically, this had the effect of tightening the relationship between Indians and Spaniards within the colony, since Spanish arms were available in defense of the Indian villages.

Some of the material goods which eventually came into their possession, directly or indirectly, from dealings with the Spaniards—tools, weapons, and especially livestock and horses—increased the mobility of the *indios barbaros*. The goods were, first, a motivation and, second, the means which inevitably led to an increase in the frequency and destructiveness of the border warfare. Such incidents affected the colonists as well as the Indians. As the numbers of the colonists increased, their sheep, cattle, horses, farm produce, and household goods were prizes tempting to the Apaches on the margins of the colony.

The numerous factionalisms and cabals within the Pueblo communities may have had roots in the pre-Spanish period, but they were certainly exacerbated by the Spanish presence. The activities of the missionaries, and the favoritism shown toward those who professed Christianity, were the basis for schisms within or between Indian groups. The existing jealousies led to power struggles between Christians and traditionalists, progressives and conservatives. In New Mexico, there were early signs of friction between the central provinces, including the Tewa, who lived and worked most closely with, and made the greatest accommodations to, the Spanish colony and outlying groups, such as the far western Hopi and the easternmost villages of Taos, Pecos, and Picuries.

Within the central Rio Grande villages, and, as Spanish rule continued, throughout most of the native communities of New Mexico, a type of compromise evolved. On the one hand, there was surface conformity with the administrative structure imposed by the Spaniards and compliance with the religious practices and other dictates of the Catholic priests. At the same time, the Indians covertly continued to practice traditional ceremonies, and to maintain a shadow government of traditional leaders. Aspects of this kind of duality still remain in Pueblo communities. This has sometimes been seen as a source of cultural stability, but it is also a point of stress to the community substructure and a double burden of responsibility on community leaders.

The antagonisms which developed between central and marginal Pueblo groups were complemented by patterns of trade and economic and political alliances. The Apache trade gained increasing economic importance. At the beginning of the colonial period, this trade was established only at peripheral northern Pueblos. These communities at times made common cause with their Apache neighbors in opposing colonial rule; the Apaches would, eventually, provide sanctuary for many disaffected individuals and families who fled the rule of the Spaniards.

> Among the pueblos of this [Tompiro] nation there is a large one
> which must have three thousand souls; it is called Xumanas, because
> this nation often comes there to trade and barter.[7]

In colonial New Mexico the Jumanos were long-time trading partners and allies of certain Pueblo groups, and also long-time enemies of the Apaches. Before Apaches invaded the southern plains, the Jumanos had been the most prominent group in the territory east of the Pueblos. They hunted bison in the Plains and had trading partners in the eastern villages, from north to south. Challenged and eventually driven from the northern part of their hunting range, they also lost contact with the northernmost villages, Taos and

Picuries, early in the century. By the 1620's, the Jumanos had also ceased to trade at Pecos Pueblo, but they were still to be found in southern villages. During this period, the Salinas area—with its "great pueblo of the Xumanas"—was the gateway for Jumano traders, who had by that time found a new market for their goods in the Spanish community (Map 6, no. 2).

> I cannot refrain from telling about the amusing remarks of an old sorcerer (native priest) who opposed me (Benavides). I was in the middle of the plaza [of Xumanas pueblo], preaching to numerous persons assembled there, and this old sorcerer, realizing that my arguments were having some effect on the audience, descended from a corridor with an infuriated and wicked disposition, and said to me: "You Christians are crazy; you desire and pretend that this pueblo shall also be crazy." I asked him in what respect we were crazy. He had been, no doubt, in some Christian pueblo during Holy week when they were flagellating themselves in procession, and thus he answered me: "How are you crazy? You go through the streets in groups, flagellating yourselves, and it is not well that the people of this pueblo should commit such madness as spilling their own blood by scourging themselves." When he saw that I laughed, as did those around me, he rushed out of the pueblo, saying that he did not wish to be crazy . . .[8]

The exact nature of the Jumano presence in the Salinas area of New Mexico has been a point of disagreement among historians and anthropologists. A traditional position, maintained by Hodge and others, held that this was simply an area of Jumano trade only, not of residence. However, the records of the Oñate conquest give clear evidence of the existence of the three Jumano pueblos of Cueloce, Genobuey, and Patoece; Abo was also partly Jumano in population. Three decades later, Benavides' *Memorial of 1630* confirmed the Jumano presence in this area. However, Benavides' references have seemed ambiguous to some scholars, and actually provided one of the bases for Hodge's interpretation.

On the other hand, Benavides left no doubt that Jumanos were to be found in large numbers in the plains, at a distance of more than one hundred leagues from the eastern pueblos, and separated from New Mexico by a zone dominated by the Apaches. Thus, in both the contact period and the 1620's, there are references to village-dwelling and plains-dwelling populations, both called by some form of the term *Jumano*. The exact relationship between the two divisions has remained unclear—were they actually a single population, residentially (or seasonally) divided between the New Mexican villages and the *rancherias* in the plains, or were they separate but related groups? The situation in and east of New Mexico seems to have been roughly parallel to that at La Junta de los Rios. Here, also, there existed a complementary relationship between sedentary village residents and a semi-nomadic population, which moved seasonally between the villages and their *rancherias* and hunting grounds in the plains.

In New Mexico Jumanos and Apaches were enemies engaged in a chronic war. It appears that the Apaches had moved into a part of what had been formerly an uninterrupted Jumano territory east of the pueblos, thus widely separating the two Jumano divisions. During this early period, it can be inferred that there was a rough division or factionalism between a northern group of pueblos (Taos, Picuries, Pecos, and perhaps Jemez) which traded with and could be considered at least loosely allied with the Apache Vaqueros, and others (Tewa, Tiwa, Keres, and Piro) who maintained a closer connection with the Jumanos. Now as earlier, the Jumanos were allied on their east through trade with a number of tribes, Caddoans and others.

The Jumanos and their Pueblo allies also seem to have had a closer and more cooperative relationship with the Spanish colony than was characteristic of the northern faction. The Spaniards, for their part, were desirous of using the Jumanos as a point of contact for economic and diplomatic relations with, and missionizing among, the distant Caddoans. Spain would avoid, however, an outright formal alliance with the Jumanos, which would have put them irrevocably at odds with the Apaches. The Spanish colonial government was obliged to maintain peaceful relations with all of these native peoples; this was necessary for the success of the missionary endeavors and for the survival and well-being of the colonists. Certainly, the Crown could not afford an outright war against the Apaches.

Almost all of the references to the Jumanos in historical sources of the early seventeenth century concern New Mexico and the regions to the east of the colony. Oñate had opened a new road—a segment of the future Camino Real—across the desert of northern Chihuahua, bypassing the Rio del Norte below El Paso. Little more is known about the Indians between El Paso and La Junta de los Rios, on the lower Pecos, or along the Colorado, until the last decades of the century.

8.

FRAY JUAN DE SALAS' MISSION TO THE JUMANOS

The Franciscan custodian Alonso de Benavides is the author of two important documents which are essential sources of information about the Spanish borderlands in the early seventeenth century, and about the Jumanos in particular. The *Memorial of 1630* was prepared as a report on New Mexico and its missions during his years in the colony.[1] Following the completion of his term of service, Benavides traveled to Spain; there, the report was first presented to the superior of the Franciscan order, then transmitted to King Philip IV. The longer and more polished *Memorial of 1634* was written in Europe for submission to Pope Urban VIII.[2]

Alonso de Benavides

Benavides was born in the Azores some time before 1580; the exact date of his birth is not known, but in 1609 he indicated that he was more than thirty years of age. In 1598, he traveled to Mexico, where he entered the priesthood. He rose quickly through a series of ecclesiastical positions and in October of 1623 was appointed to New Mexico as Custodian of the Franciscan Order and Agent of the Inquisition.

The *Memorial of 1630* describes the route over which Benavides traveled between San Bartolome, in Nueva Vizcaya, and Santa Fe; it notes climate, resources, and native peoples en route and in New Mexico, and outlines, in particular, the accomplishments of the Franciscan friars and the state of the missionary enterprise.

On the way north, accompanying the supply train which made the six-month-long trip at three-year intervals, Benavides noted the Rio Conchos as the dividing line between New Spain (Mexico) and New Mexico. Traveling the Camino Real, he took note of the Manso Indians, the southernmost of the New Mexican tribes. These Indians inhabited the region around El Paso—"since they are at the

crossing . . . (they) have always to be encountered." Benavides indicated that the name *Manso* was derived from the Spanish (*manso*,
"tame" or "peaceable"). These people were in his judgment "very
much disposed" to conversion, and "pained that they have not Religious to instruct them . . . like the other nations."[3] The Mansos,
whose language is undocumented, became culturally extinct early
in the nineteenth century. They claimed a tradition of kinship with
the southern Pueblos of New Mexico.

Benavides advocated the construction of missions for the Mansos,
as part of a plan to make the road between Mexico and the northern
colony less hazardous. Perhaps as a direct consequence of his urging, they were reduced some years later, with the founding of the
mission Nuestra Señora de Guadalupe de los Mansos near El Paso.
Benavides also suggested the development of El Paso, as a midway
stopover for the traffic between San Bartolome and Santa Fe. The
site came to play an increasingly important role in relation to Spanish New Mexico, even prior to the Pueblo Rebellion of 1680; at that
time, it became the temporary capitol of the colony.

In New Mexico, the twelve friars who accompanied Fray Alonso
on the trip north were assigned to posts, most of them in the southern pueblos which had not, until that time, been intensively missionized. Benavides himself became actively engaged in missionary
work in the provinces of the Piros and Tompiros: the second of
these included the three Jumano pueblos. By the end of his term as
Custodian, there were six mission churches in the Tompiro province. All of the Tompiros, he claimed, were converted, and he personally "began the conversion of the great pueblo of the Xumanos"
in 1627. The church in this pueblo was "dedicated to the glorious
San Isidro, because of having [begun] . . . the conversion on his
day."[4] Besides his work in the pueblos, Benavides threw his energies
into attempted conversion of the Apaches. He described the missionary efforts in some detail, claiming success in converting chiefs
of several Apache bands. A Captain Quinia of the northern Apache
was baptized, though his people then rebelled; Sanaba, of the Gila
Apache, was converted, and a priest dispatched to his territory.
And Benavides claimed personally to have pacified the "Apaches of
Navajo."[5]

The tone of Benavides' writing conveys what must have been the
prevailing impression of the strength of the Apaches, who appeared
to hem in the New Mexican pueblos.

> . . . the pueblos of New Mexico . . . are on the banks of the Rio del
> Norte, in a stretch of a hundred leagues, on one and the other bank. All

of which are surrounded on all sides by the huge Apache nation. And without exaggeration, it alone has more people than all the nations of New Spain together, even including the Mexican . . . Commencing at the beginning of it—which, as we come to New Mexico, is the province of the Apaches of the Perillo, it [the Apache country] runs on this side to the west as far as the South Sea [the Pacific] and in it are more than three hundred leagues; and continues up to the North without our having found the end in that direction, and hits the strait of Anian [the mythical Northwest Passage]. And circling New Mexico with this nation, to the side of the East, it widens more than a hundred leagues, until it returns to strike again the province of the Perillo; making in this (circuit) more than three hundred leagues of circumference for New Mexico on its frontiers.[6]

Benavides' estimates of numbers and geographical expanse are, despite his disclaimer, greatly exaggerated. The sense that New Mexico was surrounded by a seemingly limitless territory overrun by Apache bands is perhaps more accurate. But although he indicated that the Apaches held the South Plains along the entire eastern frontier, it would seem that they were not at that time in complete and exclusive control. The Plains Jumanos were still in trading contact with the eastern Tompiros, and are also known to have made several visits to the Franciscan mission at Isleta.

Toward the end of the *Memorial of 1630*, there is an account of the journey of two missionary friars—Juan de Salas and Diego Lopez—who in 1629 crossed through the country of the Vaqueros Apaches to visit a Jumano outpost in the High Plains of Texas. This is an important source of information on the Jumanos; it also reveals one of the most famous mysteries in the history of the Church in the New World. Theologians and historians have made many claims and counterclaims about the Jumanos' encounter with the "Lady in Blue."

The "Miraculous Conversion" of the Jumanos

. . . (G)oing forth from the town . . . of Santa Fe, the center of New Mexico . . . traversing the Apache nation of the Vaqueros for more than a hundred and twelve leagues, one comes to hit upon the Xumana nation. Since its conversion was so miraculous, it is proper to tell how it happened . . .[7]

According to Benavides, for several years the Jumanos of the Plains had been importuning Juan de Salas, a missionary among the

Tompiros and Salineros (the Tompiro Jumanos) to come and live among them. The custodian was unable to authorize this, because of a shortage of missionary staff; but when a number of new religious workers arrived in the colony in 1629, Father Salas and Fray Diego Lopez were "immediately dispatched," with some of the Jumanos to serve as their guides.[8] Before they left, however, the Indians were asked to explain their desire for missionaries.

> . . . [W]e asked the Indians to tell us the reason why they were with so much concern petitioning us for baptism, and for Religious to go and indoctrinate them? They replied that a woman like that one whom we had there painted—which was a picture of Mother Luisa de Carrion— used to preach to each one of them in their own tongue, telling them that they should come to summon the Fathers to instruct and baptize them, and that they should do it without delay. And . . . that the woman who preached to them was dressed precisely . . . like her who was painted there; but that she was young and beautiful . . .[9]

As the party of priests and Indians made their way across the plains, according to Benavides, the "Demon" (Satan) caused the lakes in their vicinity to dry up and the herd of buffalo to flee. Through the "Indian sorcerers" (medicine men or shamans), he "spread the word that the Religious whom they had summoned would not come." Their "captains" (chiefs) then made the decision "that they should strike their tents to go the next day at dawn." However, at the break of day, "the Holy Woman (*Santa*) spoke to each one of them individually, and told them that they should not go, for already the Religious were drawing near."[10] Twelve Jumano "captains" went out to look for the priests, and on the third day they found them. On their return, accompanying the priests, the Jumanos ". . . came out to meet them in procession, with two Crosses in front, as they were well instructed by heaven."[11]

The knowledge that the Jumanos displayed of proper religious behavior much impressed the two friars and the accompanying soldiers; to Benavides, this was evidence of the influence of the Holy Woman. When the priests took out their crucifixes, the Indians came forth to ". . . kiss and to venerate them, as if they were very old Christians."[12] A crowd of "more than ten thousand souls" had gathered, and Fray Juan de Salas told those who wished to become Christians to lift their arms; "with one great cry all lifted their arms, rising to their feet, asked for the holy baptism." The mothers even lifted the arms of their babies, "and held them upward, begging aloud for holy baptism for them."[13]

Fathers Salas and Lopez remained among the Jumanos for several days, preaching and instructing. During this time, messengers came to invite the friars to visit the neighboring nations, claiming that "the Holy Woman also had been there, preaching to them."[14] At this point, according to Benavides, the decision was made that since the "harvest was much and the laborers few, and since the people were disposed to settle down and build their churches," the priests would return to New Mexico to get assistance. Fray Salas brought the Indians together and told them that "until he returned, they should gather every day . . . to pray to a Cross which they had set up there upon a pedestal. . . ."[15] However, before leaving, the priests were implored to heal the sick; the mass healing session which followed seems quite similar to the curing rituals practiced by Cabeza de Vaca.

> . . . [I]t appears that God permitted that at this season there should be so many sick, upon whom he might well employ His divine pity. For, it being three o'clock in the afternoon when they commenced, they had to bring the sick all the afternoon, all the night, and the next day until ten o'clock. And one of the religious on one side and the other on the other, by only making the sign of the cross and saying the Gospel of St. Luke . . . and the prayer of Our Lady . . . and that of Our Father St. Francis . . . instantly they rose up cured. . . .[16]

Various neighbors of the Jumanos—the Iapes, Xabatoas, and the distant Kingdom of Quivira and the Aixaos—sent ambassadors to meet with the friars and ask for baptism and missions. They claimed that they, also, had been visited by the Holy Woman.[17] Some of these Indians accompanied Salas and Lopez, and presented their case in New Mexico. "Without fail," Benavides concludes, "they [the Friars] must by now have gone in and commenced to work in the vineyard of the Lord."[18]

Benavides in Spain

The sequence of events just described took place toward the end of Alonso de Benavides' tenure in New Mexico. It is evident that, in the autumn of 1629, he left New Mexico without knowing the outcome of Fray Juan de Salas' mission to the Jumanos, although he anticipated its successful completion. He arrived in Mexico in March of the following year, to ". . . report to the viceroy and the reverend prelates of the more notable and unusual things that were happening in their holy custodia."[19] Surely Benavides had in mind, perhaps above all other "unusual things," the recent events among the Jumanos. He immediately sought and received permission to sail for Spain, ". . . to inform his Majesty . . . and our father general."[20] He arrived in Madrid in August of 1630.

In Spain, the father general (head) of the Franciscan order transmitted the *Memorial* to King Philip IV. The report was lucidly written, conveying the author's boundless energy and optimism, and filled with lively anecdotes about the natives of New Mexico—including the story of the "miraculous conversion of the Xumanas." It was an overnight success; the four hundred copies of the first printing were soon exhausted, and a second printing was ordered. At this time, in seventeenth-century Madrid, Benavides' *Memorial* was a best-seller, and the Jumanos were one of the most celebrated peoples of all New Spain!

Besides the presentation of his *Memorial* to the superiors of his order and to the king, Benavides arrived in Spain with definite objectives in mind. He came to the royal court to promote and to raise awareness of New Mexico, its resources, and its potential for development. He obviously aimed to secure increased support for the colony. He also hoped, in Rome, to secure a bishopric, and personally aspired to appointment to that office. The story of the conversion of the Jumanos—presented as miraculous, and hinting that more wonders were yet to come—was an important part of his campaign to achieve these objectives.

The Travels of Mother Maria de Agreda

In Spain, Benavides was able to add to the growing sense of awe surrounding the "miraculous conversion." A letter which he dispatched to the Franciscans in New Mexico told of a new discovery: a Spanish nun, Mother Maria de Jesus of the town of Agreda, had reported "visions" of repeated visits to North America; she claimed to have preached to and converted the Indians of New Mexico, including the Jumanos![21] Was this the answer to the mystery?

Benavides hurried to Agreda to confront Mother Maria, armed with an order of obedience signed by the father general, which required that the nun respond to his questions. His accounts of the interview did much to establish the credulity of her claims and, in turn, served Benavides well in his own efforts to focus attention on the Franciscans' activities in New Mexico and its environs. As a result, the name of Mother Maria de Agreda is firmly linked with that region and with the legend of the "Lady in Blue."

Maria de Agreda was a cloistered nun of the Franciscan order known as the Poor Clares. Still in her twenties at the time of the interview with Benavides, she was the abbess of a small convent in what had been her family home. In the course of her life she was to become a well-known Christian mystic, a prolific writer, and a person of considerable political influence as a confidante of King Philip IV.

A field of endeavor with which Mother Maria was identified throughout her life was the encouragement of missionary activity. She frequently claimed that God had revealed to her His desire for conversion of the American Indians, and she encouraged the Franciscans to take the lead in this mission. Her own mystical "journeys" to North America, undertaken in a state of trance, can be seen as a projection of this desire: although physically cloistered in Spain, she was an avid—though vicarious—participant in the missionary work of her male counterparts.

The life of Maria de Agreda is best known through an official biography written soon after her death by Fray Joseph Ximenez Samaniego; it gives a vivid depiction of the onset of her visionary experiences.

> . . . On one occasion . . . the Lord . . . transported her in an ecstasy. Without perceiving the means, it seemed to her that she was in another and different region and climate, and in the midst of . . . Indians who, on other occasions, had manifested themselves to her by means of disembodied visions. It seemed that . . . she saw them with her own eyes, and noted the temperature of the land. . . . Preaching her faith to those people, it seemed to her that she was actually preaching . . . in her own Spanish language; and that Indians understood her as if it were their own . . . and that the Indians were converted and she catechized them . . .[22]

After Mother Maria had described experiences of this sort, recounting her impressions of traveling, preaching, and ministering to the Indians, Ximenez Samaniego indicated that other clergy and nuns became "convinced . . . that she was transported bodily."[23] Her confessor, Sebastian Marcilla, declared the experiences to be authentic, citing the nun's apparent knowledge of the country and peoples, and the vividness of her impressions. Subsequently, ". . . other learned persons to whom he communicated this were of the same opinion, and soon the news spread among the religious and nuns that Mother Maria de Jesus had been transported to the Indies."[24]

Marcilla eventually dispatched a letter of inquiry to Don Francisco Manso, archbishop of Mexico, seeking to discover if any evidences of Mother Maria's presence had been observed, and whether she had any influence among the Indians of New Mexico.

The Interview

Alonso de Benavides met with Maria de Agreda in April, approximately six months after his appearance at the royal court. With Fray Marcilla also in attendance, Mother Maria was instructed to reveal all that she knew about New Mexico. As Benavides recalled in his letter to New Mexico the nun gave him convincing evidence of her visits.

> She . . . told me all we know that has happened to our brothers and fathers, Fray Juan de Salas and Fray Diego Lopez, in the journeys to the Jumanas, and that she asked the latter . . . to go and call the fathers, as they did. She gave me all their descriptions, adding that she assisted them. She knows Captain Tuerto very well, giving a detailed description of him and of the others. She herself sent the emissaries from Quivira to call the fathers. . . . I asked her why she did not allow us to see her when she granted this bliss to the Indians. She replied that they needed it and we did not, and that her blessed angels arranged everything . . .
>
> She has preached in person our holy Catholic faith in every nation, particularly in our New Mexico. . . .[25]

For the most part, the Indian "kingdoms" attested in Mother Maria's visions are unrecognizable; the Jumanos stand out in this respect as an authentic Indian nation. Others may resemble, but do not correspond to, names recorded in North America.

> . . . She said that after traveling . . . from the east, one would come to the kingdoms of Chillescas, Cambujos, and Jumanas, and then to the kingdom of Titlas; those names are not the real ones, but something resembling them, because although when among them she speaks their language, away from there she does not know it nor is it revealed to her. . . .[26]

Although there are indications that Benavides asked leading questions, and that Maria's replies were given under some duress, Benavides left Agreda even more confirmed in his convictions. He now appeared positive not only that Maria de Agreda had been physically present in the New World, but also that her visits had continued until that same year, 1631.

From Spain, Benavides traveled to Rome, and remained there for most of 1632 to 1635, awaiting the expected appointment as bishop and lobbying on behalf of the mission establishment in New Mexico. Late in this period, he presented the revised *Memorial of 1634* to Pope Urban VIII. It may be that he returned to Spain when the bishopric was not forthcoming. Back in Spain, he addressed several petitions to the Crown, obtaining royal decrees for the protection of the Indians from various abuses and restrictions. However, in 1635, he evidently abandoned his plans to return to New Mexico, and accepted an appointment as assistant bishop of Goa, thus terminating his connection with the Americas.

The Events in New Mexico and the South Plains

Benavides' later writings, including the *Memorial of 1634*, contain details not included in the earlier account. These records, together with the information revealed in Agreda, make it possible to put together a fairly complete scenario of the circumstances surrounding the celebrated "miraculous conversion" of the Jumanos and the visits of the "Lady in Blue."

(1) The Meeting at the Chapter House

When Father Perea and the new recruits, some of them recently from Spain, arrived in New Mexico in the spring of 1629, they probably bore with them rumors about the mystical journeys of a certain Spanish nun. Perea also carried a letter from the archbishop, Don Francisco Manso, which included the inquiry which he had received from Father Marcilla.

> It is very probable that in the course of the discovery of New Mexico and the conversion of those souls, there will soon be found a kingdom called Tidan, more than four hundred leagues from the City of Mexico, to the west, or between the west and north, which it is understood is between New Mexico and La Quivira. If perhaps cosmography is at fault, it will be of assistance to obtain information concerning three other kingdoms, one called Chillescas, the other that of the Jumanes, and the third that of Carbucos, which border upon the said kingdom of Tidan. These being discovered an effort shall be made to ascertain whether or not in them, particularly in that of Tidan, there is any

knowledge of our holy faith, and in what manner and by what means our Lord has manifested it.[27]

The archbishop charged the friars to conduct an inquiry into the matter and to inform him of the results. Thus, it is clear that Benavides was well aware of the suggestion of outside influence among the Indians, whether or not he had, at this time, heard of Maria de Agreda by name.

Estevan de Perea and the other friars, traveling north with the supply train, crossed the Rio del Norte at El Paso in April of 1629, and arrived at Santa Fe at Eastertide. It is likely that they paused at Isleta on the way north, since this mission, located on the main road, was a popular overnighting place for travellers approaching and leaving Santa Fe.[28] Their formal arrival in the colony would have come in Santa Fe, with a welcome by the governor and other officials. Then the friars would have adjourned to the chapter house, the headquarters of the order, located in the village of Santo Domingo. There the new arrivals would have been introduced and given their assignments. Fray Juan de Salas, a senior and much respected priest, must have been in attendance at this meeting, as would the mission priests from all over New Mexico.

By Perea's account, the Franciscans began their chapter meeting at Pentecost, fifty days after Easter. It was at this time, in mid-June, that the letter from Archbishop Manso was finally delivered, and its content made known to the assemblage. Upon hearing this message, Fray Salas may have been reminded of the Jumanos' repeated requests for baptism.

(2) The Indian Delegation

That same summer, perhaps while the friars were still assembled, a party of Jumanos arrived at Isleta, to visit with Juan de Salas. The Jumanos had come to Mission San Antonio in Isleta at about the same time, every summer, for at least six years. In 1629, there were about fifty Indians in the party, led by Captain Tuerto.

The delegation which Captain Tuerto led to Isleta—which included a total of twelve Indian captains—may have contained representatives of other tribes, allies of the Jumanos; in fact, this is intimated in Benavides' 1630 account.[29] The Indians had come to ask for baptism and to request that missionaries be sent to their country. On each of the previous visits their petitions had been refused by the Custodian, ostensibly because of a lack of available priests. It would appear, then, that Benavides was already aware of their requests, and may have been eager to undertake the conversion of the Jumanos and the "Nations of the North" when an opportunity presented itself.

The Jumanos, according to Benavides, "had already come a few days earlier and were lodged in the pueblo."[30] This year, their meeting with Salas may have been delayed by the chapter meeting and other events attending the arrival of the friars. There was, in any event, a period of several days in which the Jumano party were present at Isleta, during which they could easily have learned what the Indian residents of that pueblo may already have been privy to—the gossip which the newcomers had brought from Mexico. They may have learned, among other things, that the Spaniards believed that a certain nun, a young woman whose appearance could be imagined from the picture which hung in the mission, had been present in their country. It was said that the woman was sent by God, and had mysterious powers, and that she claimed to have preached to the Indians and taught them how to pray. It was evident that the priests were interested in the woman and wanted to have news of her. Several days of waiting gave the Indians time to appraise the situation, and perhaps to integrate it into a scenario of their own.

Finally, some time after Bishop Manso's letter was received, an audience took place, whether at the initiative of Benavides or the new custodian, Estevan de Perea. According to Benavides, the inquiry by Bishop Manso, together with the news carried by the friars from Mexico, had already excited speculation about the Jumanos' motives: ". . . we soon noticed that the great care and solicitude with which the Xumana Indians came to us every summer to plead for friars to go and baptize them must have been through inspiration from heaven."[31]

At this juncture the clerics confronted the Indians and solicited a response which was, in its general content, already anticipated. "We called them to the convent and asked them their motive in coming every year to ask for baptism with such insistence." Some one of their number—perhaps Captain Tuerto—replied. "Gazing at a portrait of Mother Luisa in the convent, [he] said: 'A woman in similar garb wanders among us over there, always preaching, but her face is not old like this, but young.'"[32]

The effect must have been electric. Fray Salas and a young Fray Diego Lopez—possibly one of the new arrivals, who volunteered for the mission—were quickly delegated to accompany the Jumanos to their home. A military escort was secured, and the mission was under way "immediately." The actual date is not on record, but cannot have been earlier than the end of July; it may have been somewhat later.

(3) The Expedition to the Plains

An *entrada* of 112 leagues—almost three hundred miles—into territory which was not only unfamiliar but also a war zone, could hardly have been a purely religious undertaking. Since a military escort was required, a political or economic justification would have been in order.

Such a justification is not difficult to imagine. Alonso de Benavides had repeatedly argued the strategic advantages of missionizing the Nations of the North (a term usually applied to Quivira and its neighbors) in reports which he had directed to Mexico; it appears that this was, at least in part, the rationale for the large number of friars recently assigned to New Mexico. He expressed this point of view in a straightforward way in the *Memorial of 1630* when he followed the account of the "miraculous conversion" with a paragraph outlining the practical importance to Spain of the country of "Quivira and Aixaos." Believing that the coast of the North Sea was not far distant, he argued that a Spanish presence was needed to defend the mineral wealth and other resources of New Spain from "the Flemings and the English," who otherwise would come to barter with the Indians. He mentioned the trade in buffalo hides, and the possibility of developing a commercial market for buffalo wool, along with other potentially valuable regional resources such as pearls and amber.[33]

The religious community, in this case, had a clear interest in the establishment of a mission among the Plains Jumanos. The interests of the state were also served, since the regions east of New Mexico were believed to be of strategic importance. An immediate rationale for the move, however, was provided by the Jumano request for baptism. The tantalizing suggestion of a spiritual or divine presence at work served to make the invitation irresistible.

It is the motivation of the Indians which has inspired speculation, however. Why were they so eager for missionaries? Why had they gone to such efforts, made so many appeals, in order to obtain them? Benavides suggests that they took this step out of a desire for the "water of baptism," that they were influenced by the virtuous reputation of the Franciscans, and that they acted out of a special fondness for Fray Salas. Ultimately, of course, he concluded that the visits were actually initiated by Mother Maria, who had been with the Indians since 1620, repeatedly urging them to seek baptism.

But however profound the faith of the Indians, they, like the Spaniards, were moved by secular as well as spiritual considerations. The phenomenon of Indians asking for missionaries to live among them, and expressing a desire to be gathered into mission communities, was not at all unusual, especially in areas where the natives were confronted with contending forces stronger than their own, and where missions offered a degree of protection. In other areas of the Americas, missions have served to shelter Indians against both slavers and encroaching settlers. In the Southwest, too, they provided such a haven and, at times, also helped to gather and resettle the remnants of bands which were displaced or decimated by the aggression of other native groups—most notably, the several divisions of the Apaches.

The Jumanos were now in a desperate situation. By 1629, they may have been in contention with the Apaches for a century or more. They had been displaced from territory in which they had earlier been able to hunt and travel freely. Their travels across the plains must have become quite hazardous, and their ability to trade in the Pueblos of New Mexico was threatened. It seems obvious that the Jumanos were, at that time, motivated by a need to maintain access to hunting territory and to defend the remaining routes between New Mexico and the tribes located beyond the Apache strongholds to the east and south.

From the early days of exploration and colonization north of Mexico, the Jumanos had cultivated a trade relationship with the Spaniards, with whom they evidently hoped to build a stronger alliance. Captain Tuerto would have reasoned that the location of a permanent mission among his people would be one way to facilitate that goal. If there were a mission in the plains, then Spanish soldiers would be on hand to defend the priests and to keep the road to New Mexico secure. He would have known, from what he had seen and heard in the villages of New Mexico, that the presence of missionaries could bring material goods, opportunities for trade, education in new skills, and military protection.

The Plains Jumanos had kin and allies in the New Mexican pueblos; they had observed and perhaps even participated in Catholic worship there—some may already have been baptized. They appeared willing at that time to undertake the same contract that Indians elsewhere had made: religious conversion in exchange for security. The message of the "Lady in Blue" served to make the contract more attractive.

Certain Spaniards must have shared the Jumanos' aspirations. Fray Juan de Salas, at least, would have understood their situation.

Salas had worked among the Tompiros and Jumanos in the Salinas for many years, from the mission in Isleta which he founded in 1613.[34] He had a reputation for skill with native languages, and had become acquainted with Jumano leaders such as Captain Tuerto. Benavides indicated that the Jumanos admired Fray Salas, and that Salas was eager to undertake the mission.

(4) The Timing of the Mission

It is not difficult to conclude that the timing of Salas' expedition was largely contingent on the regular, seasonal movements of the Jumanos. Their trading parties came to Isleta regularly in midsummer, perhaps after wintering in the Salinas and before journeying to their base in the Plains. They remained at Isleta for a customary period of time, approximately ten to fifteen days. Over the years their leaders had cultivated the friendship of the resident Catholic priest. After the midsummer visit at Isleta, the Indians would normally have moved on eastward, making other stops and arriving in the High Plains in late summer or early autumn. These movements were part of a cycle of economic activities related to seasonal changes— largely dictated, in this prevailingly arid region, by precipitation patterns, and keyed to the annual migration of the buffalo.

In the High Plains region of western Texas, summer (often late summer) is the season of the heaviest and most predictable rainfall; similar patterns prevail in New Mexico. This period of seasonal rains and fresh vegetation prepared the way for an autumnal concentration of buffalo in the Southern Plains, as temperatures declined from midsummer highs. Following the summer rains, water remains for weeks or months in the hundreds of small *playa* lakes. This plentiful supply of water was an attraction both to the buffalo herds and to the Indians who gathered for the hunt.

Hunting parties from many tribes—including the sedentary Caddoan tribes from the eastern river valleys—converged in the region. For this reason, fall was a time for intertribal gatherings and for trade fairs. The Jumanos carried a variety of trade goods (such as mineral pigments, turquoise and other gemstones, salt, textiles, pottery, and agricultural products) from the Pueblo area: on the return trip, they would have transported pelts, meat, and other products of the hunt as well as more exotic and valuable goods.[35]

The trek of the two Franciscans, with the accompanying party of Indians, was a journey of almost three hundred miles. The friars, who traveled on foot, could hardly have covered more than twenty-five miles per day; the average may have been somewhat less. The duration of the journey, then, can be estimated at no less than ten, and perhaps closer to twenty days; arrival at the Jumanos' base would have come sometime between late August and mid-September. Messengers would surely have preceded the friars, perhaps on horseback, to inform those in the *rancherias*. The progress of the mission would have been monitored, and the priests' arrival anticipated. The "twelve captains" who contacted the Franciscans' entourage three days before arrival at the base no doubt constituted a welcoming party.

It may be that the seasonal rains had failed or were late. Benavides' narrative indicates that the land was dry and the buffalo were not yet to be seen. The arrival of the herds must have been anticipated, however, since representatives of several tribes arrived during the time of the Franciscans' presence. These tribes may have been apprised of the arrival of the padres, and aware of the importance of their visit. The Indians had assembled, Benavides believed, in anticipation of the mission; they may also have gathered in anticipation of the traders' return from New Mexico. In any event, preparations had been made for the friars' visit: flowers were gathered, and crosses and garlands were made ready for the procession. The Franciscans, who arrived apostolically, on foot, were given a grand welcome.

(5) The Encounter in the Plains

There has been a history of disagreement about locations ascribed to Jumano groups in this and other original accounts. The disagreement is related to a continuing discussion of the cultural identity and linguistic affiliation of these people.[36] The location indicated by Benavides as "112 leagues . . . to the East [of New Mexico]" has been variously assigned to areas almost two hundred miles due north and approximately six hundred miles to the southeast of New Mexico.[37] However, there seems no reason to doubt that the priests made reasonably accurate assessments of distance and direction. The Jumano camp would have been located, as indicated, between 275 and 300 miles east of Santa Fe; the trail may have followed the Canadian River for much of the distance (Map 6, no. 3).

For buffalo-hunting and trading, the two main occupations of the Jumanos, a location on the High Plains with near access to the Canadian River and to the headwaters of several branches of the Red and Brazos rivers was an optimal location. In this general vicinity, a protected site in a canyon or *barranca* such as Palo Duro Canyon—

possibly the same locale in which Coronado's party visited the "Teyas"—would have been a permanent base camp. There, buffalo pelts and other goods were accumulated and trade was conducted, especially during the autumn when members of many tribes gathered for the hunt. The indication of Quivira as forty leagues farther to the east confirms the location of the Jumano base, since the southern gateway to Quivira appears to have been the Arkansas River, near its junction with the Canadian.

The Jumanos' familiarity with Christian ritual, which so impressed Benavides, can be seen as evidence for the close ties which the Plains Jumanos maintained with those living in the Tompiro Pueblos. They knew about priests and missions, either directly or at second hand. It is impossible to know how accurately and objectively the friars reported what they saw, or what interpretations they read into the Jumanos' behavior. However, the genuflections, cheers, and the great show of hands with which the Indians responded, obviously constituted an overwhelming vote for the presence of the priests, whom the Indians may have seen as rescuers.

But if the Indians had hoped that the priests would settle in and remain among them, they were disappointed. They must have concluded that the fathers were making a tour of inspection, and they could only hope that the decision would be in their favor. After an indefinite period of time—a month at most—during which they worked at catechizing, erected a large cross, conducted healing sessions, and met with the ambassadors from neighboring tribes, the priests departed. Assuming that they were two to three weeks en route on each leg of the journey, they could have been back in New Mexico no earlier than late September, and probably just before Benavides' departure for Mexico.[38]

(6) The Aftermath

When Fathers Salas and Lopez left the Jumano camp, it was evidently their intention to return. Addressing Franciscan requests in a report written in 1631, the viceroy, the Marques de Cerralvo, still refers to "the Jumano who live a hundred leagues from Santa Fe, at the portal of the much sought-for Kingdom of Gran Quivira." He then recalls the events of 1629 and appears once more to anticipate the establishment of a permanent mission in Jumano territory.[39]

It is certain that Spain maintained contact with the Jumanos for the rest of the century. However, the High Plains area was soon, perhaps immediately, abandoned by the Jumanos, either on their own initiative or on that of the Franciscans. The friars may have made another journey, planned as a relief effort, but leading to evacuation of the Jumano base and removal of its residents to New Mexico. According to Vetancurt, the Jumanos ". . . because of the invasions and continuous wars with their enemies, the Apaches . . . accompanied the Christians to a place near Quarac where they ministered to them." Here, "many times the venerable mother, Maria de Jesus, abbess of the convent of Agreda, appeared to them. . . ."[40] Thus, some part of the High Plains Jumano population was evidently resettled in the Salinas, adding at least temporarily to the size of the Jumano element in the Tompiro province.

9.

THE JUMANOS
AT MID-CENTURY

The Pueblo Jumanos[1]

In the decades following Peralta's appointment as governor of New Mexico, new settlers arrived to join the remnants of the original colony. The Hispanic population, which had lost members by the end of Oñate's term as governor, stood at around fifteen hundred in 1630, and continued a slow but steady growth, despite periodic droughts and epidemics. At the time of the Pueblo Rebellion in 1680, there were more than two thousand Spanish citizens in the colony.

The Spanish-speaking citizenry settled into several scattered areas of concentration—Santa Fe itself; a stretch of the Rio Grande valley, down to the vicinity of modern Albuquerque; and La Canada, a region north of Santa Fe. *Encomenderos* whose holdings were located in outlying provinces usually built townhouses in the capital city as well.

By mid-century, Spaniards and Indians had interbred and even intermarried, and there was an increasingly important mestizo population. There were also Mexican Indians and mixed-bloods among the emigrants, as well as individuals of African and part-African descent. These, together with the different cultural and language groups among the New Mexican Indians, Pueblo and Apache—some Christian and others pagan—gave the colony the pluralistic quality which has continued, over the years, to characterize New Mexico. Status in this frontier region depended in part on race, in part on wealth and property. The Spanish families who received titles to lands during the colonial period remained as a virtual aristocracy for many generations.

Slavery was commonplace, the most frequent source of slaves being Indians from outside the Pueblo provinces. Pueblo Indians were often used as household servants, many of them "orphans" who were taken in and raised for this purpose by Spanish families. Those who remained in their own communities were also exploited, through the levy of a portion of their goods which was taken annually by the *encomenderos*, and through the taxes and drafts of labor imposed to meet the needs of both mission and governmental bureaucracies.

The leading male citizens of Spanish blood constituted an elite, a combination of a ruling class and a military clique. These citizen soldiers dominated the business and political life of the colony and were responsible for its defense. The core of this group was the thirty-five *encomenderos*, who made up a hereditary officer caste; these men also held power over the Indian villages, and were able to command military service as well as labor from the Indians under their control.

The divisive and wasteful rivalry between church and state continued throughout the life of the colony. In succeeding decades, the two bureaucracies, secular and religious, tended—with some fluctuations—to become even more polarized, often operating at cross-purposes. Certain secular officials, such as Governor Bernardo Lopez de Mendizabal, who held office from 1659 to 1661, openly opposed the suppression of native religious rites, and even gave official permission to certain pueblos to practice traditional *kachina* ceremonies, directly contradicting the priests' injunctions against them. Local alcaldes were sometimes permissive, quietly violating official policies; numerous disputes and court cases arose over such matters.

The economic survival of the colony, never secure, was severely threatened by several periods of drought, the worst of which occurred in the years between 1665 and 1669. The first of several lethal epidemics swept the colony in 1640; smallpox took an especially heavy toll on the native population. Their numbers declined steadily, both through death and through desertion, as residents of the pueblos fled to escape Spanish rule. At the time of the conquest, Pecos Pueblo—the easternmost of the provinces in New Mexico—was one of the largest and most prosperous Indian communities. It had a population of around two thousand people in 1622, 1,189 in 1649, and by 1694, the count had declined to 736.[2] Pecos was finally abandoned in the 1820's, when the last eighteen individuals were resettled at Jemez, the only pueblo where their Towa language remained in use (as it does today).

The decline of the Pecos community is representative of overall trends. In the course of the seventeenth century, the number of Pueblo villages fell by half, from more than 130 to around 65, and the overall population also declined by fifty percent or more.[3] Many natives left New Mexico, to join the various bands of the Apaches or to take refuge elsewhere. One large group of Tiwas from the northern pueblo of Taos fled as far as Kansas, where they established a settlement among the surrounding Apaches in an area which the Spaniards called *El Cuartelejo*. This settlement endured for several decades, until the fugitives were brought back by a military escort, in the summer of 1706.

In all parts of New Mexico, factionalisms and hostilities among the native Pueblo Indians, and between these and the colonists, were complicated by the relations of all groups with the surrounding Apaches. Autonomous Apache bands had established reciprocal relationships with their immediate Pueblo neighbors, exchanging products of their hunting and other activities for textiles and agricultural produce. However, any equilibrium which may have existed in these relationships was upset by the Spanish presence. The produce of the villages was first requisitioned and then, in subsequent years, depleted by levies and taxes. The Apaches, on the other hand, were soon drawn into a trade relationship with the Spaniards because of the apparently insatiable market for hides and pelts, and also for captives who could be sold as slaves.

Horses and livestock quickly became a temptation to the Apaches. They often stole what they could not obtain in trade. In times of shortage, raids became more frequent. The theft of livestock was a frequent cause of hostilities between groups. The Apaches themselves, as well as captives from more distant tribes, sometimes found their way into the slave trade and were often transported to Mexico (from whence they could be shipped to Spanish colonies in the Caribbean or elsewhere).

The colonial government incited new enmities and intensified existing factionalisms through the policy of using pacified Christian Indians as militia in making war against rebellious groups. Where hostilities already existed, they were sometimes exploited and, in the process, exacerbated. The Tompiro Jumanos must frequently have been among the Christian Indians deployed against the Apaches. Considering the historical pattern of Jumano-Apache relationships, they were probably quite willing to serve in this capacity.

In the southeastern Tompiro province (Map 6, no. 2), many of the problems that affected the colony would have been at their worst. The drought of the mid-1660's devastated the population of the Salinas, a region which may never have been really self-sufficient in agriculture. The Salinas villages had, in the best of times, a very limited water supply drawn from wells and *pozos* (cisterns or tanks for the storage of rain water). One of the mysteries surrounding the Salinas region, puzzling to both historians and archaeologists, is the existence of these large communities—perhaps three thousand people at Las Humanas alone (the archaeological site called Gran Quivira)—in a region of such prevailing aridity. Not only was rainfall inadequate, and the subsurface water supply meager, but such wells as existed must have produced highly mineralized, virtually unpotable water.

The province of the Tompiros was one of the last to be entered by Christian missionaries. Little is known about the population of this region during the decades immediately following the conquest. The first missionary active there was Fray Alonso de Peinado, who began his duties in Chilili in 1613. During Alonso de Benavides' tenure as custodian, additional priests were assigned to New Mexico. Mission churches were built in the Tompiros, including the one at Las Humanas. Several additional priests were sent to this province out of Estevan de Perea's group, which arrived in 1629. In his *Memorial of 1634*, Benavides wrote with obvious gratification about his own success in proselytizing among the Jumanos in the Salinas, in view of their "extremely rebellious nature."[4] This is an apparent reference to the resistance movement which developed in the region during Oñate's reign, leading to the punitive measures taken against Salinas villages in 1599 and 1600.

The Plains Jumanos

It was under Benavides' leadership also, that efforts were made to convert the Plains Jumanos, beginning with the mission led by Fray Juan de Salas in 1629. The relationship between the colony and more distant Jumano groups continued in the following decades. Following Juan de Salas' visit, no more is heard of Jumanos in the plains due east of New Mexico. In later decades, the site 112 leagues east of Santa Fe would have fallen well within the territorial range of the Plains Apache. Perhaps this entire band of Jumanos eventually departed or were evacuated as the Apaches increased in number; or, perhaps the Apaches attacked and defeated the Jumanos, exterminating or incorporating any remnants of their population remaining in the area. The evacuation may have consisted of the Franciscans' removal of several hundred Jumanos, mentioned by Vetancurt in 1698; the refugees, according to this source, were brought to New Mexico and settled "near Quarac (Quarai)," where the priests continued to minister to them. According to one churchman's account, the refugees were a useful source of information about the Indian nations to the east, providing the missionaries with accounts of "the Aixas, the Excanxaques, the Uracas, the Lupies, the Chillescas, the Tulas, and the Quiviras."[5]

What became of these refugee Jumanos? They could have been taken into one or more of the Salinas villages. However, the phrase "near Quarac" suggests that they were resettled in camps or *rancherias* of their own, and that the mission church at Quarac (probably the Acolocu of the Oñate period) was the closest to their settlements. Their presence, in any event, would have increased the population on the Mesa Jumanes.[6]

The area of Apache dominance gradually expanded southward and eastward, through the Plains. Jumano traffic across this region, bringing goods to and from the eastern pueblos, would eventually have been disrupted. As conditions grew increasingly troubled, any Jumanos living on the margins of the Salinas region would have been situated in a kind of pincers, threatened both by the Apaches of the Sacramento and Guadalupe Mountains (Benavides' "Apaches del Perillo") and those in the Plains. Some may eventually have moved from outlying *rancherias* into the pueblos for protection; others may have retreated southward, and made their way to join more distant Jumano communities beyond the Pecos, along the lower Rio Grande, or on the Rio de Las Nueces (Concho).

It might be noted at this point that, some time after 1630, an infant was born in the Tompiro province, in or near the village of Las Humanas, who would become the most famous Jumano leader of all time. His name was Sabeata (sometimes written as Xaviata); when he was baptized as an adult at Parral, in Nueva Vizaya, he became Juan Sabeata. It is tempting to imagine that Juan Sabeata could have been a son, or perhaps a grandson, of the earlier Jumano leader, Captain Tuerto. In any case, his mother could have been a woman from the Plains, perhaps one of those who took refuge in the Salinas region following Fray Salas' mission.

Fray Ortega's Mission

In 1632, there was a second Franciscan mission to a distant Jumano base, planned in the aftermath of the 1629 expedition and probably assisted by Jumanos living in the Tompiro province. Some of the refugees from the Plains may have accompanied the friars to this base, which was located farther south and out of the combat zone. They could have been the source of information about this distant location and served as guides for the missionaries. The friars who set out in search of the distant Jumano settlement had a much longer trek ahead of them than those of the previous mission. They were Fray Pedro de Ortega (who had earlier tried, but failed, to reach Quivira at about the same time that Salas visited the Jumanos) and Fray Ascension de Zarate. There has been confusion about the relationship between the two successive expeditions to the Jumanos: some writers appear to have merged the two, or to have associated Fray Juan de Salas with both.[7] But Fray Salas himself apparently did not undertake the journey in 1632, though he undoubtedly played a role in planning it.

The Jumano location toward which the friars, Ortega and Zarate, made their way, is specified by Posada, in his *Report of 1686,* to have been "two hundred leagues southeast of Santa Fe, on a stream called the Nueces." This, as Bolton painstakingly demonstrated, was identical (or at least very close) to the site visited by several subsequent Spanish expeditions, later in the century (Map 6, no. 4).[8] It is at the same crossroads, near the confluence of the Concho and Colorado of Texas, where Cabeza de Vaca, a century earlier, found the "village of a hundred huts." This is another indication of the enduring importance of the native highway along the Colorado, Concho, and Pecos rivers.

The missionary friars again were afforded a military escort and must have been guided by Indians who were knowledgeable about the location and route. Of the two Franciscan friars, Pedro de Ortega remained among the Jumanos for at least six months. Benavides, who must have learned about this event while in Europe, stated in his *Memorial of 1634* that Fray Ortega died among the Jumanos ". . . worn out by the long and severe hardships of the march, the evangelical preaching, and the catechizing of the Indians in the Christian doctrine." The friar, according to Benavides, "deserved the palm of martyrdom" because of having worked at the conversions until his physical strength gave out.[9] However, in another report written the same year, addressed to the Congregation of the Propagation of the Faith, Benavides told a somewhat different story: he stated that Ortega achieved martyrdom in the "Xumana nation, where . . . they poisoned him with the most cruel poison."[10]

In the *Memorial of 1634,* Benavides also praised the "apostolic zeal" with which Pedro de Ortega pursued his missionary labors. In fact, Ortega seems to have had chronic difficulties in his relationships with the Indian communities in which he worked—perhaps reflecting, in part, his parishioners' response to an excess of "apostolic zeal." Benavides went on to recount the friar's earlier, and equally zealous, missionizing at Taos, where the Indians finally "illtreated him . . . (and) gave him tortillas of corn made with urine and mice meat."[11] Might Ortega have received similar treatment from the Jumanos? That, in itself, could have been the basis for the report of poisoning. Posada, writing in 1685, stated (perhaps pointedly, to dispel the rumor) that "Father Fray Juan [sic] de Ortega . . . was with them [the Jumanos] for a period of six months without their having treated him badly or doing him any injury."[12]

The contradiction between the two accounts of Ortega's death may seem to be a minor point of difference; however, the accusation—or rumor—of murder against the Jumanos could be of significance for Spanish-Jumano relations in the years immediately following. We have no way of knowing how many different divisions of Jumanos, in how many separate communities or locations, there were during these years, or whether the population of the group visited by the two friars, Ortega and Zarate, included any part of the group contacted in 1629. There must have been, at the very least, some relationship, perhaps a kinship connection, between the two. Thus, carrying out the second mission would mean that earlier contacts were renewed or re-established, between New Mexico and the Jumanos east of the Rio Pecos.

The First Mission at Las Humanas

After arriving in New Mexico in 1629, as one of Estevan de Perea's contingent of friars, Francis Letrado was the first Franciscan priest to be stationed in the Salinas pueblos. It was evidently he who supervised the building of the small chapel in the pueblo of Las Humanas, mentioned in Benavides' *Memorial*, which was dedicated to San Isidro. But Letrado left, by his own request, in 1632 to work among the Zuni. The reason for his departure is not known; however, it may not be a coincidence that it roughly coincides in time with the reported death of Pedro de Ortega among the Jumanos on the Rio de Nueces. If, as Benavides suggested, Ortega was poisoned (whether or not deliberately)—or if he received treatment by the Jumanos which seemed to belie the earnestness of their recent appeals for missionaries—this could have brought the work of the missionaries among the Jumanos to a temporary halt.

It seems, at any rate, that there was a period of cooling or alienation in relations between Franciscans and Jumanos, both in the Tompiro pueblos and in the Plains. However, the Jumanos in New Mexico remained, until 1643, under the provincial supervision of Fray Juan de Salas, who appears to have dealt with them sympathetically.

New Expeditions to the Nueces

In 1632, the only group of outlying Jumanos with which Spanish New Mexico is known to have had direct contact was in a situation which was more remote from the colony, more secure (for a time) from Apache attack, and perhaps closer to some of their Texas trading partners than was the earlier locale, in the High Plains. However, the fact that the Rio de las Nueces was located so far away from New Mexico may have meant that there were now fewer direct contacts in that direction. There may, therefore, have been a weakening of ties between the Jumanos in New Mexico and those in the Plains. From the Nueces, the trip to New Mexico was not only long, but was growing more hazardous because of the increased Apache presence. By mid-century, the Jumanos may have found it unfeasible to make this journey for trade purposes.

However, by 1650, Spaniards from New Mexico were making trading trips to the Nueces (the Rio Concho) on a regular basis. The Concho, near the point of its confluence with the Colorado of Texas, was an ideal location for a trading post (Map 6, no. 4). The forks of the Concho provided routes leading westward toward the Pecos and the mountain trail to the Rio Grande near La Junta. The upper course of the Pecos was the natural route to the eastern pueblos and Santa Fe. Downstream, the main course of the Colorado leads to the Gulf of Mexico; it also gives access, via its many tributaries, to a network of streams and trails by which tribes on neighboring river systems—the Brazos, Trinity, Guadalupe, etc.—could be reached. There is reason to believe that the Rio de las Nueces base had been long occupied by the Jumanos; and it was not a location which they would have willingly abandoned.

The Martin-Castillo expedition of 1650 was the first not to be formally initiated by religious personnel, but by the secular government of the colony; it had no overt religious mission. The *entrada* was authorized by the current governor of New Mexico, Hernando de la Concha. A military party, accompanied by Christian Indians— probably Jumanos from the Salinas—traveled to the Nueces from Santa Fe, by way of the Rio Pecos. It is evident that their aim was to strengthen or re-establish the relationship between New Mexico and the outlying Jumanos, and to use the Jumanos to make contact with the Indian nations to the east and south. High in the Spaniards' priorities at the time were the Caddoan Hasinai, or Tejas, a large Indian confederacy which was the most powerful in Texas and with whom the Jumanos maintained an amicable and important trade relationship. In view of the subsequent dispatching of a second Spanish party in 1654 which included troops and undertook a military action, it seems likely that Martin and Castillo found a situation which seemed to call for the use of military force, with an eye to improving Spanish access to the Hasinai trade.

The *Informe* of Alonso de Posada, written in 1686, is the most detailed source of information on the *entrada* of 1650, as well as the subsequent one led by Diego de Guadalajara.

> This river they call the Rio de las Nueces because it has along its banks and meadows many trees of this kind, besides mulberry trees, plum trees, wild grapes, and other fruits, and attractive resources all along it. In its vicinity there are many wild cows which they call buffalo and many chickens of the land which in Spain they call turkeys, and all kinds of deer.
>
> . . . In the year 1650 Captain Hernan Martin and Captain Diego del Castillo set out from the villa of Santa Fe at the order of General Hernando de la Concha who was then governor of the provinces of New Mexico. Having marched . . . some two hundred leagues they arrived at the above-mentioned place on the Rio de las Nueces and nation of the Jumanas. There they remained both because the Indians showed them affection as well as because of having found in that place more than enough food supplies. During this period of six months they took out of the river a quantity of shells, which, having been burned, yielded some pearls, which if they were not finer than those of the Orient because they came from sweet water, they seemed to be . . .[13]

The pearls were a commodity which Jumano traders had brought to New Mexico, where they excited the interest of the Spaniards. It would seem that one objective of the expedition was investigation of the source of the pearls, and the appropriation of this resource for potential Spanish exploitation. Specimens were carried back to the governor, and subsequently shipped to Mexico for appraisal. The quality was judged to be inferior to salt water pearls, but sufficiently fine to justify the second investigation, which was made in 1654.

From their base of operations at the Jumano village on the Nueces, the Spanish captains explored eastward following the river and traveled through or near the territories of the Cuitoas, Escanjaques, and Aijados. At some fifty leagues distance, they reached the limits of the country of the Tejas, but did not continue because of the size and population of that nation. The Tejas were said to border Quivira on the north.[14]

The nation of the Texas runs from south to north a distance equal to that between the Rio del Norte and the Rio de las Nueces, which will be about one hundred leagues and about the same in width from east to west. From the far side of this nation to the coast and Gulf of Mexico there will be another fifty leagues to the east. Occupying this expanse of fifty leagues are single groups of Indians [Karankawas] who neither sow nor reap, because, according to information, the vicinity of the coastal region is covered with sand and dunes throughout this part of Texas.

This nation borders the Quiviras on the north and both are said to have native chiefs or caciques who govern them; they sow and reap their crops of maise; their lands are fertile and abundantly irrigated by streams from the north. They utilize the wild cows which they call buffalos and the rest of the products provided along the Rio de las Nueces which is their boundary . . .[15]

Whatever degree of enthusiasm the pearls of the Nueces may have excited in Mexico, the reports which Captains Martin and Castillo had brought back to Santa Fe describing the many resources including—perhaps cspccially—peltries, along with the prospect of contact with the Tejas, evidently kept New Mexican interest in the Jumano middlemen at a high pitch.

The next documented entry into Jumano country and beyond was made by order of Governor Juan de Samaniego, in 1654. This time the expedition was under the command of Captain Diego de Guadalajara, *maestre de campo* (chief military officer) of the colony. Guadalajara took a party of thirty soldiers and over two hundred Christian Indians, and followed the same route as the previous party, descending the Pecos and following the overland trail to the headwaters of the Nueces. Again, it can be assumed that the New Mexican Indians in the party were Jumanos; they could have come from Guadalajara's own hacienda. Captain Guadalajara, it may be noted, was an *encomendero* with holdings in the Salinas; a few years after this expedition, he was charged with using native labor illegally in working the salt mines of that region. His contacts with the Jumano population in New Mexico may have influenced him to undertake—or because of those connections he may have been selected to lead—what now appears to have been a military intervention in support of the Jumanos on the Rio de las Nueces.

One junior member of Guadalajara's company was a young officer named Juan Dominguez de Mendoza, whose family holdings extended east from Isleta Pueblo to lands beyond the Manzano Mountains. Like Captain Guadalajara, he had vested interests in the Salinas region; some years later he was granted a fractional interest in

THE JUMANOS AT MID-CENTURY

an *encomienda* there. Thirty years later, Dominguez de Mendoza himself, holding the position of *maestre de campo*, would lead another military expedition to this same riverside location in Texas.

> Having marched some two hundred leagues, they reached the Rio de las Nueces and found along it a considerable number of Indians of the Jumana nation. When he [Guadalajara] wished to continue his travel, these Indians advised (him) . . . that he should note that the Cuitoas, Escanjaques and the Aijados were at war. The commander and captain, to learn if this were true, sent Captain Andres Lopez with twelve soldiers and some christian Indians and many of the [local] Jumanas who went willingly to reconnoitre those nations, while the captain and commander remained in that spot with the rest of the soldiers . . .[16]

In the process of reconnoitering, the party commanded by Captain Lopez became involved in a day-long battle with the Cuitoas. The Escanjaques came to the aid of the Cuitoas, and so apparently did the Aijados (although their role is not clear). However, the combined Spanish-Jumano force administered a crushing defeat to the Cuitoas and their allies.

> After the battle had lasted almost all day, with the victory for our forces and the loss of very few of our Indians, but many of the enemy, the victors collected their prisoners and their spoils, which totaled two hundred bundles of deer skins and buffalo hides, and returned to the place of the Jumanos on the Rio de las Nueces, where Don Diego de Guadalajara had pitched camp. As soon as the soldiers joined him, he returned to the villa of Santa Fe.[17]

Considering the outcome of Guadalajara's *entrada*, one is tempted to suspect that from the beginning it was a mutually beneficial connivance of Spanish and Jumano economic interests. The Cuitoas and their allies may have blockaded or in some way interfered with Jumano trade access to the Tejas. If this were the case, then the Jumanos—either those on the Rio Nueces or their trading partners in New Mexico—may have sought Spanish military support in breaking through or pushing back the Cuitoas. The victory yielded, for the Spaniards, a large quantity of deer and buffalo pelts (which probably had been accumulated by the Cuitoas as trade goods). They also gained an unknown number of prisoners, who were taken to New Mexico as slaves—perhaps serving, *en route*, as porters for the cargo of peltries. It seems reasonable to believe that the primary purpose of the military foray had to do with defending or strengthening the position of the Jumanos in their role as middlemen between New Mexico and the Tejas confederacy. The Jumano trade at this date must have been of considerable importance to Spanish entrepreneurs, such as Captain Guadalajara, in New Mexico. On a political level, of course, the strategic importance of the territory of the Tejas had long been apparent to Spain, just as Benavides had earlier pointed out.

Sometime in the decade which began with the Martin-Castillo junket to the Nueces, if not earlier, direct and regular Spanish traffic between that region and New Mexico was established. By 1660, ". . . groups of soldiers and traders visited the same area, sometimes making annual excursions for the purpose of exchanging New Mexican products for buffalo hides."[18] In other words, scheduled expeditions by New Mexican traders, with military support, had replaced the annual comings and goings of the Jumano traders to New Mexico. It would appear that their visits had become too risky to undertake because of the increasing control which the Apaches exerted along the eastern frontier of the colony. During this period the only Jumano presence east of the Pecos for which there is direct evidence is that on the Rio de las Nucces. However, further to the south, the trail linking La Junta with the Pecos and the Concho (Nueces) was still securely under Jumano control.

Hard Times in the Salinas

In the Tompiro province, religion continued to be a political issue, as it was throughout the colony; it was a frequent basis for factional cleavages, cutting across ethnic and class divisions. Church, state, and private interests all contended for the loyalty and the labor of the Indians. In the pueblo of Las Humanas, Letrado's church was for some time administered by the minister stationed at the neighboring village of Abo, Francisco de Aceveda. By 1660 this original church, dedicated to San Isidro, had fallen into neglect after being despoiled several times in the previous decade during Apache attacks on the village. Finally, Diego Santander received an appointment as resident priest in Las Humanas; he enlarged and rebuilt the church from the foundations with Indian labor. At this time, San Buenaventura was adopted as the patron saint.[19] Las Humanas, in 1660, was referred to as a "new conversion"—a community which had not previously, at least for some time, had a resident minister. Once more, parallel developments—perhaps connections—may be seen in Spanish-Jumano relations in the Plains and in New Mexico, as the interest evidenced in trade on the Rio de las Nueces is closely followed by new overtures to the Pueblo Jumanos.

According to Fray Santander, Governor Lopez de Mendizabal attempted to prohibit the Indians of Las Humanas from working on the project, "but the Indians continued at great risk in the construction of the edifice, for they had no church."[20] A tremendous amount of native labor was obviously involved in the construction of this imposing church and its adjoining convent. The recorded history of the town of Las Humanas, during the 1660's, is marked by recurrent friction between Fray Diego Santander and the alcalde of the Salinas jurisdiction, Nicolas de Aguilar. Much of the disagreement focused on the exploitation of native labor. Santander was eventually forced to remove the large herds of sheep and cattle belonging to the mission, which were being watered, by native labor, from the limited supply in the village wells.

Governor Lopez, for his part, became notorious for his profiteering. He used the alcaldes, including Aguilar, to commandeer the Indians' crops, wool, woven textiles, and piñon nuts for his own storehouses—anything, apparently, that could be sold at a profit. The *encomenderos* also exploited the natives, though perhaps more paternalistically, since they usually had a more enduring relationship with them.

The most important product of the Salinas area was salt. According to charges brought by Santander, the Jumano Indians of the hacienda of Captain Diego de Guadalajara were held "as slaves" by their *encomendero*, who kept them "in such oppression that he did not even allow them to recognize their minister, but kept them busy carrying to their pueblo the salt which they get for the governor every year, it being in the cordillera of Las Salinas."[21] Like various other products, most of this salt, transported by oxcart over the Camino Real, would eventually reach market in the mining region around Parral. There was a steady market for salt, used in the refining of silver.

Throughout the Lopez administration, 1659–1661, Nicolas de Aguilar actively carried out the governor's campaign against the authority of the Franciscans in the Salinas. In one incident, Aguilar is reported to have caused a choir of native cantors, who had come from nearby Abo, to be lashed and driven out of the church of Las Humanas, apparently in an effort to put an end to the performance of the mass in that village. There were other incidents of the same sort.

> Nicolas de Aguilar had sent out a public notice . . . This notice, in the name of the alcalde mayor himself, was cried in Spanish by an Indian named Andres, who was well versed in that language, and who repeated the notice in the Tumpira language. He told the whole pueblo of

Indians—and that pueblo [Las Humanas] is the most populous one in those provinces, whither they gather together from all parts, to trade antelope skins and corn—that they might live just as they chose, and that they should be punished for no fault, either by the father, the *fiscales*, or the captains . . . And, so that it may be made plain that what Nicolas de Aguilar ordered to be announced was put into execution . . . in the pueblo of Tabira, a visitation of Humanas, in the jurisdiction of Las Salinas, the Indian captains, who are the judges of the Indians, brought before Nicolas de Aguilar two Indians who had been taken in illicit intercourse. Nicolas de Aguilar, scolding the captains for bringing them to him, set them at liberty without punishment.[22]

For these and other actions, Aguilar was arrested in 1662 by Garcia de San Francisco, the Franciscans' vice-custodian and head missionary among the Piros and Tompiros. Eventually, both Lopez and Aguilar were taken under arrest to Mexico, to stand trial before the court of the Inquisition. Lopez died in the course of the trial, and the charges against him were dropped posthumously; Aguilar was found guilty and prohibited from holding future public office in New Mexico.

The Indian villages east of the Manzanos were repeatedly evacuated and reinstated, and their populations were repeatedly reduced and relocated, for reasons of convenience and strategy. At one point, during the administration of governor Juan Manso (1656–1659), the far southern Piro village of Sevilleta was ordered evacuated, and the population was moved to nearby Alamillo. Within a year, his successor ordered their return, on the grounds that the village was needed to serve as a buffer against the Apaches, who had been entering the province through abandoned farmlands. The overall population of this village, like others, must have been on a steady decline through the effects of famine, disease, warfare, and desertion.

As was seen earlier in the century, it seems that in the sixties there was no sharp distinction to be drawn between Tompiros and Jumanos in the Salinas. By mid-century, however, a large part of the Jumano population of the Tompiro province must have consisted of fairly recent arrivals, refugees from the Plains bands and their descendants.

Scholes has summarized seventeenth-century sources—some from the period just after the conquest, but some extending to the later years as well—which indicate that the Jumanos did differ from other residents of the Pueblos in appearance, primarily in being *rayados* (or *pintados*); some of them, at least, painted their faces in a distinctive manner. He concluded that ". . . the *rayado* element constituted a large part of the total population of the Jumano pueblos, and that it was not a transient element . . ."[23] But even though the Jumanos may have been distinctive in appearance, in facial decoration and/or costume, they evidently spoke the same language as the Tompiros. As was indicated at an earlier date, public announcements in villages such as Abo and Las Humanas were made in the Tompiro language, to Tompiros and Jumanos alike.[24]

After direct contact between the Plains and Pueblo Jumanos was broken around 1660, it can be assumed that the latter group would be increasingly acculturated to and submerged in the Tompiro population. When their distinctive economic role came to an end, there may have been no reason for the Jumanos to maintain a distinctive social identity. Archaeologists describe slight, seemingly insignificant, differences in material culture among population groups in this province, based on comparative study of the ruins of both Tompiro villages (e.g., Abo) and those identified as Jumano (Las Humanas, now called Gran Quivira).[25] The one community which can with confidence be identified as a Jumano center at mid-century is Las Humanas (Cueloce). There was also evidently a large Jumano element in the villages of Abo, Quarai (Cuarac), and Tabira (sometimes called Las Salinas). Fray Alonso de Benavides had specifically described Las Humanas, or "the great pueblo of the Xumanas," as a trading center where "this nation come to trade and barter."[26] In 1660, Las Humanas was still a trading center, but trading visits by Jumanos from beyond the Pecos had dwindled and may have been completely discontinued. Instead, there are repeated indications of the presence of Apaches, visiting and trading in the Salinas villages. Here, just as was the case earlier at Pecos Pueblo, the Apaches displaced the Jumanos and gained another foothold in eastern New Mexico.

Las Humanas itself had suffered repeated raids by the Apaches of Los Siete Rios, the region between the Guadalupe Mountains and the Pecos, southeast of the Salinas. In the 1650's, the town had been invaded, and the old mission of San Isidro despoiled. A decade later, after the church had been rebuilt and dedicated to San Buenaventura there were more incidents.

> . . . the Apaches of the Seven Rivers district made an attack on the Jumano village and left a trail of ruin behind. The church was profaned and laid waste, images were smashed, the sacred ornaments were broken in pieces, and many other atrocities were committed. Eleven persons were killed, and thirty prisoners were seized.[27]

As visits by the Plains Jumanos decreased, Apache trade and other contacts in the area increased. East of New Mexico, Apache control extended ever farther toward the south; the Jumanos were in retreat. After 1660, the Apaches were increasingly in evidence at Las Humanas, arriving in greater numbers, on both peaceful and hostile errands.

Tensions between the Apaches and the Tompiro villagers, which would have arisen in any case, were exacerbated by the presence in these villages of the Plains Jumano refugees who had a longstanding enmity toward the Apaches. Spanish authorities had to deal with several violent encounters between Salineros and Apaches. These were recounted in the testimony given at the trial of the alcalde, Nicolas de Aguilar.

> . . . two heathen Indians [Apaches] from Los Siete Rios having arrived at nightfall at the pueblo of Cuarac, the Indians of that pueblo, understanding that they were enemies, killed one of them and wounded the other. Thereupon the Apaches of Los Siete Rios who had been friendly made demonstrations, desiring to come and attack the pueblo to avenge the killing. Gov. Don Bernardo [Lopez] sent the accused [Aguilar] to wage war on them, or pacify them before they could fall upon the pueblo of the Christians. He went, taking with him a squadron of Spaniards and another of Indians; he worked hard to reduce the enemy, for they were very much determined on war. But God willed that they should be reduced to peace, and a pact was made with them that they should not pass beyond the pueblos of Humanas and Tabira, where they come to barter; nor should the enemy of the same nation in the jurisdiction of Casa Fuerte and Navajo come, because it is from there that the whole kingdom receives hurt, because they [the Apaches] are all one people, and it is impossible to tell whether they are friends or enemies. This pact has been observed, and the Indians of Cuarac have been ordered not to go to the pueblos of Humanas and Tabira at the time when the Apache nations of Los Siete Rios should come to trade, for, if the nations would avoid seeing each other there would be no war . . . [otherwise] they might again start trouble, for this is the usual thing among them.[28]

The region, at the same time, was suffering the prolonged effects of drought and famine. In 1669, Fray Juan Bernal described its death throes in one of the last official reports on the Tompiro province.

> . . . this kingdom . . . is nearly exhausted from suffering two calamities which were enough to put it out of existence . . . One of these is that the whole land is at war with the widespread heathen nation of the

Apache Indians . . . The second misfortune is that for three years no
crops have been harvested. In the past year, 1668, a great many Indians
perished of hunger . . . There were pueblos (as instance Humanas) where
more than 450 died of hunger.[29]

Removal of population from the Salinas pueblos was under way by
this time. Soon after missionaries began their efforts around El Paso,
the Mansos were reduced to a single settlement at the mission of
Nuestra Señora de Guadalupe. The Franciscans judged these Indians
to be "so barbarous and uncultivated that all its members go naked
and . . . they have no houses in which to dwell."[30] To deal with this
situation, some of the Christian Indians of the eastern Pueblos were
transported to that area, to assist in religious instruction, house
construction, and other matters. This contingent included a number of Jumanos, and may have marked the beginning of a deliberate
attempt to move Jumanos out of the Tompiro province.

The relocation of Indians from the Salinas increased, as the problems of famine and war continued. During the decade of 1670–
1680, the region became steadily depopulated, and was largely deserted by 1678. It seems that Las Humanas and Tabira were the first
communities to be abandoned, though one or the other may have
been briefly revived before the final demise. There were, according
to Scholes, many Indians from Humanas Pueblo at El Paso as early
as 1670. It appears that when full-scale evacuation of the eastern
Tompiro province got under way, the Jumanos were usually sent to
the Manso mission at El Paso, while Piros were often taken into
Piro villages along the Rio del Norte. Later, many of these were
again removed and transferred to El Paso.[31]

The Jumanos who settled at El Paso may have been able, once
more, to make contact with and perhaps to join their relatives
further east or south. Any who remained eventually became inter-
mingled with the mission Indians of Manso and Piro descent and
other refugees who arrived there along with the Spanish colonists,
at the time of the Pueblo Rebellion of 1680. Over the course of the
following centuries, this native population lost whatever ethnic
and cultural distinctions were earlier present.[32]

10.

THE PUEBLO REBELLION OF 1680 AND ITS AFTERMATH

Through the decades of the 1660's and 1670's, the Tompiro province had grown ever more impoverished and depopulated. At the same time, hardship and internal dissension appeared through all of the provinces of New Mexico. The Indians' rankling resentments surfaced in repeated attempts at revolt, inevitably followed by Spanish reprisals. Most of the incidents were local or regional, and were quickly put down. The Indian agitators, when they could be apprehended, were usually executed. The momentum continued, however, and the Indians learned from their failures. To the Spanish population, the rebellious movements were probably most frightening when they seemed to involve the complicity or cooperation of the Apaches, who were never effectively under Spanish control. The colonists had gradually come to see themselves as the protectors of the Pueblo Indians against Apache encroachment: at the same time, they were able to use fear of the Apaches as a threat, to keep the Pueblo communities in line. Like the long-existing factionalisms among the Pueblos, hostile relations between Pueblos and Indians outside of New Mexico played into the hands of the colonial power; therefore, the Spanish rulers found it especially disturbing when there were signs of Pueblo-Apache cooperation.

Don Esteban Clemente, an Indian governor in the Tompiro Pueblos, who was known as a Christian and was trusted by the Spanish administration, was found to be the leader of one of the most serious of the Indian liberation movements. The plan involved Christian Indians in the Salinas, and therefore probably had Jumano participation. It called for a coordinated assault on the herds of Spanish horses, which would be turned loose and driven off into the mountains; immobilized by the loss of their horses, the Spaniards were to be massacred. The elaborate scheme is evidence of the growing ability of Indians throughout the provinces to plan and coordinate such efforts. However, it did not succeed; the plot was discovered, and

Don Esteban was hanged. Although he had been a prominent native Christian, objects were found among his possessions which indicated that he was also, in secret, a practitioner of the native *kachina* religion.

Indian resentments were highest in periods when the suppression of the Pueblo religion (an elaborate form of ancestor worship) was carried out most rigorously. The administration of Governor Juan Francisco de Trevino (1675–1677) was a period of extremely harsh repression of native religious practices and persecution of the *kachina* priests, who were labeled as *hechizeros* (sorcerers). In one such campaign, forty-seven men of the Tewa province were arrested; four of them—probably *kachina* priests as well as political leaders—were hanged and the others were lashed and imprisoned. At this point, over seventy armed Indian men forced their way into the governor's office, ceremoniously presented him with tobacco and food, and formally demanded the release of the prisoners. Governor Trevino acceded, addressing the Indians as "my children" and attempting a bold show of paternalistic condescension. He later learned—as he must have sensed at the time—that the men were prepared to kill him on the spot, had he refused their request, and that a massacre of Spaniards was to follow.

One of the prisoners whom the governor released was Popé, a Tewa medicine man, who retreated to the far northern pueblo of Taos. Here he prayed, communed with the spirits, and made plans. Popé—to become famous as the mastermind of the Pueblo Rebellion—worked for five years to put together the coordinated attack which began in August of 1680. This time, the Indians succeeded; those Spanish colonists who did not die in the initial uprising were driven from New Mexico. Spanish rule was overthrown, and the Pueblo Indians were free, although for little more than a decade.

The program of the leading clique among the Pueblo insurrectionists assumed the character of a nativistic movement. Their followers were enjoined to break up and burn crucifixes and religious images, to raze churches, to destroy the vestments and other possessions of the priests. The use of the Spanish language was forbidden, baptismal names were to be abolished, and Christian marriages dissolved; a ritual washing with yucca-root was prescribed, to remove the taint of baptism. The objective was to return to a purely Indian way of life, with all traces of Spain and Catholicism eradicated.

In the frenzy of the early days of the insurrection, there was tremendous destruction of property, most especially religious property. Many churches, such as the great mission church at Pecos Pueblo, were totally destroyed; in some cases, the walls were torn down brick by brick. Others—as at Isleta—were desecrated by being used as pens for animals.

The desecration of the churches might be undertaken with enthusiasm; other commands, however, were harder to obey. Many things that the Spaniards had introduced were already familiar and had become part of the Indians' way of life. Few Pueblo Indians would have been willing to give up the metal tools, food plants, sheep, goats, and horses which had transformed their subsistence economy.

In most of the outlying Pueblos, where there were no Spanish soldiers to protect them, the Franciscan friars were slain. A few escaped, with assistance from their converts, and made their way toward Santa Fe. The colonists of upper New Mexico quickly assembled in the capital, where the militia organized a defense. Santa Fe was under siege from August 12 to 20; then, under the direction of Governor Otermin, the survivors began an orderly retreat. They followed the road southward, finally overtaking the residents of the lower villages, who had gathered at Isleta and were now also in flight. From Isleta, around twenty-five hundred colonists eventually made their way toward the mission settlement at El Paso. Almost four hundred had been killed, including twenty-one Franciscan friars.

The refugee colonists would have had a more difficult passage downriver had not Isleta and the Piro villages to the south been slow to join the revolt. Several hundred Indians from these villages accompanied the Spaniards in their retreat. There may have been divided loyalties throughout New Mexico, but in most villages the rebels prevailed; families and individuals who had shown signs of pro-Spanish sympathies were suspect.

Since the Jumano pueblos had been abandoned a decade before the rebellion, we hear virtually nothing about Jumanos in New Mexico during this period or after the reconquest. There is an occasional mention of individual Jumanos, as servants or retainers of Spanish officials; however, there was no longer a cohesive Jumano community. A substantial portion of the Pueblo Jumano population had already been removed and resettled elsewhere, principally at El Paso. Any who remained would eventually lose their distinctive identity and merge into the Piro population, which was also declining.

At a place called Sevilleta, about ten miles north of El Paso, the fleeing colonists made camp for several days in late September. Here, Governor Otermin counted heads and assessed the situation. Considering his options, and awaiting the reply to a letter which had been dispatched to the viceroy in Mexico, he decided to set up temporary headquarters at El Paso, near the mission of La Señora de Guadalupe de los Mansos.

El Paso in 1680

At the end of the year 1680, the colonial government of New Mexico was at its lowest ebb, and its fate rested in El Paso del Rio del Norte. This border settlement must have been an unprepossessing place, both before and after the arrival of the refugees from upriver.

El Paso was a part of territorial New Mexico, as was a stretch of northern Chihuahua, as far west as Casas Grandes. The early attempts at missionizing the Indians between El Paso and La Junta had come mainly from the Franciscans in New Mexico. Fray Alonso de Benavides had made contact with the Mansos near El Paso, as he traveled to and from New Mexico. Like the Jumanos, these Indians seemed to him to be eager for resident missionaries, and they had requested baptism. Benavides recommended that a mission station, defended by a military post, be established near the river crossing, and that the region be developed; he thought mining and ranching were good possibilities. More visits by missionaries soon followed, but the earliest permanent mission, which was named Nuestra Señora de Guadalupe, was founded in 1659 by Fray Garcia de San Francisco.

> In the name of the most holy and indivisible Trinity, Father, Son, and Holy Ghost . . . on the eighth day of the month of December, of the year 1659, I, Fray Garcia de San Francisco of the order of the minor friars of the regular observance of our Seraphic Father San Francisco . . . of the holy custody of the conversion of San Pablo of New Mexico, minister and guardian of the convent of San Antonio del Pueblo de Senecu: whereas the captains and old men of the heathendom of the Mansos and Zumanas Indians went to the said custody to supplicate me to descend to preach them the Holy Evangel of Our Lord Jesus Christ and succeed in quieting them and baptizing them . . . and having received the patents from my superior, in which he orders me to descend for the instruction and conversion of this heathendom, and license from . . . Señor Don Juan, Manso governor; and having descended, with no little labor, to El Passo [sic] del Rio del Norte . . . and having congregated most of the rancherias of the Manso heathen on said site; and having offered them the evangelical word, and they having accepted it for their catechism, and permitted me to build a little church of branches and mud and a monastery thatched with straw . . . I took possession of this conversion of the Mansos and Sumanas, and of all the other surrounding

heathen which might be assembled . . . and I named and dedicated this holy church and conversion to the most holy Virgin of Guadalupe with the above name of El Passo . . . Fray Garcia de San Francisco, apostolic commissary of the Mansos and Zumanas . . .[1]

The mission was located near the ford of the river, on the west bank. As indicated by Fray Garcia, it was originally designated to serve the Mansos and Sumanas (or Zumanas). By far the greater number of Indians baptized at this mission in its early years seem to have been Mansos (though many are listed without an indication of tribal affiliation). The listings of those at the mission before 1680 actually include Mansos, Piros, Sumas, Tanos, Apaches, and Jumanos. The church had a large convent, and there were usually several missionaries in residence there. From this mission, two others were subsequently founded; the exact dates are unknown. One of these was Nuestro Padre San Francisco de los Sumas, about twelve leagues south of El Paso. Here, according to Vetancurt, there were ". . . some Christians of the nations which they call Zumas and Zumanas."[2] The other, La Soledad, was considerably farther to the west and ministered primarily to the Janos; though technically in New Mexico, it was close to Casas Grandes, and eventually became a *visita* of San Antonio de Casas Grandes.

The Mansos were the indigenous people in the immediate vicinity of El Paso. The presence of Piros, Tanos, and Jumanos at the mission of Guadalupe reflects the removal of population from the southern Pueblos. According to Hughes, ". . . there were present in El Paso in 1670 many Indians from the Jumano pueblos."[3] There were also Indians from the pueblos of Abo, Senecu, Galisteo, and Isleta. The source of such information is principally in baptismal records, and so probably would not include the already Christianized Indians who came as assistants to the missionaries (including the six Tewas who accompanied Fray Garcia from Senecu).

There was a very small number of Apaches settled at the El Paso missions. The Janos—who may possibly have been Apachean[4]—were present only at La Soledad; the broad territorial range of this tribe extended west from the vicinity of Casas Grandes. The Sumas, too, were primarily desert-dwellers whose presence is noted over a tremendous area west of the Rio del Norte, generally somewhat south of the Janos.

It is clear that the Sumas and Jumanos were related peoples; the actual variation in the form of the names makes it difficult, at times, to distinguish between them. Sauer made the general observation that the Suma (Zuma, Yuma, etc.) seem usually to have been found west of the Rio del Norte and the Jumano (Xumana, Humana, etc.) to the east.[5] The Sumana (Zumana) mentioned by Fray Garcia and others may possibly have been part of the Sumas; however, in some cases (as in the reference by Vetancurt, quoted above) Suma (Zuma) and Sumana (Zumana) are mentioned together, as separate "nations," indicating that some distinction between the two was made by contemporary observers. Further, at least in the records of La Señora de Guadalupe, the Jumanos also seem to have been considered a separate group.

It may be that the Jumanos in the missions at El Paso were those who had removed from the Pueblos. Occurrence of the closely related names Suma and Sumana suggests that members of both western and eastern populations were found in the vicinity of El Paso, on or near the Rio Grande. The western group, the Sumas, may have been pushed toward the east by the advances of Apachean groups from further west. The Sumanas then, may be tentatively identified with the Jumano group earlier called *Caguates* by Luxan, *People of the Cows* by Cabeza de Vaca, and usually, in later references, known as *Cibolos* or *Cibolo-Jumanos*.[6] Their range lay toward the east, at least as far as Rio Pecos.

From their base at El Paso, the Franciscan friars began around 1670 to make visits to La Junta de los Rios, where the Julimes (earlier called *Cabris* or *Abriaches*) were the dominant people. It was already obvious, a century earlier, that the Indians around La Junta were strongly affected by the development of Spanish industries and settlements along the upper Rio Conchos. Well before 1680, much of the native population had been drawn into the labor force, as permanent or seasonal workers, but it was only after this date that a resident enclave of Spaniards became established at La Junta.

At El Paso, the arrival of the refugees from the upriver colony put a tremendous strain on the mission installations and on the small community of Spaniards already in residence. Initially, three small refugee settlements were laid out, and makeshift huts were thrown up. It was hoped that the bivouac at El Paso would be brief, and that the settlers could quickly return to their homes and lands upriver. After getting both Spaniards and New Mexican Indians settled into temporary quarters, Governor Otermin began to formulate plans to suppress the rebellion and reoccupy New Mexico.

Six months later, in the autumn of 1681, Otermin himself led an expedition which ascended the Rio del Norte and entered the southern Pueblos. His second in command was Juan Dominguez de Mendoza, who had led numerous punitive expeditions against Apaches in New Mexico, and now held the high rank of *maestre de campo.* The governor managed to assemble a company of fifty soldiers, some of them recruited from colonists who had fled to such places as Parral and Sonora. With servants and accompanying loyal Indians, the expedition numbered around three hundred.

In predicting a quick return to Santa Fe, Otermin apparently expected that the rebel Indians would be repentant and eager to surrender. However, for the most part, they were still defiant. After ascending the river road as far as the southern Pueblos, the Spaniards inspected the damage done to their properties and to the churches, salvaged a number of religious artifacts, and burned some of the abandoned villages. Captain Dominguez de Mendoza, leading a party to reconnoitre in the vicinity of his family holdings near Isleta, came very near being captured by the defiant Indians. However, as the dejected company returned southward a group of Christian Tiwas from Isleta—which was now under attack by rebel forces—followed, to join the loyal Indians already settled at El Paso.

After the failed expedition of reconquest, efforts were reluctantly made toward establishing permanent accommodations at El Paso. Eventually, the main Spanish settlement was built at San Lorenzo, about twelve leagues below the river-crossing, and fairly near the mission of San Francisco de los Sumas. The New Mexican Indians were settled in three pueblos, one made up of Piros and Tompiros, one of Tiwas, and one a mixed group which included Tano and Jemez. A presidio was built, centrally located, for the defense of the now greatly increased population at and below El Paso.

In 1682, Governor Otermin requested permission to leave the colony for medical reasons. Late in the summer of the next year, his successor, Don Jironza Petris de Cruzate, arrived, bringing some of the fifty soldiers authorized for the new presidio. Traveling with the new governor was Fray Nicolas Lopez, to assume the position of Custodian of the Franciscan Order and to supervise work at the missions and in the newly established Indian villages.

11.

THE EXPEDITION TO
THE RIO DE LAS NUECES

In August of 1683, a group of Indians—mainly Jumanos, but very likely accompanied by one or more representatives of the Tejas confederacy—visited El Paso in order to meet with the governor of New Mexico, Antonio de Otermin. The Jumanos requested that the Spaniards grant them a resumption of trade, that missionaries be sent to their communities, and that they receive Spanish military help against the Apaches. There are in the Jumanos' efforts—in their repeated appearances in El Paso, the petitions they presented, and in the Spaniards' response—remarkable parallels to the events of 1629. It will be useful to recall that earlier encounter between Jumanos and Spaniards, while examining the one which took place in 1683–1684, for which more detailed and possibly more accurate information is available.

Governor Otermin may or may not have been favorably impressed by the Indian emissaries' petitions. In any event, his term in office was expiring, and he deferred to his successor, Don Gironza Petris de Cruzate, whose arrival was imminent. This was not the first time that the Jumanos had appealed for aid in El Paso; their visits had begun during the early years of the mission. Jumanos had, moreover, journeyed as far as Parral, returning to El Paso when their efforts there met with no success. During this same period similar Indian delegations had been seen in other Spanish frontier towns. The historian Bolton noted, in a discussion of missionary work among Coahuiltecan tribes, that "for several years some of the Indians of Coahuila and even from beyond the Rio Grande had been asking for missionaries, and, under what influences we do not know, had sent messengers to Saltillo, Parral, Guadalajara, and Mexico City to seek them."[1] This great surge, through the 1670's and 1680's, of Indians begging for baptism and mission protection— all reminiscent of the High Plains Jumano of the 1620's—seems to have been a widespread reaction to essentially the same primary cause: the accelerating southward and eastward expansion of the Apaches.

Two months later, in mid-October, another delegation of seven Indian leaders came to El Paso, accompanied by an escorting body of approximately two hundred individuals. The Indians came to petition once more for ministers for the "more than 10,000 souls of the Jumanas and Julimes who were jointly sending the request." This time, Governor Cruzate was on hand, together with the new Franciscan Custodian, Fray Nicolas Lopez. According to Lopez, in a report submitted in 1686, "a number of nations" had been asking for the "water of baptism" at El Paso; the Jumanos' plea was given special attention because "they had always maintained friendship with the Spaniards."[2]

The Jumano spokesman, on this occasion, was their captain, or chief, Juan Sabeata, a figure who appears prominently in historical records over the next decade. According to Cruzate's account of this encounter, Sabeata (or Xaviata) had been a member of the earlier delegations; he had probably also been among those who visited Parral.

> In the pueblo of Nuestra Señora de Guadalupe del Paso, on the twentieth day of the month of October in the year 1683, I, Don Domingo Gironza Petris de Cruzati, governor and captain-general of this kingdom and province of New Mexico and its presidio for his Majesty: In view of the fact that there had arrived at this pueblo an Indian of the Humana Nation, called in his language Sabeata and in Spanish Juan—he was baptized in San Jose del Parral, according to what he says; and before I reached this town he had been here and had returned to his land which, according to what he says, is about six or eight days journey from this said pueblo, from where he was sent by all the captains of different nations who have their territories in the direction of the east; and in order that the most excellent señor viceroy of this New Spain may be informed concerning the report which this Indian, named Don Juan, and his companions who number six, made, I commanded him to appear before me. Through the interpretation of Captain Hernando Martin Serrano, a citizen of these provinces, and very well versed in the language which the said Indian, Don Juan, speaks . . . I received his oath in behalf of God, our Lord, and the sign of the cross in proper form, under burden of which he promised to tell the truth concerning all that he might know; by whom sent and for what; what he had seen and heard in all those territories; the distance which there is from one to the other; what nations are those which have commercial relations and amity with his.

He spoke as follows: He is a Christian and knows that God aids the one who speaks the truth and punishes the one who does not speak it; that where he lives at present with many of his Humana Nation is at the junction of the Rio del Norte and the Conchos, which must be from here about eight days' journey; that from there he was sent by six captains who are Christians and are named Don Juan, Alonso, Bartolome, Luis, Don Francisco and Jose; that these captains, with this witness, seeing themselves disconsolate because, being Christians, they do not have a minister to teach them the things of God, resolved in a *junta* which they convoked, that this witness should come to this pueblo of El Paso to ask for a minister so that when they were sick he might comfort them, and those who would die he might bury as Christians and the rest of the people he might baptize. According to what this witness says, there must be more than ten thousand souls who are asking for baptism, and these are the Julimes and Humanas. At the same time, he says that he was sent by the said people to seek favor of the Spaniards in order that they may defend them from their enemies, the Apaches, who have a rancheria very near theirs, and that the friendship so ancient which his nation of Humanas has enjoyed with the Spaniards from New Mexico moved them to come to present this petition.[3]

Juan Sabeata presented his request in religious terms; he had, it would appear, mastered the conventions of Spanish officialdom. At the same time, he made no secret of the Jumanos' primary objective—they had promised the Julimes and the other allies "to bring the Spanish to aid them against the Apaches." He went on to inform Governor Cruzate about the "nations" in whose interest he was speaking. Although many of the names are now unrecognizable, it is clear that the majority were located east of La Junta and pertain to the Concho-Colorado drainage system, the Tejas confederacy, and other regions of central and southern Texas.

Having been asked how much of a journey it probably is from where this witness is [lives] at present to where the other people of his Humana nation are, he said that it is about a six days' journey; that the buffaloes are a three days' journey from the *rancheria* where this deponent is [lives] at present; that the river which they call Las Nueces is a three days' journey from that place; that there are nuts in such abundance on this river that they constitute the maintenance of many nations who enjoy friendship and barter and exchange with his. These are those of the Miembro Largo which is a very extended and unnumbered nation; another nation which is called the Nation that Grinds; another that of the Ugly Arrows; another which is called the People of the Fish;

another which they call the People who Eat; another which they call
the People of the Dirty Water; another called Texuxa; another, the Pe-
nunde people; another, the Tixemu people; another which they call
Janaque; another called Tohojo; another nation called Emit; and another
which they call the People of the Caimanes.

Another nation is called Toapa; another, Quiovoriqui; another, Toa-
pari; and another, Geobari. Another is Borobamo; Cocuma; Obozi;
Comocara; Bean; Arihuman; Utaca; Tumpotogua; Mano; Los Surdos;
Quide. Also, the Great Kingdom of the Texas; those who make Arrows;
the Great Kingdom of Quivira; the very extended Nation of the Yutas;
and the extended Nation of the Humanas. There are thirty-six nations,
not counting a very great many others with which the Humanas trade
and have established friendly relations. He knows without doubt that
they will receive the ministers and Spaniards with very great affection
because they have been awaiting them for years, and that by not going
on this occasion they all might be low-spirited to such a degree that all
might be dispersed.

He said that where [he] now lives, he left two Indians of the Texas nation awaiting the reply which this deponent will carry in order to take
the information to those of their nation. These have told the declarant
that into that eastern region Spaniards are entering by water in wooden
houses, and that they barter and exchange with the said nation of the
Texas.[4]

The last point, seemingly an afterthought, may well have been
intended as a clincher: a hint of the presence in eastern Texas of
other Europeans—all "Spaniards" to the Jumanos—approaching by
ship and trading with the Indians.

At about the same time, but in a separate audience, Juan Sabeata
stated his case to Fray Nicolas Lopez. According to Lopez' account,
there were present at this audience "twenty-six captains of different heathen, and of three Christian nations, who were asking for
the second or third time for the water of baptism." The Indians,
most of whom resided for at least a part of each year at La Junta,
maintained that they had been ". . . serving the king in the mines
and in the fields of the inhabitants of Parral, and that the latter had
never given them ministers, although they had asked for them
many times." For this reason, the Indian captains indicated to
Lopez, they had turned to El Paso, "being acquainted with the lo-
cality, and knowing that Spaniards were settled there."

The Custodian, "in order to learn at once whether their petition
was sincere," indicated to the Indians that, should the fathers come

to La Junta, it would be very inconvenient for them to say mass, since there was no church on the lower river. "On the following day, the captains sent messengers to take the measurements of the altars of the church of El Paso, and they themselves set out to give orders to build a church. Within twenty days the messengers returned to the number of more than sixty persons, both men and women, saying that all the people were employed in building two churches."[5]

It was apparently at an audience after returning from this errand that one of the Jumanos—probably, once more, Juan Sabeata—told Fray Lopez about the Miracle of the Wonderful Cross.

> Impelled by the fact that they [the Jumanos] were about to engage in a great battle, and distressed because they were few in number and their enemies totaled more than thirty thousand, they had invoked the aid of the Holy Cross, of which they had learned from their forefathers. Instantly there had descended through the air a cross adorned with colors, with a pedestal two *varas* long . . . With this cross placed on their standard, without the loss of a single person they had conquered their enemies, winning many spoils of war. Knowing this to be a miracle, they had come to beg for holy baptism.[6]

This eleventh-hour invocation of a miraculous apparition—so reminiscent of the earlier appearance of the "Lady in Blue"—reveals, once more, the astuteness of a Jumano leader who grasped the importance of providing the Spanish authorities with both material and spiritual incentives for action. However, the story of the cross was dismissed as fiction—as it was apparently revealed to be, by some of the Indians involved. It should not be doubted, however, that Fray Lopez was impressed at the time. Just as in 1629, the Jumanos' final appeal—spiced with intimations of heavenly intervention—was followed immediately by action on the part of the Franciscans. A trio of priests, including the Custodian himself, set out for La Junta within a fortnight (Map 6, no. 1).

Governor Cruzate, for his part, had sent off his report to the viceroy, the Count de Paredes, containing a transcript of Juan Sabeata's declaration, which pointed out the apparent threat of foreign intrusion into Texas. An *entrada* into the Jumano country would be, he predicted, an opportunity to win two kingdoms—Quivira and the Tejas—with very little investment, and thus to secure a very large territory as a bulwark against the French threat. After the messengers' departure, without waiting for the viceroy's reply, he ordered the *maestre de campo*, Captain Juan Dominguez de Mendoza, to proceed immediately to assemble a company of twenty volunteers for the expedition.

The Mission to La Junta de los Rios

Father Nicolas Lopez recruited two Franciscan friars for the mission, Antonio Aceveda, and Juan Sabaleta (or Zavaleda) who was then the Commissary of the Inquisition. The three clerics departed from El Paso on December 1, 1683. They chose to make their journey apostolically—that is, walking barefoot in traditional Franciscan fashion and without an accompanying military escort. They were accompanied by the large body of Indians who had been awaiting their departure.

Two years later, after returning from his travels, first to La Junta de los Rios, and then to the Concho and Colorado valley of Texas, Lopez traveled to Mexico to petition the offices of his order for funds and personnel to carry on a full-scale missionary campaign among the Indians of Texas. In that document, he gave an account of the earlier *entrada*.

> The supplicant [Lopez] . . . resolved to set out on foot with two apostolic religious, in company with these heathen Indians . . . He spent thirteen days on the journey, traveling by easy stages, and found a great number of heathen Suma Indians.
>
> He continued in this manner until arriving at La Junta de los Rios. Having reached the first nations, the supplicant found erected a large church of grass, with its altar made according to the measurements taken by the Indian messengers, and so arranged as to enable him to say mass. Passing on six leagues farther, he found another church much larger and more carefully built, where he halted. There was also a house which the Indians [Julimes] had built for the minister to live in . . .[7]

The priests immediately began the tasks of baptizing infants, catechizing adults, laying out garden plots, supervising the sowing of crops, and settling or resettling the Sumas and Julimes in compact communities around these missions. By the next summer, several additional "nations"[8] had begun building churches, and had forwarded to Fray Lopez their requests for religious personnel to assist in a similar reorganization of their communities under Spanish missionary supervision and protection.

The Franciscans called themselves "barefoot friars"; their apostolic way of travel was a doctrinal matter, emphasizing poverty and humility. By mentioning this in his report, Fray Lopez may have intended to emphasize the religious aspects of the expedition. This was also Juan Sabeata's intention, with his tale of the miraculous cross. Both Jumano and Spanish leaders were fully cognizant of the military and political exigencies; however, all parties seem to have found it important, as strategy, to formulate the project and to put it on record with an appropriate religious rationale.

Nevertheless, in his request that assistance be sent to the Rio de las Nueces (Concho), Juan Sabeata emphasized not only the large number of souls to be saved there, but also the potential wealth of natural resources in the area—the large number of buffalo, great abundance of nuts, fruits, and other products. He also described the wealth of the "great kingdom of the Tejas," and indicated that this nation had a close affiliation with Quivira, which had long been another objective for Spanish diplomatic connections. Finally, of course, he dropped the hint of those other "Spaniards" in the east, entering by water in "wooden houses" and trading with the Indians. Governor Cruzate rose to the bait—the expedition to the Nueces was to be undertaken "for the best interest of both Majesties"—i.e., the Spanish Crown and the Church of Rome.[9]

The measured progress of the priests on the river trail to La Junta gave Captain Dominguez de Mendoza time to organize the military arm of the undertaking. The company of twenty volunteers departed on December 15, 1683, from the Real of San Lorenzo, the Spanish settlement some twelve leagues below El Paso (roughly in the location of modern Juarez, Chihuahua). The actual point of bivouac before departure was San Bartolome, a hacienda established by Thome Dominguez de Mendoza, former *maestre de campo* and father of the commander of the expedition. Three generations of this important colonial family were represented in the undertaking, since both Juan the Younger and his cousin Balthazar, the son of the captain, were among the volunteers. The military party included, it might be noted, Hernan Martin Serrano,[10] the El Paso resident who had served as translator during Juan Sabeata's audience with Governor Gironza. The citizen-soldiers were to rendezvous with the missionary party at the Julime settlements, near La Junta de los Rios.

Along the route south, both Father Lopez and Captain Dominguez de Mendoza noted the presence of many scattered *rancherias* of Suma Indians. After leaving the Real de San Lorenzo on December 15, Dominguez de Mendoza reported seeing Sumas on December 16, 17, 19, 21, and 22; these Indians, he commented, were "poor people who live chiefly on mescal, which is baked palms." Although some of the *rancherias* were small, others were quite large; he observed that "a considerable portion (of the Sumas) were already reducing themselves to settlements and alleging that the Hapaches (Apaches) did not allow them in their lands." Further, ". . . all of these *rancherias* asked of me aid and help against the common enemy, the Hapaches nation, alleging generally that most of them were already disposed to becoming Christians." The commander erected crosses at his stopping places, and promised the Sumas "all help and protection" on his return journey. However, he did not pass that way again.[11]

The passage of the mounted military party downriver actually took one day longer than the barefoot trek of the friars. Dominguez de Mendoza and his men joined the three religious on December 29, their progress having been delayed several times by rough ground and the loss of some of their animals. As the party approached the mission where Fathers Lopez and Sabaleta were at work, settlements of Julimes were seen on both sides of the river. Because of numerous crosses which had been planted in these villages, the Spaniards named the place La Navidad en las Cruces. The Julime communities were, as they had been a century earlier, clustered at the confluence of the Rio del Norte and the Conchos. According to Captain Dominguez de Mendoza, these Indians "are versed in the Mexican (Nahuatl) language, and all sow maize and wheat."[12]

Fray Acevedo had established himself seven leagues distant from La Junta, in the mission named El Apostol Santiago; this was situated near an arroyo, at the point where the trail turned toward the north, away from the river, and leading, by way of the mountains, to the Salado (Pecos). When the rest of the party departed on this road, Acevedo remained behind, to supervise the mission work; in this, he was undoubtedly assisted by Christian Indians whom the friars would have brought from the missions at El Paso. On January 1, 1684, the other two clerics, Lopez and Sabaleta, joined the company of soldiers and the large escorting group of Indians, to begin the journey through the mountains.

The March Across Texas

The detailed itinerary recorded by Juan Dominguez de Mendoza is the essential document for tracing the route and establishing the location of the Jumano post on the Rio de las Nueces; it gives a daily accounting of leagues traveled, the direction of march, and several landmarks for the identification of each day's bivouac site.

After leaving the Rio del Norte the party traveled northward at first, and proceeded for several days through a series of arroyos, finally to emerge on a level plain, where they turned toward the east. With the help of the Jumano guides, they were able to end almost every day's march at a spring or water hole. The entry for January 3, 1684, is typical.

> . . . we set out from this place, which was named San Nicolas. It is distant from Nuestro Padre San Francisco [the previous camping place] about seven leagues . . . It is at the extremity of a mesa which extends to the north. It is a watering place consisting of a beautiful reservoir which is supplied by the rains. The passage through the rocks forms two steep crags on the sides; on one of them I had a holy cross placed. There are in the environs of the reservoir some ash trees . . . and in the cavities made by the rocks adjoining the reservoir there is a great quantity of maidenhair fern and most beautiful grape-vines. Toward the west there is a beautiful plain, with plentiful pastureage of couch grass. The direction which we were following was toward the north.[13]

The party at this time would have been entering the Davis Mountains. The march was broken on several occasions for the purpose of hunting, to provide food for "the Indians of the Jumana nation and others who came with them," as well as for the soldiers. The Indians did the hunting, in traditional style; they ". . . arranged to surround the deer and other kinds of animals, in order to relieve the necessity which we all shared."[14] After the party had traveled for ten days, some tracks of buffalo were sighted, but none of the animals was encountered until January 15, two days after reaching the Rio Salado (Pecos). Every day, as the company moved along, crosses were erected, except when lack of suitable timber made it impossible; the priests celebrated mass on auspicious days, including January 13, the day of arrival at the Salado.

This river was followed for three days more, until they reached a Jediondo (Cibolo) *rancheria*, located on the eastern bank; this was the main way station on the road to the Rio de las Nueces (Map 6, no. 6). The *rancheria* was situated "at the foot of a great rock that serves it as protection against the hostile Apaches."[15] The Jediondos had built huts for the military party, but the commander would not consent to their lodging in the *rancheria*; declining Jediondo hospitality, the Spaniards pitched camp on a nearby hilltop.

An advance party of Indians, led by Juan Sabeata, had ridden ahead of the main body of the expedition, to announce and initiate preparations for the Spaniards' arrival. Sabeata rejoined the party as they approached the Jediondo *rancheria*, which the Spanish captain promptly gave a new name, San Ygnacio de Loyola. On January 17,

the Spaniards were greeted with a reception which, once more, is
strangely reminiscent of that staged for Fray Salas in 1629.

> Their chiefs and other people came out to receive us with much re-
> joicing, most of them on foot, others on horseback, carrying a holy cross
> very well made, which apparently must be two and a half varas long, of
> somewhat heavy timber, painted red and yellow, and fastened with a
> nail which they call *taxamanil.* They also brought forth a banner of
> white taffeta, a little less than a vara long; in the middle of the banner
> were two successive crosses of blue taffeta, very well made. At the time
> of meeting us they fired several shots, Don Juan Sabeata firing with a
> fuse an arquebus barrel without a lock; and I ordered the salute returned
> on our part with two volleys.[16]

It might be noted that, despite strict controls which the Spanish
authorities officially endeavored to maintain on the possession of
guns by Indians, the captain was willing to overlook the Jumano
violation, and returned Sabeata's salute. The cross, which may have
been intended to represent the one which had miraculously de-
scended to earth, was kissed by the clerics and military officers; and
the priests were embraced enthusiastically by women and children,
who kissed the hems of their habits. The "well-made banner" with
two crosses of blue taffeta may have been a French flag, showing the
cross of Lorraine.[17]

At this "place of San Ygnacio," the Jediondo *rancheria,* Captain
Dominguez de Mendoza was told of the Indians' fear of "a great
ambuscade which the enemy [Apaches] are coming to make on
them, in order to carry off many horses."[18] Two days after their
arrival, the Spanish officers were invited to an assembly to confer
with the Indian governor, Juan Sabeata, and "all the chiefs" of the
different nations.

> For this purpose, I [Dominguez de Mendoza] on my part ordered all
> the chiefs of squad and soldiers of rank to assemble, in order that they
> might be present. This being done, I commanded Governor Don Juan
> Sabeata and all their chiefs to say what it was they wished; and all, in
> one voice, asked that for the love of God I should make war on the hos-
> tile Apaches, who were enemies of theirs and of the Spaniards. Because
> this was true, and because the said governor and the chiefs protested
> that it was not wise to leave them behind, on account of the many dan-
> gers which might follow, and seeing that they petitioned forcibly, I
> granted that war should be made upon them, with which the governor
> and other chiefs were pleased.[19]

The Spanish commander acceded with little enthusiasm, evidently under some duress because of the large numbers of the assembled Jumanos and allied Indians. On the day following this meeting, January 20, Juan Sabeata immediately had deer skins distributed to the Spaniards, in order to provide them with protection against Apache arrows. Four more days were spent at the Jediondo *rancheria*—possibly for the purpose of preparing shields or armor from the deer skins—and then the entire party, including the Jediondo warriors, moved on toward the Nueces. A day later, they were joined by "the people whom they call the Arcos Tuertos (Twisted Bows)"; Dominguez de Mendoza observed that their "wearing apparel and all the rest" were "after the fashion of the Suma nation."[20]

For the next several days, scouts were out searching for Apaches, and several rumors of their proximity went through the company. Some horses were stolen around the twenty-fourth of the month, some were lost on the twenty-ninth, and there was an Apache raid, with the loss of nine horses, around the sixth of February. On the last occasion, the Jumano scouts reported sighting an Apache camp, but it would seem that no Apaches were seen in the flesh, or engaged in battle.

> The hostile Apaches stole nine animals, seven from the Jumana Indians, and the others, a horse and a mule, from the chief and Ensign Diego de Luna, respectively. Because of carelessness, these animals joined those of the Indians. It was not possible to follow them because of the great advantage which they had.[21]

On the nineteenth of February, after a four-day halt during which the Jumano scouts undertook a futile search for the Apaches, and one day after a violent thunderstorm which destroyed a part of the expedition's supplies, Captain Dominguez de Mendoza evidently lost his temper and lashed out at the Jumano governor. Irritated by the time spent waiting for the return of a scouting party, the commander leaped to the conclusion that Juan Sabeata—"who in nothing had told us the truth"—was misleading him with false reports and deliberately slowing the pace of the expedition.

Actually, the commander may have been miffed by some disruption or interference with the great buffalo hunt which the Spanish officers were enjoying. At about this point, just before reaching the Rio Concho, the officers, with Indian assistance, began to slaughter large numbers of buffalo—sixty-six one day, forty-three the next, and, soon after, eighty in a single day. There was little or no movement toward their objective; they camped for days at a time, apparently for the purpose of hunting.

According to his own account, the *maestre de campo* confronted the Jumano governor, accused him of deceitfulness, and either dismissed him outright or humiliated him into leaving: "From this place [a tributary of the Rio Concho], under this date [February 19], I dispatched the Jumano spies [scouts] together with the said Sabeata, because of the frauds in which he had been caught. There went in his company two Piros Indians." No more is seen of Juan Sabeata, who clearly had departed. Later, Dominguez de Mendoza writes, for the benefit of Governor Cruzate, that "Juan Sabeata . . . had plotted with some nations to kill us," and suggests that for this reason Sabeata had fled *from the other Indians* in order to escape their retribution. "His conduct having been so bad, he was perhaps afraid they would kill him, for he remained in bad repute with all those nations." [22]

The commander's protestations ring distinctly hollow: considering the number of incidents of Apache harassment which did occur, including the repeated theft of horses, Juan Sabeata's fear of Apache attack was justified, and his caution appears to have been judicious. Captain Dominguez de Mendoza's account never makes clear the nature of the "frauds" with which he charged the Indian leader. Moreover, in the following years there is no indication that Juan Sabeata was in ill repute with other Jumanos, or that his influence among the Tejas and other Texas tribes was diminished to any degree. However, he seems never again to have attempted to deal with the Spanish colony of New Mexico.

On the Rio de las Nueces

Those remaining in the party reached the main course of the Concho on February 24. Dominguez de Mendoza refers to the river, on this occasion, as the Rio de las Perlas. He recognized the location (probably in the vicinity of San Angelo, Texas) as being "about eight leagues further down the river than the place where Don Diego de Guadalaxara arrived," referring to the expedition of 1654, in which he had been a participant. This river, he stated, was the one named in his order from Governor Cruzate, "which order is now executed." [23]

The party stayed at or near this spot from February 24 to March 15, with the priests celebrating mass every day and twice on holidays, and the soldiers killing large numbers of buffalo. There is no clear indication of the size or disposition of the group of Indian allies at this point, though Dominguez de Mendoza mentions the presence of representatives of "sixteen nations." However, the list which he later gives of the nations accompanying the expedition—most probably from the vicinity of La Junta—contains nineteen names. The count of sixteen would, at this point, obviously exclude the Jumanos, who had already quit the expedition, perhaps along with some others whose departure is not mentioned.[24]

> . . . First, the Jumano nation; the Ororosos, the Beitonijures, the Achubales, the Cujalos, the Toremes, the Gediondos, the Siacuchas, the Suajos, the Isuchos, the Cujacos, the Caulas, the Hinehis, the Ylames, the Cunquebacos, the Quitacas, the Quicuchabes, Los que Asen Arcos, the Hanasines. These nations are those who are accompanying us.[25]

Between the end of February and the beginning of May, there is very little accounting for the disposition of the expedition's time. The camp established on February 27, called San Isidro Laborador, was only eight leagues from the previous stay near the Rio Concho; and the move to the Rio Colorado, to which they shifted on March 15, was an advance of a mere five leagues. The expedition was in residence on the "glorious San Clemente" (the Colorado), from mid-March to the beginning of May. According to Bolton, the spot was a short distance below the junction of the Colorado with the Concho, near present-day Ballinger, Texas (Map 6, no. 5).[26]

> The San Clemente River flows toward the east. In this place there are no shells whatever; but I learned that six days' journey below the place on the same road there was a great quantity of large shells, and that most of them had pearls. The bottom lands of the river are luxuriant with plants bearing nuts, grapes, mulberries, and many groves of plums; with much game, wild hens, and a variety of animals, such as bear, deer, and antelopes, though few, but the number of buffalo is so great that only the divine Majesty, as owner of all, is able to count them.[27]

This was the place where the Spaniards were to await the representatives of forty-eight additional Indians nations who had been hoping to formalize an alliance with Spain. Here, Captain Dominguez de Mendoza ordered the construction of a combination chapel and bastion atop a hill. In the chapel, mass was sung daily, with all the Christian Indians assisting in the services for the benefit of the "barbarous nations" which were present. Buffalo hunting, which was pursued throughout the entire sortie, continued here. The Spaniards also explored the area, and some pearls were taken from the river.

The Apache raids and attacks increased, and the Apaches were joined by "bandit Indians from [Nueva] Vizcaya, whom they call the Salineros," who killed two Jediondos.[28] These Salineros may also have been Apaches; more likely, they were Chizos bands from near La Junta, with whom the Jumanos and Julimes were in a chronic state of war. Don Juan Sabeata's vigilance was vindicated, although Captain Dominguez de Mendoza continues to accuse him of treachery.

> . . . being without forces, and with only few munitions, I considered it best to return (to El Paso), in order to give an account to Captain Don Domingo Xironsa Petris de Crusate, governor and captain-general of New Mexico and its presidio, that his lordship may do in the case what he may consider best for the service of both Majesties.[29]

On the first day of May, Dominguez de Mendoza aborted the mission. Although messengers had earlier arrived from some of the eastern tribes, the ambassadors had not appeared. Both the commander and Fray Lopez indicate that a commitment was made, through the messengers, for the Spaniards to return in the following year. Dominguez de Mendoza recorded a list of the nations who were awaited on the San Clemente; like the list of the escorting nations, it bears very little resemblance to the list which was given to Governor Cruzate by Juan Sabeata.

> They will be set down with their names, although curious . . . Those for whom we are waiting are the following; People of the Rio de los Tejas, who had sent me a message that they would come, the Huicasique, the Aielis, the Aguidas, the Flechas Chiquitas, the Echancotes, the Anchimos, the Bobidas, the Injames, the Dijus, the Colabrotes, the Unojitas, the Juanas, the Yoyehis, the Acanis, the Humez, the Bibis, the Conchumuchas, the Teandas, the Hinsas, the Popjues, the Quisabas, the Paiabunas, the Papanes, the Puchas, the Puguahianes, the Isconis, the Tojumas, the Pagaiames, the Abas, the Bajuneros, the Nobraches, the Pylchas, the Detobitis, the Puchames, the Abau, the Oranchos.[30]

The Franciscans appear to have had little to do other than to celebrate mass at least once a day, with the assistance of the faithful Christian Indians. Curiously, Father Lopez' writings devote more attention to the building of the missions at La Junta and to the needs of the hard-pressed Indians there, than to the period of time spent in Texas.

The stay on the San Clemente was evidently a military, religious, and diplomatic disaster. On May 2, the Spaniards finally departed, having waited in vain for the arrival of most of the tribes who had promised through their messengers to attend. It may be that Juan Sabeata had already spread the word about the calumny of the Spanish captain. The departure from the riverside camp was precipitous; the party hurried west, by a different and more direct route to La Junta, accompanied by very few Indians: "There remained with us only some families." The Jediondos left quietly and unceremoniously, when the party neared the Salado.[31]

One of the more intriguing aspects of Juan Dominguez de Mendoza's journal is the running count of the number of buffalo killed, which is reported almost daily. The total recorded, for the entire six months between departure on January 1 and the final entry on May 25, 1684, is 5,156. Of these, 4,030 were slaughtered during the six-week stay on the San Clemente; the commander specifically noted that this number did not include "those which they left lost in the fields, only removing the pelts from them, nor the little calves which they brought to the camp, which were many."[32] Thus, the count given was evidently lower than the actual number killed; the take in pelts could have been six thousand or more.

Since we do not know the number of persons in the combined expedition party—Spaniards and accompanying Indians—it is difficult to assess the figures. However, when bison were being killed primarily for food, during the march eastward, the several days when one or two were killed seem typical. It is obvious that much of the time that the party was encamped on the Concho and the Colorado was devoted to hunting simply for taking pelts.

At the end of the hunt, Dominguez de Mendoza did distribute a share of the meat to the departing Indians, but—whether the actual killing was done by Indians or Spaniards, or both—the Spaniards took home the cargo of pelts loaded on the wagons which had carried their provisions into the field. It is clear that Captain Dominguez de Mendoza and his officers were able to return to the Rio del Norte with a very large cargo of buffalo pelts; elimination of the Jumano participants may have increased the size of the Spaniards' profit. It should not be forgotten that Juan Dominguez de Mendoza was one of the members of the 1654 expedition to the Nueces, which also yielded a cargo of pelts taken under distinctly questionable circumstances. It is no surprise then, that his participation in

the expedition of 1683–1684 seems to have had a covert profiteering motive; this motive may have been shared by some or all of the
Spanish volunteers.

Some historians have trivialized the expedition to the Nueces
and San Clemente, by treating it simply as a hunting expedition and
by putting the onus for its failures on the Indians.[33] However, to put
things in perspective, one should recall the status of the chief Spanish participants in the expedition: Nicolas Lopez, the chief religious
official of New Mexico; Juan Sabaleta, the head of the Inquisition;
and Captain Juan Dominguez de Mendoza, a prominent *encomendero* and the colony's highest ranking military officer. The expedition was an extremely expensive undertaking, considering the state
of military and economic emergency which prevailed in New Mexico at the time; it was, however, given priority at the highest levels
of both the church and the secular government.

Further, the political importance of the Jumanos should not be
underestimated. These Indians had a long connection with New
Mexico. Outside of the Pueblo provinces within the colony, the
greatest diplomatic efforts of the Spanish administration in New
Mexico, over the years, had been directed toward the Jumanos. The
Jumano trade was important to New Mexico from the beginning;
and the idea that the Jumanos could be the key to contacting and
eventually establishing rule over the Nations of the North was still
a tantalizing possibility.

The geopolitics of the situation—the view of the Texas country
as a buffer against France and other nations potentially desirous of
invading Mexico—always had to be considered; indeed, as time
went on, the French threat seemed ever more imminent. For the
Church, the idea of making a new beginning in missionizing,
among the Tejas and Quivira, was especially attractive in view of
the recent fiasco in New Mexico.

From the point of view of the two majesties, however, the religious and political objectives of the expedition, though they seemed
compelling at the outset, were not well served. The effort to establish mutually beneficial trade and diplomatic contacts with the
Tejas and their neighbors could not have been less competently carried out. The evident eagerness of the Franciscans to proselytize
among the Indians had to be counterbalanced by a commitment to
military support—however, the military commander apparently assumed no obligation beyond the safe conduct of the priests. Further,
even if the Spanish representatives made serious efforts to negotiate
with the Indians—as Fray Lopez at least may have wished to do—it

seems unlikely that this could have been accomplished in the absence of their leader and spokesman, Juan Sabeata.

All the diplomatic efforts of Juan Sabeata and the other captains, the repeated petitions to Spanish governors and religious officials, the elaborately planned rendezvous between Spaniards and Indians on the San Clemente, and the Jumanos' long-term hopes for peace and the survival of their trade routes were in vain. All were apparently sacrificed to the short-term financial gain of the Spanish citizen-soldiers, including their commander, Juan Dominguez de Mendoza—who had, in the process, alienated Juan Sabeata, one of the most remarkable American Indian leaders of this or any historical period.

For the Jumanos and their allies, the experience was but the latest in a long string of frustrations. Their efforts to maintain long-established relationships by appealing to Spanish self-interest as they perceived it, to form an alliance and to stem the tide of Apache expansion, was a failure. Juan Sabeata had good reason to be bitter, and he can hardly be blamed for his efforts, a few years later, to ally himself with the very power which the Spaniards feared the most.

Aftermath

Father Nicolas Lopez had promised to return to Texas within a year. He may well have been distressed by the collapse of all the avowed goals of the mission. He was, to be sure, serious in his aspirations for a campaign of mission-building among the Tejas, and he had high hopes of making his way to Quivira. After returning to El Paso, Lopez proceeded to Mexico, to solicit sponsorship for a major missionary campaign in that direction. In a letter to the king, appealing for personnel and funds for this project, Lopez claimed to have "trod the lands of . . . the Aijados, adjacent to the great kingdom of Quivira," and to have reached the "threshold of the extensive and powerful kingdom of the Texas." His account, at this point, reads remarkably like the reports written earlier by Alonso de Benavides, and could have been directly inspired by that source. In 1684, it does not seem likely that Fray Nicolas actually traveled very far from the Spanish blockhouse on the Colorado, which was constantly endangered by the hostile Apaches.

It would seem evident that the Spaniards' parting with the Indians on the San Clemente was not completely amicable. This is evidenced by the rather precipitous departure and the evident haste with which Captain Dominguez de Mendoza conducted the party

to La Junta. Fray Lopez seemed to hint to this effect when he wrote
to the viceroy in 1686 that "... [a] compact ... had been made with
those nations to return to their country within a year. This was
the reason, Sir, *that they permitted us to leave their country* and
now ... it is necessary ... to repeat once more the manifest dangers
that are threatened by delay in putting the remedy into effect, especially when danger threatens from every side."[34] In his report to the
king, written in the same year, Lopez again indicated that "... in
order that they remain assured of our friendship, a pact was made
with them that we would return within a year and bring priests to
minister to them and *with this contrivance they let us leave* ..."[35]

Fray Lopez immediately began to work toward this objective,
pleading with his superiors for twenty new missionaries for the
Texas field. Later, he increased this to sixty-six, the maximum
number which the New Mexican custodia was allotted. Lopez' reports emphasized, once more, both the wealth of resources to be
found in the Texas country, and also—perhaps more urgently—the
importance of establishing a Spanish presence in order to block the
entry of France into the region.

> Now the petitioner [the Franciscan custodian, Lopez] represents again
> to your Lordship [the viceroy, the Count de Paredes] in the name of his
> Order ... that if the Most Christian King [of France] attracts these na-
> tions whose docility the petitioner had experienced, to his friendship—
> for it appears that he has had dealings with them for years—their com-
> plete ruin is threatened, and it cannot be repaired afterwards with
> millions, although at this time the ingress [of the French] may be pre-
> vented with two hundred men.
>
> There are now friendly to us seventy-five nations, which are asking
> for aid against the Apache nation, and all this can be accomplished by
> his Majesty at this time at very little cost ...[36]

The Spaniards arrived at La Junta to find that an Indian rebellion
had begun on the Rio del Norte below El Paso. The country was in
turmoil. Perhaps in an effort to hold the allegiance of those groups
that were still friendly, Captain Dominguez de Mendoza "took possession of the north bank of the Rio Grande as part of New Mexico
and delivered rods of justice to four native chiefs." These probably
were Jumano Cibolos.

Because of native unrest in the Rio Grande valley, Lopez and
Dominguez de Mendoza were forced to make their way to El Paso
by ascending the Rio Conchos and the Rio del Sacramento—a long
way around, taking them to the vicinity of Casas Grandes. Fray

Juan Sabaleta remained behind, along with Antonio Aceveda, to supervise the newly established missions at La Junta. The Sumas, who had repeatedly addressed desperate appeals for help to both Lopez and Dominguez de Mendoza a year previous, had reached the breaking point, and soon many of them would join forces with the Apaches in waging war against Spain. However, Christian Sumas and Julimes would help the two friars to make their escape to Parral, carrying with them the sacred artifacts from their mission churches.

The combined effects of the Pueblo Revolt in New Mexico, the rebellion near La Junta, and the protracted Spanish efforts to combat these insurrections and to complete the reconquest of New Mexico led to a virtual cessation of Spanish involvement in Texas for more than two decades. Nicolas Lopez' recommendations were not implemented. The French colonists and traders who soon made their presence felt in Texas may have benefited from the Spaniards' default, just as Lopez had predicted.

12.

ALONSO DE POSADA'S REPORT: THE JUMANO WORLD IN 1685

In his *Memorial of 1630* Alonso de Benavides had expressed a growing Spanish conviction of the importance of Texas as a buffer zone. He made specific recommendations for development and settlement of this area, designed to defend New Mexico and northern New Spain against the encroachments of other imperial powers. Benavides had urged, in particular, the selection of the Bay of Espiritu Santo (Matagorda Bay) as the future port of entry for trade and communication between Havana and New Mexico, noting the potential savings, in terms of distance and the dangers to be encountered en route, as compared with the overland trail between Mexico and Santa Fe.

Over subsequent decades, Benavides' concerns were still echoed; however, after 1665, they were given a new sense of urgency in the wake of a series of events involving a former governor of New Mexico, Don Diego de Peñalosa.

The Peñalosa Affair

In New Mexico, the scandal-ridden governorship of Bernardo Lopez de Mendizabal came to an end in 1661. A newly installed Franciscan prelate, Alonso de Posada, presented charges against Lopez during the *residencia*, the official review held at the end of his term in office.[1] Lopez' successor was Don Diego de Peñalosa, another scoundrel, who had earlier fled to Mexico to escape criminal charges in South America. Peñalosa proceeded to build a political career in Mexico, and in 1661 arrived in Santa Fe to begin a term of office as governor, while his predecessor was returned to Mexico in chains.

Near the end of a four-year term of unparalleled corruption, Peñalosa managed to avoid the obligatory *residencia* by precipitously departing the colony for Mexico. However, Fray Alonso de

Posada pursued him, and brought charges before the tribunal of the Holy Office in Mexico. Peñalosa's trial dragged on over three years, but ended with the imposition of a fine, public humiliation, and perpetual banishment from New Spain and the West Indies.

Having the good judgment not to return to South America, Peñalosa traveled to England, where he remained only a short time before proceeding to France. There, he married a socially prominent woman and soon gained acceptance to the royal court. In France, Peñalosa began a swashbuckling career of self-promotion. He published an account of an expedition which he claimed to have led, from Santa Fe across the Great Plains to the kingdom of Quivira. It is for this tale—which was later exposed as a fraud—that Peñalosa is most notorious.

This fabricated account of his own exploits was, however, only a part of Peñalosa's larger scheme. The book was intended to raise interest in a daring proposal, which he had earlier put forward in England, although without success. In France, with greater confidence, Peñalosa approached King Louis XIV with his plan for invading and seizing New Spain; the port of Espiritu Santo, together with the Texas country, was crucial to this plan.

Peñalosa himself intended to lead the invasion, which would enter and take possession of the "provinces of Quivira and Teguayo";[2] these were undefended and were, he claimed, rich in silver and gold. These provinces constituted, roughly, the area of Texas, from the Gulf Coast to New Mexico; they were to be his base of operations for an invasion of the interior. This was precisely the danger against which Benavides had warned, half a century earlier.

When reports of Peñalosa's intrigues, and of the attention he had received at the court of France, reached Spain, a royal *cedula* (letter patent) was dispatched to the viceroy in Mexico. The Crown[3] requested information and advice as to the degree of danger posed by Peñalosa's scheme and inquired about the defense measures which should be taken. Apparently there was no timely response to this *cedula*, which was dated 1678; a second was sent out in 1685, during the vice-regency of the Count de Paredes. Enclosed in this letter, it might be noted, was a copy of Benavides' *Memorial of 1630.*

It will be recalled that two years earlier this same viceroy, the Count de Paredes, had received a report from the governor of New Mexico. The report recounted the visit of the Jumanos and their allies to El Paso, where they petitioned for Spanish help against the Apaches. The viceroy could have recalled that on that occasion the Indian leader, Juan Sabeata, intimated that foreign ships had made landfall on the Texas coast. At the time, the viceroy responded by approving an expensive military mission into the interior of Texas. One of the primary objectives of this mission was the establishment of an alliance with the Indian nations of the region, as a defense against further foreign inroads. Unfortunately, this objective was not accomplished.

The viceroy, in the present case, had every reason to take the threat of invasion seriously, and he responded to the royal *cedula* with due haste. To his credit, he appointed one of the best qualified and most experienced men available, to prepare the response: Fray Alonso de Posada.

Alonso de Posada

Posada is known to have gone to New Mexico for the first time in 1651, as a Franciscan missionary. He spent most of the next decade in the colony, working for periods of time at the Hopi village of Awatobi, and at Jemez, Pecos, and Senecu. After a brief return to Mexico, he was appointed custodian of the New Mexican missions, and arrived to assume this position in 1660, just in time to prepare the case against Governor Lopez. Posada must have been shocked by the continuing corruption in Peñalosa's governorship; as already noted, he led the opposition to Peñalosa, and successfully brought him to trial. At the conclusion of the trial, he remained in Mexico. In the autumn of 1685, when asked to prepare a report as background on the Peñalosa matter, Fray Alonso was serving in an administrative position in Mexico City.

Posada's *Report* was completed in March of the following year. The friar set out to respond methodically to the list of queries contained in the royal *cedula:* ". . . [W]hether it is suitable or not to open the communication which Fray Alonso de Benavides proposed by way of the Bay of Espiritu Santo; what conveniences or lack of them it will have, what they are and for what reason; what means and measures can be used to achieve the communication with . . . Quivira and Tagago [Teguayo], and the conversion of their natives . . . ; whether in that kingdom there will be religious who long to make these conversions . . . or whether this may be done more easily through the provinces of Florida; and whether . . . any injury may be feared from the proposal Don Diego de Peñalosa made to his most Christian Majesty [Louis XIV] . . ."[4]

The body of Posada's report falls into three main sections. First, after briefly stating his own background and experience in New Mexico, he recounts the history of exploration out of the colony into the Plains and the Texas country. Second, he presents an extensive review of the geography of New Mexico and neighboring regions; this actually touches on most of North America, as far as the continent was known to Spain, treating the physical features of the land, and the Indian nations in their relations to one another and to New Mexico. Finally, he returns to deal, point by point, with King Louis' inquiries relating to Quivira and Teguayo, and to the development and defense of the area around the Bay of Espiritu Santo. For present purposes, Posada's *Report of 1686* is of great interest, both because it make specific reference to the location and movements of the Jumanos, and because of the broad view which it gives of lands, peoples, and lines of communication.

North American Geopolitics in 1685

A. B. Thomas has observed that Posada's knowledge of geography is remarkably accurate when he is dealing with New Mexico and other regions which Spain had occupied, explored, and mapped. Beyond the limits of the Spanish territories, he reveals some interesting—though typical—misapprehensions. For example, Posada envisioned a large mountain range, which he called the Sierras Nevadas, extending from east to west across the North American continent somewhere north of Quivira, at fifty-four degrees of latitude (roughly, the latitude of central Saskatchewan). This range was thought to form a bridge between the northern Rockies and the Appalachians. The existence of such a chain of mountains was a commonly held belief; its presence served to explain the drainage pattern in the southern latitudes, as the height of land from which the "Great River" (the Mississippi) and numerous other streams flowed southward, into the Gulf of Mexico. Lying north of the Sierras Nevadas was the famed Strait of Anian, the waterway which was thought to bisect the continent, stretching from the Pacific coast to the northern reaches of New France.

Closer to Santa Fe, Posada's central point of reference, the Rio del Norte (Rio Grande), and its two large tributaries, the Conchos and the Pecos, are located accurately. Posada traces the lower course of the Rio Grande in detail, giving reasonable estimates of distances, as it flows past the mining country of Quencame, the Spanish settlements at Parras, and the province of Nuevo Leon (where it becomes known as the Rio Bravo), to enter the sea at twenty-six degrees, between the Bay of Espiritu Santo and the port of Tampico. There is, however, no mention of the several leagues of narrow, winding canyons through which the river passes as it flows through the maze of mountainous country in the Big Bend region;

this stretch was yet to be explored, and was very likely considered impassable.

Posada is also on fairly firm ground as he recounts Coronado's exploration, and traces the course of the Colorado river (which he calls El Grande) as it rises in the mountains north of Santa Fe and flows to the Western Sea. However, looking toward the east, it seems remarkable to realize that—despite the long history of Spanish interest in the Texas country—Posada actually had a very hazy and overly simplistic view of the land mass, the physical features and, especially, of the river systems of that region. This can be seen in his depiction of the famed Rio de las Nueces.

> . . . in the region northeast of the pueblo they call Pecos, another river forms on those slopes whose current flows directly southeast. At a distance of two hundred leagues from its origin, equal in size to the Rio del Norte, and running through the interior part of the plains of Cibola, it is eighty leagues north from the spot which we call the Junta de los Rios . . . This river they call the Rio de los Nueces because it has along its banks and meadows, many trees of this kind, besides mulberry trees, plum trees, wild grapes and other fruits . . . In its vicinity there are many wild cows which they call buffalo and many chickens of the land which in Spain they call turkeys, and all kinds of deer.[5]

It is Thomas' editorial interpretation that Posada has here confused the Rio de las Nueces (the Concho-Colorado system of Texas), with the Rio Pecos. However, Posada has already accurately identified the Pecos as a tributary of the Rio del Norte, and has shown that he is familiar with its course. It appears, rather, that he has mistakenly identified the headwaters of one of the several streams which originate in the southern Rockies—perhaps the Canadian[6]— as the source of the Rio de las Nueces. He was vague about its downstream course, but an important stretch of the river, the part which had been visited by various Spanish expeditions to the Jumanos, is quite accurately located in relation to La Junta de los Rios. Below this point he was aware that the river—the Colorado of Texas—flows south and east, to empty into the Bay of Espiritu Santo.

The several Spanish parties which had traveled to the Jumano settlements on the Rio de las Nueces had either followed the mountain trail from La Junta, or had traveled south from New Mexico along the Pecos: in either case, they would have used an overland route from the Pecos to the Concho. Posada's lack of familiarity with the complexities of the river systems and other features of the geography of Texas was undoubtedly typical of the Spanish colonial population. Outside of the few well-known routes which Spaniards had used in travel and trade, Texas was *terra incognita*. An obvious reason for this ignorance is the fact that, to a great extent, the colonies had relied on the Jumanos and other Indian middlemen as their agents in dealings within this region.

A map drawn to Posada's specifications would show, east of the Pecos, only two important rivers. One of these, the Rio de las Nueces, is a long, circuitous river which would arise near the source (on a modern map) of the Canadian River, and flow south-by-southeast to assume the lower course of the Colorado, eventually emptying into the Gulf of Mexico at the Bay of Espiritu Santo (Matagorda Bay).

The Bay of Espiritu Santo also figures prominently in Posada's geography. Just as the interior of the Texas country seems to be dominated by the Rio de las Nueces, the coast of La Florida is dominated by the Bay. The Rio de las Nueces drains into the Bay of Espiritu Santo; and so, according to Posada, does the other major stream, the Great River. This river arises in the north, converges with the Arkansas and then turns southward, assuming the general aspect of the lower Mississippi. It enters the sea through an imagined northern extension of the Bay of Espiritu Santo.

> . . . [L]et it be grasped that on the Sierra Blanca [the southern Rockies], which is between the sierras of New Mexico and the Sierras Nevadas, a river (the Arkansas) is formed . . . which runs directly east, and from the Sierras Nevadas, comes another [the Mississippi] with its current running to the south until it joins the former. This there is formed a large full-flowing river called accordingly the Great River. This stream continuing some two hundred and fifty leagues to the east with declination to the south, makes a turn to the south for some thirty leagues, turns again to the right, while passing through the center of La Quivira so that, according to the direction of its current, considered in relation to the Bay of Espiritu Santo, which is on the coast, it appears that it is the same river which debouches into that bay.[7]

Thus, in Posada's view, the Gulf Coast would be drastically foreshortened, telescoped to the degree that the mouth of the Mississippi is thought to be so close to that of the Colorado of Texas that the rivers almost converge near their mouths and drain together into the Bay of Espiritu Santo.[8]

The Apaches and Jumanos

Alonso de Posada's account is of great interest in relation to the history of Spanish contacts with the Jumanos. It has already been cited as a source of information concerning expeditions to the Jumanos which occurred between 1632 and 1654, the year of the Guadalajara junket. Further, Posada provides documentation of later movements and relocations of the Jumano and other Indian nations, which occurred during the years of his missionary service. Like Benavides, Posada was most impressed by the strength and territorial dominance of the Apache, and the impact on other Indian nations of this tribe, which continued to expand its territorial holdings during the middle and later years of the century.

> . . . [I]t must be noted that there is a nation which they call the Apacha which possesses and is owner of all the plains of Cibola. The Indians of this nation are so arrogant, haughty and such boastful warriors that they are the common enemy of all nations who live below the northern region. They hold these others as cowards. They have destroyed, ruined or driven most of them from their lands. This nation occupies and has its own lands and as such they defend them, four hundred leagues from east to west: from north to south, two hundred leagues, and in some places more.[9]

Posada takes us through a circuit of Apache territories, from the central point of the Plains of Cibola (where a few decades earlier, the Jumano had been in residence). The lands of the Apache are bordered on the east by Quivira and the nation of the Tejas (Hasinai); along the south, by the Tejas and the Ajijados, Cuitoas (or Caytoas), and Escanjaques; the last three, he indicates, have been driven back from the Rio de las Nueces to the Rio del Norte. He reveals that the Jumanos have also been forced from the Rio de las Nueces to take refuge at the junction of the Rio del Norte and Conchos; the Apache are at war with them and their allies—Sumas, Mansos, and others from the Rio del Norte below the mission of Nuestra Señora de Guadalupe, at El Paso.

The Apache holdings extend toward Sonora, where they have driven back the Janos; they conduct raids into Sonora, and are at war with the Sipias nation (the Sobaipuri). In the mountains in this direction, Posada makes a puzzling reference to an Apache stronghold, which he calls El Cuartelejo. This is a mountainous region on the north side of the Sierra Madres, where ". . . for a distance of fifty leagues, the Apacha nation has some meadows and small plots of land, very pleasant and fertile. In this place is a considerable number of inhabitants of this Apacha nation."[10] This stronghold must have been in and around the Chiricahua Mountains, in Arizona and northern Sonora, later known as the heartland of the Chiricahua Apaches.

From El Cuartelejo, the Apache lands extend west to the lower Colorado, where they dominate the Coninas (Havasupai): "This nation the Apacha hold complete in vassalage." The Colorado appears to form the Apache western frontier; further north, the same river separates the Apaches from the Yutas (Utes), whom Posada holds to be their equal in bravery: ". . . those of this nation, valorous in campaign, alone are equal in manliness to the Apacha with whom they war."[11]

Proceeding eastward, crossing the Sierra Blanca (Rocky Mountain range), the Apaches fronted on Quivira; the dividing line was the Great River (here, the Arkansas), a frontier of perpetual warfare. As to Apache relations with New Mexico, Posada gives roughly the same picture as Benavides, describing Apache encroachments on both the Pueblo Indians and the Spanish colony.

> All the sierras that are within and those which surround the province of New Mexico the Apacha nation claims as its own. . . . They have made many attacks from prepared ambushes on Indian pueblos, killing atrociously the warriors, carrying off the women and children alive, considering them as legitimate captives, laying waste usually the irrigated fields of maize, running off day and night the horseherds of the Spaniards and inflicting all the rest of the injuries which the force of their fierce arrogance imposes. With special care all the Indians of this nation who live on the eastern side of the province of New Mexico have always maintained peace with the Spaniards to trade and exchange their hides and chamois, but protect on the other hand the very Indians who live in the mountains surrounding New Mexico and who war on the Spaniards.[12]

A trade relationship between the eastern Apache bands, the predecessors of the Jicarillas, and Pecos Pueblo, had been in effect since the period of the Spanish conquest. This may always have been, as Posada intimates, an uneasy alliance for both parties. However, over the years since Benavides surveyed the situation, the region of Apache dominance had expanded and become more sweeping. This expansion is indicated in Posada's references to the displacement of the Southern Plains tribes, recently relocated to the south or given refuge in the missions at La Junta and El Paso.

Fray Posada concludes his report by listing several positive and negative aspects of the proposal to open communications by way of the Bay of Espiritu Santo. On the positive side, he mentions the opportunity to win converts among the "great number of Indian barbarians," and he predicts that God will provide ministers willing to undertake the task.

Turning to secular considerations, he asserts the most obvious strategic purpose for Spain of any move to settle on the Gulf Coast: "Colonizing that port . . . will prevent enemies of any other nation . . . from taking possession of that coast and making themselves owners of the lands and kingdoms which border upon it. If that were done there would follow very serious injury and even danger of our losing lands and kingdoms already acquired."[13] Additional arguments relate to the ready abundance of food supplies in the area—here are buffalo, fish, corn and other crops; there may also be minerals, and there are the famous pearls of the Rio de Las Nueces. The port would serve as a sentinel, to watch for invaders, and to provide a refuge for Spanish ships, when needed.

On the negative side, Posada has doubts about the suitability of the bay for large ships. He knows there are reefs and shallows, and he wonders whether the Great River might not deposit silt and cause the formation of dangerous marshes around the bay. He urges that a survey of the coast be undertaken—a project which had already been recommended by the viceroy, but never executed. A large garrison of soldiers would be necessary, both for defense against pirates, and for protection against the "many barbarous Indians, with whom no arrangements can be made because, naturally, from the beginning they must try to defend their lands and liberty."[14] Finally, Posada fears that the port would be so remote that it would be impossible, in case such problems develop, to obtain help from any other place. There would be logistical problems in supplying such an installation: the threat of pirates along the sea lanes, the length of the lines of communication, and the danger of attacks by hostile Indians en route. All things considered, however, Posada feels the Spanish garrison to be necessary; the "foreign nations who are colonized to the northeast of Florida [the French, British, Dutch, et al.] could easily occupy, settle, and trade at the port without opposition, if it were not garrisoned by Spain.[15]

At the end, Posada's practical recommendations are that the "Texas and Quivira nations" should be settled at the port, along with a "sufficient garrison of soldiers and settlers" to defend it against pirates and other threats. Secondly, there should be a presidio further inland on the Rio de las Nueces, with one hundred soldier-settlers, at a spot which is appropriate for farms and pasturage. From this base, the soldiers would undertake the subjugation of the hostile Indians (principally, no doubt the Apaches). In this project, writes Posada, the Jumanos can surely be enlisted.

> They [the soldiers] will undoubtedly have the support of the Jumana nation and the other ten or twelve [nations] which are near the Jumana along the Rio del Norte. They will go and settle on the said river [Nueces] because it is their land which the Apacha nation took away from them and whom they hold as enemies. Their desire for vengeance together with the inclination which they have shown to become Christians will impel them to remain faithful. The same consideration applies to the Ahijados, Cuitoas, Escanjaques and Texas Indians because they suffer from the same oppression of the Apacha nation . . .[16]

From the time of Benavides' writing in 1630 to that of Posada's in 1685, it is evident that the Bay of Espiritu Santo was seen as a natural gateway to northern New Spain, and that the Rio de las Nueces was the main highway linking the bay and the interior. Posada seems less concerned than Benavides about the problem of maintaining lines of communication between the port and New Mexico. However, he suggests that once Spanish forces are established on the Rio de las Nueces, a new, shorter route could be opened, linking the bay with Nuevo Leon, and thence directly with Mexico City.

Posada's recommendations, like those of Benavides, were never carried out. The logistics of such a plan were probably too complex, and undoubtedly too expensive, to be mounted at the time. The lines of communication between Mexico, Parral, Nuevo Leon, and other frontier establishments were already overextended, and there were problems of Indian discontent or outright rebellion to be dealt with on almost every front—not to mention the difficulties attending the anticipated reconquest of New Mexico.

Ironically, by the time Posada's report was complete, and well before it could have reached the royal court in Spain, foreign encroachment on the Texas coast was no longer simply a possibility. It had become a reality, with the arrival of a French colony at the Bay of Espiritu Santo.

PART THREE

JUMANO CHRONOLOGY, 1685–1700

THE DECLINE AND FALL OF THE JUMANO TRADE EMPIRE

13.

LA SALLE'S COLONY: THE FRENCH CONNECTION

In 1683, Juan Sabeata was able to tell Governor Cruzate about strange "Spaniards" in floating "houses" who were visiting the coast of Texas and trading with the Indians. The Spanish governor's suspicions immediately fell on the French, who already had a stake in the north of the continent, and were making a claim on the mid-section as well. France and Spain were in contention for possession of La Florida, the Gulf coastal plain east of Mexico. Alonso de Bena-vides, whose *Memorial of 1630* was still given serious considera-tion by Spanish strategists, had invoked the spectre of French ad-vances into the Texas country; he had warned against the Flemings as well, and English privateers were always a threat in the waters of the Gulf of Mexico and the Caribbean. In the 1680's, however, there was a new reason for strong apprehension in New Spain concerning the intentions of their French neighbors—the intrigue which was inspired and led by the former governor of New Mexico, Don Diego de Peñalosa.

It is very likely that several intrusions by unofficial representa-tives of France into territory claimed by Spain had already occurred, prior to any documented instances. Commerce of the sort inti-mated by Juan Sabeata was familiar to the Indians of Texas, al-though in open violation of a Spanish ban on international traffic in the Gulf of Mexico and thus a cause for alarm. However, the first documented French presence in Texas was a short-lived settlement which was established two years after Juan Sabeata's warning to Governor Cruzate, at the bay which the Spaniards called Espiritu Santo (Matagorda Bay).

La Salle's Colony

In the summer of 1684, while Fray Nicolas Lopez and Captain Juan Dominguez de Mendoza were returning from their sojourn in central

Texas, Robert Cavelier, Sieur de La Salle, sailed from France with a little fleet of four ships, authorized to plant a colony in the New World. La Salle, whose name was already prominent in New France, had been actively engaged in the northern fur trade for many years. He had dealt with Indians throughout the Great Lakes and the rivers of the northwest, where he established a series of trading posts, including Fort St. Louis, a strategically important post on the Illinois River.

In 1682, together with his friend and close associate Henri de Tonty, La Salle followed the course of the Mississippi River to its mouth, where he planted the French flag and declared the claim of France to Louisiana. Some years later, in the wake of La Salle's abortive venture into Texas, Tonty would build a post at the mouth of the Arkansas. From there, *coureurs de bois* recruited in Canada would begin explorations leading to the establishment of trade relations with the Siouan, Caddoan, and other Indians of the Great Plains.

La Salle's voyage of 1684 had the announced objective of establishing a French colony on the lower Mississippi, to regulate access to the mouth of that river. This would give France effective control, north to south, of a massive waterway system dominating the interior of the continent. However, either by error or by design, his ships made landfall on the Texas coast, at the Bay of Espiritu Santo. Historians still disagree as to whether La Salle's landing, hundreds of miles past his announced objective, was a simple mistake, the result of an apparent error in calculating latitude, or whether it could have been a deliberate covert move, aimed at an invasion of Spanish territory.[1]

In 1684, Spain and France were at war, and both were jealous of their respective territorial rights in the New World. In an appeal for royal support, La Salle put forward a proposal which argued that the designated site, on the lower Mississippi, could be used effectively as a base for launching an invasion, via the River Seignelay (Red River), into the Spanish mining province of Nueva Vizcaya. The idea was absurdly impractical, and La Salle's proposal grossly misrepresented the distances, direction, and terrain involved. However, the geographical errors were not obvious to the court—though some may at least have questioned the feasibility of his plan to accomplish the task with six thousand French troops and fifteen thousand Indian recruits. It seems possible that La Salle put forward the proposal to seize the Spanish mines simply as a ploy, a way of gaining sponsorship and funds. King Louis was, in any case, evidently persuaded. He granted La Salle a commission for expeditions into ". . . the country which will be subject anew to Our dominion in North America, from Fort St. Louis, on the River of the Illinois, unto New Biscay . . ."[2]

In France, La Salle recruited a hundred soldiers and a number of other volunteers—men, some with families—along with a half-dozen clergy, of the Sulpician and Recollet orders. The "principal persons" of the colony included the three Sulpician priests, one of whom was La Salle's brother, M. Cavelier; the Recollet friars, Membre, Douay, and Le Clercq; and La Salle's young nephews, Moranget and Cavelier. Henri Joutel, an ex-soldier from La Salle's native city of Rouen, came to be regarded as one of the most trustworthy of the colonists. Joutel and three of the clerics kept the journals which provide the main body of information on events in the colony. The personnel also included several Canadian Indians, among them La Salle's trusted Shawnee scout and hunter, Nika.

La Salle's colonizing efforts were plagued by problems from the beginning. He and the ship's captain, Beaujeu, were at odds throughout the voyage. One of the ships, loaded with supplies, was seized by a Spanish patrol ship in the Caribbean. After landing the colonists, Beaujeu immediately sailed back to France with the largest of the ships. A third vessel foundered soon after, while being unloaded, causing the loss of a large part of the food and supplies. However, with all the problems, La Salle managed the construction of a small fort at the Bay of Espiritu Santo, which he immediately renamed Saint Louis Bay. The fort, like the earlier one in Canada, was dubbed Fort St. Louis.

There seems to be no compelling evidence to indicate that La Salle deliberately made landfall on the Texas coast, inside Spanish territory. However, when he discovered his error, and realized that he was, in fact, far from the Mississippi, it appears that he may have revised his plan, hoping to make the best of a bad situation, and devoted some time and effort to scouting and reconnoitering in the direction of Mexico.[3]

Explorations

After Beaujeu's departure, in March of 1685, La Salle devoted most of a year to exploring the vicinity of the bay. The local Karankawan Indians, the Ebahamos (or Bracamas), were initially friendly, but difficulties arose; there were skirmishes when Indians were apprehended making off with some blankets and other supplies salvaged from the shipwreck. Several colonists were killed in Indian attacks, and La Salle's Shawnees reciprocated by killing and scalping an

Ebahamo chief. Before leaving the colony on his explorations, however, La Salle determined to make peace with this tribe, reasoning
that this was necessary for the security of the fort. By the end of
July, peace seemed secure; the colonists and Indians exchanged visits, and feasted together. The colonists, in the interim, proceeded to
plant gardens, care for their small stock of domestic animals, and
improve their living quarters.

Going farther afield, La Salle and his men undertook to follow the
many rivers and streams in the vicinity of Matagorda Bay, the
largest of which are the Guadalupe and the Colorado. In the fall, he
led a party of fifty men on an exploring trip lasting almost six
months. By the time they returned, the following March, La Salle
surely must have been convinced—if he had any remaining doubts—
that the Mississippi was nowhere in the vicinity of the bay.

In the course of these explorations, Father Cavelier noted an encounter with Indians who wore "large pearls hanging from the car-
tilage between the two nostrils."[4] This would have been on or near
the Colorado River; the pearls may have been from the pearl fish-
eries on that river and its tributaries, though Cavelier assumed they
were from the sea. The party searched the courses of the major
rivers, and so must have ascended the Colorado.

It could have been around this time, during a long and relatively
optimistic period of exploration, that the approaches toward Mexico were made which Jumano and other Indian witnesses later reported to the Spanish authorities in Parral (see Chapter 15). If the
Indians' accounts were accurate, there is little doubt that the Frenchmen were gathering information and scouting out the route toward
Mexico, as well as trading with the natives along these streams.

During one sortie in February of 1686, Father Cavelier described a
remarkable reunion between La Salle and three Shawnee Indians,
who had, four years earlier, disappeared from the expedition down
the Mississippi River. The Shawnees said that they had been taken
captive; they were led away by their kidnappers to the village where
they were now living. There, they had married, learned the language, and had been highly honored because of the effectiveness of
their guns; their reputation had faltered somewhat, when they ran
out of ammunition.

> It was from these three Indians that we learned . . . that the Indians
> among whom we were made war on others who had intercourse with
> the Spaniards, distant about 130 leagues from the sea [and] . . . that
> there was a river . . . more beautiful than the Mississipiy, and two oth-
> ers . . . in which gold was found in large grains and in dust. . . .

They added: We have been to war against the nation that has intercourse with the Spaniards and took some prisoners, who were neatly dressed in silk. They told us that the Spaniards furnished them their clothes and many other things in exchange for certain stones which they prized highly . . .[5]

The Shawnees described trade between this nation and the Spaniards in gold and precious stones, and, according to Cavelier, led La Salle's party to a large hill, where there were mines; the Frenchmen were able to obtain samples of the ore, which eventually were assayed in France.

This hill lies about forty leagues from . . . [the captive Shawnees'] village and is near a little river which empties in a larger one, which, coming a great distance and passing between two ranges of hills, empties into the Gulf of Mexico. The Spaniards have several villages on the southern part of this river, and the Indians who make war on them cross over and make captures along the road, which they frequent with little precaution.[6]

La Salle asked several questions about the possibilities of attacking the Spaniards, and was told about certain native rebellions, either in New Mexico or on the lower Rio del Norte. They learned, however, that the Spaniards were well established "on the southern part" of the river (the reference may be to El Paso or La Junta), on a road where the Indians sometimes took captives.

They assured us that there was not a nation for a hundred leagues around but feared the inroads of the Spanish; that they dreaded them on account of the frightful stories told of their firearms; that this consideration alone had prevented their leaguing together to undertake to carry a town, lacking neither desire, courage nor means of uniting . . . They convinced us that they needed only good leaders and some regular troops to instruct them, arms, saddles, bridles and ammunition. On this my brother [La Salle] asked them on which side they would attack the Spaniards, they replied that it was beyond the great river of which they had spoken to us, where there were several cities and villages, some open and others fortified merely by palisades . . . That the year before they had killed or taken over two thousand persons and forced them to send religious to exhort them to peace.[7]

Admittedly, it is difficult to interpret this information, since the identity of the tribes and the geographical locations are uncertain. It would appear possible, however, that the Shawnees had been captured by and were living among Apaches, and that the location was on or near the Pecos (the little river), which empties into the Rio del Norte (the larger one). The Apaches, then, were still at war with the Jumanos, who must have been the "nation that had intercourse with the Spaniards." It certainly would appear, from Father Cavelier's account, that La Salle asked questions aimed at determining the location and vulnerability of the Spanish settlements.

In the spring of that year, 1686, La Salle returned to the bay and supervised the removal of the colony to a new location, which had been under construction for some months. It was during this period that the colonists discovered that their only remaining seagoing vessel, a small ketch, had drifted away; searching for it, they finally discovered that it had sunk. La Salle had planned to use the ketch to navigate some of the larger rivers which drained into the Gulf and eventually to sail to the Indies for supplies and assistance for the colony. They now realized that their only link to the civilized world was lost. The mood of the colony, which had until then persevered, despite many blows in the form of death, disease, crop failure, and other hardships, became very bleak.

A Visit to the Cenis

In April, La Salle departed with a group of around twenty men, setting out this time in a determined effort to make his way to the Mississippi, as the only certain route to the Illinois country and Canada, where he knew that he would be able to get help for the colony. The accounts of this journey and of that of the following year, during which La Salle was killed, provide the richest descriptions of the Indians of Texas, including the Hasinai and the Jumano.

Aiming for the Mississippi, La Salle's party traveled northward past the Robec River (the Colorado) and the Maligne (the Brazos), and then turned toward the east. As they approached the Trinity River, the party entered the territory of the Cenis. These people, the Ceni or Hasinai, are, it should be noted, the same that the Spaniards on the Rio Grande called Tejas. The records of La Salle's visits give us our earliest firsthand views of that great confederacy which the Spaniards, at the time, knew only at second hand, mainly through their contacts with the Jumanos.

After their time among the simpler Karankawan bands of the Gulf Coast, the Frenchmen were impressed by these people who, according to Fr. Douay, "had nothing barbarous but the name." The

Frenchmen were greeted ceremoniously by the Cenis, and given "presents and all kinds of provisions."[8]

> This village . . . is one of the largest and most populous that I [Douay] have seen in America. It is at least twenty leagues long, not that it is constantly inhabited, but in hamlets of ten or twelve cabins, forming cantons, each with a different name. Their cabins are fine, forty or fifty feet high, of the shape of beehives. Trees are planted in the ground and united above the branches, which are covered with grass. The beds are ranged around the cabin, three or four feet from the ground; the fire is in the middle, each cabin holding two families.
> We found among the Cenis many things which undoubtedly came from the Spaniards, as silver coins and other money; silver spoons; thread, lace, and point lace of silk, gold, or silver; clothing; and horses. We saw, among other things, a bull from Rome, or of the Holy Inquisition, which excused the Spaniards of new Mexico from fasting during the summer. Horses are common; they gave them to us for an axe; one Cenis offered me one for our cowl, to which he took a fancy.[9]

The Frenchmen learned the source of these things: the Choumanes (Jumanos), through whom the Cenis had intercourse with New Spain. La Salle had the villagers draw a map, showing the position of the various nations, and the location of the Mississippi. The Cenis indicated that they were about "six days journey from the Spaniards, of whom they gave us so natural a description that we no longer had any doubts on the point, although the Spaniards had not yet undertaken to come to their villages, their warriors merely joining the Choumans to go war on New Mexico.[10] At this point, La Salle appears to have courted favor with the Ceni chiefs, by speaking in glowing terms of his own exploits and of the power of France—"He told them [the chiefs] that the French was the greatest chief in the world, as high as the sun, and as far above the Spaniard as the sun is above the earth."[11]

While in the Ceni village, the French party finally came face to face with representatives of the Jumanos.

> On that occasion, ambassadors were there from the Choumanes. They visited us, and I was agreeably surprised to see them make the sign of the cross, and fall upon their knees with their hands joined, which they raised from time to time toward the sky. They kissed my robe, making me understand that some people, dressed like ourselves, taught the people in their vicinity; and that they were not distant more

than two days' journey from the Spaniards, where our religious had large churches were everybody assembled to pray. They repeated to me plainly the ceremonies of the holy mass. One of them made me a sketch of a picture that he had seen of a great woman, who wept because her son was nailed to a cross. He told us that the Spaniards cruelly slaughtered the Indians, and finally, that if we wished to come with them, or if not, to give them muskets, it would be easy to overcome them, because they were cowardly people; that they had no courage; and that they caused people to walk before them with a fan, to cool them when they were warm.[12]

Father Douay was most impressed by the piety expressed by these Indians. He might have considered—but of course did not realize—that the Jumanos had at least a century of experience at this sort of thing: whatever their other accomplishments, they were past masters at manipulating Catholic priests. Neither would they have known, at this date, about the recent alienation between the Jumano leader, Juan Sabeata, and the government of New Mexico, which is reflected in the attitudes expressed by both the Jumanos and the Cenis. The Ceni village was full of evidence of peaceful trade which the Jumanos had long conducted between the Spanish colonies and the Cenis and their neighbors; their warlike posture was undoubtedly an expression of their present angry state of mind. It may also have been calculated to appeal to the Frenchmen; by this time, having observed their scouting parties, the Indians must have had ample reason to believe that the French were interested in an invasion into Spanish territory.

However, La Salle and his men, while assuring the Cenis and Choumanes that they were enemies of the Spaniards, were now in no position to get involved in border warfare with New Mexico. They bartered for as many horses as they could, either from the Cenis or from the Choumanes, and after four or five days of rest and relaxation in the Ceni village, continued their march doggedly eastward. However, while among the Nassonis, a neighboring division of the Hasinai confederacy, both La Salle and his nephew Moranget suffered an attack of fever, which caused them to remain for more than two months. By the time they had recovered their strength, ammunition and other supplies had run short, and it was thought necessary for the party to turn back to Fort St. Louis; they arrived there in October of 1686.

La Salle returned to his colony with a fresh supply of horses, but without having made significant headway toward the Mississippi.

Joutel—who had not accompanied La Salle on this expedition—indicates that "M. de la Salle had penetrated very far up into the country, inclining toward the northern part of Mexico [i.e., New Mexico]. He had traveled through several nations . . . and had concluded a sort of alliance with them, and particularly with the Cenis . . ."[13] Such a western inclination does not seem indicated by the firsthand accounts, including Douay's; Joutel's remarks seem more suggestive of the earlier period of exploration, and especially of the events of early 1686 described by Cavelier. On the other hand, further explorations toward the west may have occurred during the next few months, the interval between the two major expeditions in search of the Mississippi.

La Salle's Final Journey

There followed a period of several months during which the colonists argued, vacillating between staying where they were, on the possibility that someone—perhaps Tonty—might come to search for them, and making further efforts to save themselves. Still, there was a continuation of explorations out of the fort.

> [W]e visited together all the rivers that empty into [the bay] . . . I am sure that there are more than fifty, coming from the west and northwest . . . On every side we saw prairie on which the grass is, at all seasons of the year, higher than the wheat with us. Every two or three leagues [there] is a river skirted with oaks, thorn, mulberry, and other trees. This kind of country is uniform until within two days' march of the Spaniards.[14]

It is possible that trading and information-gathering sorties were once more made up the Colorado during this period, the winter of 1686–1687. At any rate, as in this passage from Douay's journal, there are clear indications that at some time—either that year or the previous one—the Frenchmen had approached the Spanish colonies, reaching (as earlier indicated) at least as far as the Rio Pecos.

Early the following year, La Salle set out again for the Mississippi, along the same route as before, with a party of seventeen. This time the group included Henri Joutel, who to that point had been left in charge of the fort and of relations with the neighboring Indian tribes. The colony was now in dire straits, and La Salle was desperate in his efforts to find a route to the Illinois country in order to bring reinforcements and aid or a vessel to evacuate the survivors.

Some members of the party did, in fact, eventually find shelter fairly close at hand, at the post which Tonty was just then building on the Arkansas River.

During this final expedition, travel and communication were facilitated by the experiences of the earlier ones. La Salle always made notes on the speech of the Indians he came in contact with, and he had gained some knowledge of the language of the Hasinai. This helped the party in dealing with most of the tribes along their route, although at times it was necessary to use sign language, in which it appears that La Salle was also quite fluent.

Father Douay mentions several nations of Indians who were encountered as the men made their way once more toward the Ceni villages: the Ebahamos and Quinets, who were neighbors of the fort, and, further on, Konaras and Anachoremas. At the River Robec (Colorado), there was a people with "many populous villages" who "have a language which is so guttural that it would require a long time to form ourselves to it. They are at war with the Spaniards, and pressed us earnestly to join their warriors."[15] There is no way of knowing whether these villagers were those who wore the pearl ornaments earlier described by M. Cavelier; situated as they were on the Colorado, they could have been a tribe allied with the Jumanos. Because of wet weather, travel was painfully slow; many days were spent sitting through thunderstorms and waiting for swollen creeks to subside. Having left Fort St. Louis on January 12, the party reached the banks of the Maligne (Brazos) in mid-February, and a month later had not yet got as far as the Ceni territory.

Near the Maligne, the Frenchmen visited a village of the Teao, who told La Salle once more about a "great nation called Ayona and Canohatino, who were at war with the Spaniards, from whom they stole horses." They passed on a rumor to the effect that "one hundred Spaniards were to have come to join the Cenis, to carry on that war, but that, having heard of our march, they turned back."[16] Some of the Teao indicated that they had been to the country of the Spaniards. Apparently still hopeful of eventual success for the French cause, La Salle made his own partisanship clear: he ". . . gave them to understand that we were at war with the Spaniards and that we feared them not, and that he was sent on their account by the great captain of all the world, who had charged him to do them all good and to assist them in their wars against such nations as were their enemies."[17]

At most of the settlements through which the French party passed, some trading occurred; most often, knives were exchanged for foodstuffs. The Indians offered buffalo pelts, which the Frenchmen were obliged to refuse, as they were unable to transport them in quantity; they put off the Indians with a promise to buy pelts when they returned. The Frenchmen, for their part, made repeated efforts to buy horses, offering hatchets in exchange; the Indians had horses, but not in sufficient numbers, and were unwilling to sell.

A few days past the Maligne, Indians were encountered who spoke the language of the Cenis. One of them, whose name (or nation) was Palaquechaune (or Palaquesson), indicated that his people were allies of the Cenis; that "their chief had been among the Choumans with the Spaniards;" and that "the Choumans were friends to the Spaniards, from whom they got horses . . ." La Salle was informed that ". . . the Choumans had given their chief some presents to persuade him to conduct us to them; that most of the said nation had flat heads; that they had Indian corn, which gave M. de la Salle grounds to believe that these people were some of the same he had seen upon his first discovery."[18] The reference here is uncertain, but it probably concerns the meeting with the Jumanos which occurred the previous year, among the Cenis, which was described by Father Douay.

Very soon after this visit, and before reaching the Ceni villages, a group of conspirators led by Heins, an English buccaneer whom La Salle had recruited in Santo Domingo, ambushed and murdered La Salle's nephew, his footman, and his Shawnee hunter. Three days later, when La Salle himself went out to search for those three, he met the same fate. It is unnecessary to go into the details of the events following La Salle's death. The surviving "principal persons," fearing that they would be dealt with in the same way, were forced to make their peace with the perpetrators of the plot. Eventually, however, the assassins fought among themselves, and two of them were killed. Heins and several others then determined to stay in Texas, among the Cenis.

En route to the Cenis, following La Salle's death, Joutel was alarmed to encounter three horsemen, one of them in full Spanish dress. Joutel momentarily mistook this individual to be a Spaniard, and feared that "if we fell into their hands we must never expect to get away, but be condemned to serve either in the mines or in the quarries in the kingdom of Mexico." Attempting to bluff it through, Joutel addressed the man in his best Spanish (laced with Italian); however, the reply was a Ceni word, "*coussica,* which . . . signifies *I do not understand you.*" The man was a Ceni, sent to invite the Frenchmen to visit the chief's house. Joutel learned that he had been to the Spaniards' country, and that his clothes and horse had been brought from there. Many men among the Cenis, Joutel

observed, had Spanish swords, the hilts of which had been orna-
mented with "great plumes of feathers and hawks' bells."[19] It is
safe to assume that much of this finery had been transported by the
Jumanos.

In the months since the founding of La Salle's colony, several
men had been lost or had deserted; half a dozen had disappeared
during the expedition the year before. Joutel found three of them
living among the Cenis, and was able to obtain supplies through
their intervention, as well as information about the country ahead
and the location of the Mississippi and other rivers. These renegade
Frenchmen, their gunpowder exhausted, had already become skilled
with the bow and arrow, and had taken Ceni wives.

Before Joutel and his companions took their leave, several of
them (not, apparently, including Joutel himself), together with two
of the "half-savage" Frenchmen, participated in a Ceni assault on
the Canoatinno. The attack was a success: "Their enemies . . . had
expected them boldly, but . . . having heard the noise and felt the effects of our men's firearms, they all fled, so that the Cenis had either killed or taken forty-eight men and women."[20] Most of the
captives had been killed on the spot; Joutel graphically described
the torture and killing, followed by ritual cannibalism, of those
brought back to the village.

The Canoatinno (or Canohatino) appear several times in the narratives; their identity presents a special problem. There is repeated
reference to this people as a warlike tribe, carrying on raids against
the Spaniards to the west and also warring with the Cenis on the
east. They are first mentioned under this name by Douay in 1687;
they are said to "lord it over" their neighbors.[21] Cavelier also mentions the "Kanoutinoa," describing what is probably the same encounter, roughly two weeks after departure from Fort St. Louis, on
La Salle's first expedition to the north; the location would have
been south of the "Maligne," probably just beyond the "Robec" or
Colorado. Cavelier indicates that there was a troup of around 150
of the Indians, "all on horseback, armed with lances tipped with
sharpened bone, well tied and encased, each of whom attacked a
bull . . . They made us mount, the more conveniently to witness the
close of the bull fight, which seemed to us the most diverting thing
imaginable, and I am convinced that there is no chase as curious in
Europe."[22] After the hunt, these Indians treated the French party to
a feast of roasted meat and fish, and then sold them thirty horses in
exchange for a quantity of knives, hatchets, and needles.

The same year, La Salle heard of the Canoatinno from the Teao,
who mentioned their war with the Spaniards; and Joutel took

seriously the possibility that Spanish troops may have been on their way to join the Cenis against the Canoatinno. Finally, through Joutel's eyes, the reader witnesses the Ceni attack on the Canoatinno, to which Frenchmen give their support.

Who were the Canoatinno? One scholar, Swanton, thought they were Wichitas. Another, Hyde, disputed this identification and suggested that they were Apaches who had occupied the country around the head of the Colorado River.[23] Assuming that the Maligne was, indeed, the Brazos, it seems reasonable to accept Hyde's suggestion. The Apaches would by this time have reached the upper course of that stream, as well as the Colorado. At the same time, the Jumanos were still struggling to maintain a foothold on, and passage along, the Colorado. By 1700 the Apaches were established throughout the region, and were clearly in control of the upper courses of both the Colorado and Brazos. Thus, it does seem possible that the Canoatinno represent the easternmost branch of the advancing Apaches.

Soon after the return of the Ceni war party, a group of seven Frenchmen—including the MM. Cavelier, La Salle's brother and nephew, Father Augustin Douay, and Henri Joutel—were permitted to continue on their way. They left Ceni country, accompanied by guides who saw them as far as the Caddodacho, on the Red River. There, they learned of Tonty's new fort on the Arkansas; they reached the fort in late July of 1687.

The group of seven, now led by a Sulpician friar, the senior Cavelier, next made their way to Canada and thence to France, where they arrived in October of 1688. Henri Joutel had hoped to find a ship there, and to return to rescue the colony. However, the king, although he issued a warrant for the arrest of the murderers, refused to concern himself any more about the colonists, who were, after all, deep inside the borders of an enemy power. In fact, an effort at rescue, at this time, would have been in vain. Although the news had not yet reached France, the fort had already been destroyed by an Indian attack, and most of the remaining colonists, numbering only about twenty, were dead.

Aftermath

In the spring of 1686, after waiting months for some word from La Salle, Henri Tonty made a journey down the Mississippi to search for the colony. The effort was futile, since the fort was on the Texas coast, nowhere near the Mississippi. Tonty then returned north to build his post in a strategic location, at the mouth of the Arkansas, and stationed six men there to watch and wait for some sign of La Salle. Tonty himself was not present when the seven survivors finally passed that way, and for reasons of their own, they chose not to reveal the fact of La Salle's death or the actual plight of the colony.

Tonty only learned about the misfortunes which had befallen La Salle in the fall of 1688. At that point, he set out to go to the aid of Fort St. Louis, also hoping to recruit a band of Indians and to take up La Salle's objective of leading an invasion into Mexico. However, he made little progress; rains and swampy ground slowed him down, a number of his men deserted, and when he finally reached the Ceni village, he fell into an altercation with the Indians. Ill with fever, he was forced to turn back to the Arkansas.

In the meantime, the call to seek out and destroy the French colony had become a *cause célèbre* in New Spain. Several sea searches were initiated out of Vera Cruz, scouring the Gulf Coast. The wreckage of the ship was found, but the fort was so far inland, on the edge of the bay, that it was not sighted. After rumors about the Frenchmen at the fort and the deserters living among the Indians had filtered into the neighboring Spanish colonies, new investigations were launched. From Nueva Vizcaya, Jumano scouts were dispatched to search out the location of the fort and to confirm its destruction.

At about the same time, Spanish forces out of Nuevo Leon made several forays across the Rio del Norte. In the spring of 1689, a party under the leadership of Alonso de Leon, guided by a captured French deserter, finally reached and razed the ruined fort. Captain de Leon also found and interviewed two Frenchmen living among the Hasinai, and learned that they had gone to Fort St. Louis in the wake of the Indian attack and buried the bodies of the victims.

In the short, unhappy story of the French colony in Texas, there are several points which relate to the Jumanos. For one thing, the narratives of the French colonists provide the most graphic evidence available testifying to the unique and important role of the Jumanos as intermediaries between east and west. Horses, tools, and weapons, and many other Spanish goods were seen in the possession of the Caddoan village tribes. Again and again, reference is made to the Jumanos as intermediaries, and to the closeness of the alliance linking the Cenis and their neighbors with the "Chouman."

As for the goods which were carried on the return trip, it can be concluded that buffalo and other peltries were a very important part of this cargo. During the last visit of the Frenchmen, the Texas Indians appear to have had large supplies of pelts on hand. In this

Figure 2. A mounted Jumano, circa 1680 (illustration by Andrew Hall)

period of the mid-1680's, the recent alienation between the Jumanos and New Mexico had left the Indians with a surplus, which the Teao and other tribes were eager to dispose of to their visitors. It can also be noted that, at that time, the Cenis were reluctant to sell their horses; this could be another indication that the western trade was in decline. Within the next quarter-century, French traders from the Mississippi valley would become active among the Caddoan tribes, quickly replacing the earlier trade with Spain which was conducted through agency of the Jumanos.

The French narratives raise questions about the nature of the relationship between the Jumanos and the Spanish colonies. The French were told on several occasions that the Jumanos were allies of Spain, and they heard repeatedly of trips to New Mexico which Cenis and others made in Jumano company. Yet, at the Ceni village, a Jumano spokesman—probably Juan Sabeata himself, although his name is not mentioned—appealed to La Salle's party for help in an attack against the Spaniards. The Jumanos' disaffection would no doubt have dated from the debacle of the Lopez–Dominguez de Mendoza expedition, two years earlier. Perhaps more significantly, however, Juan Sabeata and the Jumanos had recently witnessed both the rout of the Spaniards from New Mexico and the onset of rebellion at La Junta. The most recent hostilities involved the Sumas and Julimes, who were, respectively, kinsmen and allies of the Jumano. The repercussions of these events were felt by all the Indian tribes in Texas, but they may have been felt most immediately and directly by the Jumano.

Thus it was not necessarily simply opportunism which led Juan Sabeata to represent himself to La Salle as an enemy of the Spaniards. Sabeata himself was personally disaffected from New Mexico. He must also have realized that Spanish sponsorship, however often it had been solicited and promised, was vacillating and ineffective; the trade at La Junta could not be maintained for long, in the face of Apache advances. Juan Sabeata would gladly have joined forces with France, if France had been willing to do what Spain had not—to give real support to the Jumanos and their allies, and to wage an all-out and effective war against the Apaches.

14.

APPROACHES FROM COAHUILA

There was a third point of entry for seventeenth-century Spanish missionaries and colonizers, from whose records an additional perspective can be gained concerning the place of the Jumanos among the Texas Indians. This was Coahuila, the terminus of an eastern corridor, where explorers penetrated the interior after becoming established on the gulf's coastal plain.

The province of Nuevo Leon was founded in 1517, claiming territory in a two-hundred-league radius around Panuco; this included much of present-day Texas. Mining began within a few leagues of the lower Rio Bravo in the 1580's. By 1590, there was a settlement at Almaden, the point of departure for the illegal *entrada* led by Gaspar Castaño de Sosa. After Castaño's departure, however, Almaden was abandoned, and the mines were not reopened for half a century.

By 1650, settlements had sprung up in what was to become the province of Coahuila. Prospectors seeking silver and other minerals soon came into conflict with the Cacaxtles and other tribes in northern Coahuila. Military expeditions of reprisal against the Indians reached and crossed the Rio Bravo by 1660. Around 1670 Franciscan missions already established near Almaden began efforts to enter the country beyond the river. The priests stationed in northern Coahuila—like those in other frontier posts such as Parral—were, at this time, receiving petitions from Indians seeking baptism and mission settlement. Some of the petitioners had come across the Rio Bravo from the Texas side, where there were a multitude of small bands and tribes, many of them refugees from more distant regions.

The Bosque-Larios Expedition

Fray Juan Larios was one of the missionary friars who responded to requests from this quarter. Larios, assisted by other clerics and lay personnel, visited the Coahuila frontier several times, founding native settlements in that border area. After taking formal possession of the country beyond the Rio Bravo, the initial goal of the Spanish policy was—as always when dealing with Indians living in small, widely scattered bands—the reduction of the population to compact communities clustered around missions, accessible to civil and religious authority. The efforts of the priests, working toward this goal, quickly revealed factions and alliances among the many small groups of Indians which would undoubtedly have made it difficult to entice them to live together in a single settlement.

In 1675, Larios joined in an expedition which had military support under the leadership of Captain Ferdinand Bosque, intending to make an organized push to the north. The party included Larios and a second priest; Bosque, with ten soldiers under his command; and a large number of Christianized Indians. One of these, the governor of an already settled Coahuiltecan tribe, served as interpreter. The Bosque-Larios expedition set out specifically to survey the Indian groups along and north of the Rio Bravo and to make recommendations as to how many missions would be needed, and where they should be located in order to accommodate the existing native factions. The journal of the military commander, Bosque, is especially valuable because tribal names and locations were noted with an obvious effort at accuracy. This information is a cornerstone body of data for the ethnography of the Coahuiltecan Indians and their neighbors.

> In the province of Nueba Estremadura de Quaguila [Coahuila], on the 30th day of April, 1675, I, Fernando de el Bosque, lieutenant alcalde mayor of the province . . . set out this day from the city of Our Lady of Guadalupe . . . in fulfillment of the orders of Captain Don Antonio de Valcarcel Riba Niera Sotomayor, alcalde mayor of said province [Nueva Estremadura, or Coahuila] . . . arising from the petition of Pablo, Indian chief of the nation of Manosprietas and the other nations from the Rio del Norte and its vicinity . . .[1]

Governor Balcarcel had planned to lead the *entrada* himself, but due to ill health entrusted it to Bosque, his second in command. The party traveled north along the Rio de Monclova and Rio de Nadadores, taking possession of the country and planting crosses as they made their way toward the Rio Bravo. At each stop, Indians were gathered together and given religious instruction by the two priests. Around the twelfth of May, they built a raft and crossed the river at a place where it was broad and shallow, evidently in the vicinity of Eagle Pass, Texas. On the other side, on May 13, the Spanish party encountered Indians hunting buffalo; they are identified as Yorica and Jeapa, and their enemies as the Ocane, Pataguaque, and Yurbipiame nations.

[May 14, 1675] I, said lieutenant alcalde mayor, certify and testify that in my presence there were killed by said Indians [Yoricas and Jeapas] and Spaniards three buffalo bulls and two buffalo cows for the people to eat. The meat is very savory. The form of the buffalo is very ugly. Although large, they resemble cows and bulls. Their hair is shaggy. The withers are very high, making them appear humpbacked, and their necks are large. The head is short and very shaggy, so that the wool covers the eyes and prevents them from seeing well. The horns are small and thick, like those of the bull. The hips and haunches are like those of a hog, and the tail is bare, except at the end, where there are long bristles. The hoofs are cloven, and at the knees and from there up to the shoulder there is much bristle-like hair, like he-goats. They gaze at the people sidewise like wild hogs, with hair abristle . . .[2]

The hunting Indians offered to lead the Spaniards to "the place where the Indian nations of the Sierra Dacate y Yacasole [Sacatsol] are, and [to] send to their *rancherias* to have them come out to a place where they might be given Christian instruction."[3] The expedition progressed northward in several stages, stopping to convene and proselytize regional clusters of Indians as they advanced to Sierra Dacate (or Anacacho Mountain), and about ten leagues beyond (Map 6, no. 7). All told, this *entrada* moved almost due north approximately one hundred leagues from its starting point. On the way back, the route veered somewhat to the west.

[May 15] . . . [There] appeared before me . . . the chiefs Xoman [Jumano], Tercodan, Teaname, and Teimamar, with their people. I had them examined through sworn interpreters who understand their language, Mexican, and Castilian . . . Various questions having been asked of these chiefs, each one separately, they said unanimously and in agreement that they were heathen . . . and had lived as heathen without knowledge that there was a God . . . that they wished to be Christians and be baptized, with their children and wives, and to live as such in a pueblo or pueblos . . . so that while they, being old, would not enjoy it, their children would enjoy it and be reared as Christians . . . and that at once they were rendering and did render obedience to his Majesty the king our lord Don Carlos the Second; and that they would be friends of the Spaniards . . .[4]

The priests returned to their mission, Nuestra Señora de Guadalupe, in June, after contacting and interviewing many Indian leaders. Although the population of the region would, in earlier times,
no doubt have consisted primarily of small, independent, widely
scattered semi-nomadic bands and tribes, by the 1670's the situation had become considerably more complicated.

T. N. Campbell, who has attempted to sort out the hundreds of
band and tribal names recorded in southern Texas and northern
Coahuila, indicates that this marginal region had become a refuge
area. Gathered there were displaced populations and refugee groups
fleeing from Apache expansion in the north and west, and others
moving north ahead of advancing Spanish settlements. In this situation, there was a heightened competition for territory, which must
have led to a great increase in inter-group rivalry and warfare. There
is uncertainty about the identities of many of the ethnic groups involved, since remnant band segments frequently joined and became
incorporated in related bands, small groups merged and acquired new
identities, and many of the earlier named entities had disappeared.[5]

Bosque's report indicates that the Indians of the entire area fell
into "three tiers of settlements," ranging roughly from west to east;
each group appeared to acknowledge the leadership of a chief. The
easternmost group, which was very numerous, included Catujanos,
Tilijaes, Apis, and Pachaques. The middle tier was made up of
Bibits, Yoricas, Geniocanes, and others, under the leadership of a
Bobole chief. The western tier, "the least numerous, although wild
and the most bellicose," consisted of "the following of Don Esteban
Gueiquisal," and ranged in the mountains around Sacatsol.[6]

Fray Larios seems to have spent the most time in this area, where
there were—besides the petitioning Manos Prietas and the Guei-
quesal—other groups which he called Pinanaca, Xaeser, Tenimama,
Cocama, Tercoda, Teaname, Teimamar, and finally, the Xoman. Besides the *Xoman* or Jumanos, a number of these bands were evidently based in Nueva Vizcaya; the names of the Pinanaca, Cocama, Teimamar, and Manos Prietas, at least, appear in a list of the
Indian nations in that province some twenty years later.[7] Their rep-
resentation here, at Sierra Dacate, would indicate the existence of
an east-west route of travel skirting the Rio Bravo south of the canyons of the Big Bend region, with a crossing at or near Eagle Pass.

All three of the segments defined by Bosque fall within, and in
the western portion of, a much larger cultural province usually labeled, on the basis of prevailing language affiliation, as Coahuiltecan. However, it must be noted that in the western group as given
by Bosque there are several of unknown or questioned linguistic

classification; in the judgment of J. Forbes, for example, the "Terco-dame, Tripas Blancas, Gueiquesales . . . Babosarigames, Coahuilas, and many other bands were apparently non-Coahuiltecan."[8] The Jumanos, certainly, did not fall under that rubric.

Thus, Sierra Dacate was located in a transitional or marginal zone, which formed an enclave between the predominantly Coa-huiltecan populations to the south and east, and the linguistically complex valley of the Rio del Norte on the west. Further, it was easily accessible to the Tonkawans of the Edwards Plateau; the Chisos and others, predominantly Uto-Aztecan in language, of Nueva Vizcaya; and the predominantly Caddoan area of central Texas. This region of low mountains was apparently a gathering place, a center for Indian activities and intertribal contacts. It was also a center for trade, which might explain the presence there of the Jumanos, on that and later occasions. (Doubt might possibly be cast on the identification of Bosque's *Xoman* as Jumano, if there were not clear evidence a decade later of the presence of the Ju-manos and their leader, Juan Sabeata.)

The Search for La Salle's Colony

The expedition of Bosque and Larios was a prelude to the growth, in the next decade, of a more intense Spanish interest in Texas. This interest was, to a great extent, linked to the presence of La Salle's colony at the Bay of Espiritu Santo. At about the same time that Governor Pardinas of Nueva Vizcaya learned of the appearance of foreigners on the Texas coast, the same news reached authorities in the capitol of Mexico, and those in Coahuila as well.

Immediately, ships were dispatched from the port of Vera Cruz to sail the coast in search of the French fort. From Coahuila, Captain Alonso de Leon was dispatched to lead land expeditions, beginning in 1686 with an attempt to reach the Bay of Espiritu Santo by fol-lowing the Rio Bravo to the sea. However, De Leon failed to make his way past the mouth of the river; in a subsequent attempt, he was deterred by a maze of streams and lagoons as he attempted to ascend the coast. De Leon was appointed governor of Coahuila in 1687; still, he continued to lead expeditions personally to find the remains of Fort St. Louis in east Texas and to discover and appre-hend survivors of the colony.

In his last two expeditions, De Leon was joined by Fray Damian Mazanet (or Massanet), a Franciscan from Spain, who was stationed at Caldera, near Monclova, in Coahuila. It might be noted that Mazanet's own desire for a ministry among Indians in the New

World was originally inspired by his acquaintance with writings of Mother Maria de Jesus de Agreda.[9]

Unhappily for Fray Damian, the missionary yearnings of the Franciscans at the College of Queretero had been for some time temporarily frustrated by the policies of a custodian who discouraged members of the order from proselytizing among unconverted heathen tribes. At the time of De Leon's *entradas* into Texas, however, a change in administration made it possible for Mazanet, along with several other friars, to join in missionizing among the Indians beyond the Rio Bravo. In the spring of 1687, according to his own account, Damian Mazanet came in contact with an Indian convert of the Quems nation (a Coahuiltecan-speaking tribe, from beyond the Rio Bravo). This man claimed that he had visited the French colony and had been ". . . even in the very houses of the French . . ." He gave a very convincing description of the settlement, and offered to guide Mazanet to the place, where ". . . we should also find priests like myself, and that . . . the people were sowing maize and other crops."[10]

At about the same time, Captain de Leon paid a visit to the mission at Caldera, where Mazanet was in residence. After the two men had conferred, De Leon suggested that Mazanet try to obtain more substantial evidence to confirm the claims of the Quems convert. Mazanet's account indicates that he then learned from a captain of the Pacpul tribe that there was a Frenchman living in a *rancheria* some sixty leagues from the mission. The priest dispatched the Pacpul captain to this *rancheria*, where ". . . having come close to the sierra of Sacatsol . . . he found an assembly of many Indian nations composed of the following: Mescales, Yoricas, Chomenes, Machomenes, Sampanales, Paquachians, Tilpayay, Apis."[11] Along with these Indians, the Pacpul also found the Frenchman, whom he brought out to a more accessible spot; he then returned to inform Mazanet. Since Juan Sabeata is believed to have visited Sacatsol just before joining General Retana in the summer of 1687, it is possible that he was one of the Chomenes contacted there by Mazanet's emissary.[12]

In May of 1688, Captain de Leon went, with twelve soldiers, to this same *rancheria* and brought back ". . . the Frenchman, painted like the Indians, old and naked."[13] The man was later identified as Juan Jarri, a native of Chablis, who was evidently one of the deserters earlier encountered among the Cenis by Joutel. The Frenchman was put under arrest, used as an unwilling guide in De Leon's journey in search of Fort St. Louis, and eventually dispatched to be incarcerated in Mexico.

The next year, 1689, Fray Damian joined an expedition, led by De Leon, which advanced to the Bay of Espiritu Santo and beyond, in search of the numerous Frenchmen who were believed to have established themselves in the Indian villages and *rancherias*. De Leon had heard that "among the Tejas there were eighteen Frenchmen, and that houses had been built; that they had flocks of goats and sheep, and that some of the Frenchmen had gone to their country for women and more men." [14]

The expedition of 1689 included Captain de Leon, Fray Damian Mazanet, and three companies of men drawn from Nueva Vizcaya, Nuevo Leon, and Coahuila. On their way north, just before crossing the Rio del Norte, they passed through a village where the French prisoner greeted certain of his friends—De Leon called them the "Indians of the Frenchman." In this village, there were "five nations joined together . . . entitled Hapes, Jumenes, Xiabu, Mescale, and another. We distributed among them some cotton garments, blankets, beads, rosaries, knives, and arms, with which they were very much pleased." [15] This reference to Jumanos well south of the Rio Bravo, in Coahuila, may be the southernmost location on record.

Captain de Leon's army finally crossed southern Texas and reached the Bay of Espiritu Santo, where they found the ruins of La Salle's settlement. From Indians in the vicinity—Tonkawan Emets and Lavas—they also learned about several Frenchmen still living nearby. As the Spaniards pushed further north, they found two of the Frenchmen in a *rancheria* of the Toaa (likely the Teao of the La Salle accounts), together with a party of nine Tejas (Hasinai) Indians, one of whom Mazanet understood to be a "governor" of that tribe.[16] Although they were several individual survivors from the French colony who were apprehended on this and De Leon's next expedition, it seems that the rumors about the existence of thriving French settlements may have been inspired in part by the presence of Henri Tonty's post on the Arkansas. They may also have reflected the growing interest of the Texas tribes, including the Hasinai, in the possibilities for trade in that direction.

Father Mazanet took advantage of his meeting with the Tejas headman to undertake to proselytize and to secure the promise of an opportunity to introduce missions in Tejas territory. He returned to Coahuila full of plans for this enterprise.

Encounters with the Jumanos

In March of 1690, De Leon led a party of soldiers to the Texas coast, this time with orders to burn the remains of the fort and to seek out whatever additional Frenchmen might still be living with the Indians. On this occasion, he once more escorted Fray Damian Mazanet, along with the five priests who were to establish what were intended to be permanent missions among the Tejas.

Once again, De Leon mentions a meeting with the "Indians of the Frenchmen," near the crossing of the Rio del Norte; there is no indication of whether any Jumanos were present on this occasion. Very few Indians were encountered en route to the Bay of Espiritu Santo, where the Spaniards quickly set fire to what was left of the French habitations. Making their way north, they retrieved several French children, who had been rescued at the time of the attack on the fort and cared for in nearby Indian villages.

Mazanet and his group of friars were cordially received by the Nabadaches, the southernmost tribe of the Hasinai confederacy. Here, Mazanet installed the priests in two pole-and-thatch missions situated between the Trinity and the Neches Rivers. He himself traveled back to Coahuila with De Leon's party, promising to return the next year with supplies and reinforcements.

During the winter of 1690-1691, a smallpox epidemic swept the Hasinai villages, and latent hostilities surfaced between the Catholic priests and the Indian religious leaders. The Grand Xinesi held the Franciscans and their God responsible for the sickness. The missionary enclave—which was protected by only three soldiers—became alarmed as well about rumors of the impending arrival at the missions of parties of Frenchmen from the north.

In the fall of 1690 one of the Franciscans, Fray Foncuberta, encountered Juan Sabeata, who was making the rounds on an annual visit to the Hasinai villages. The Jumano leader was on his way westward, toward the Rio del Norte, and offered to carry a letter, which Foncuberta addressed to the Custodian of New Mexico, at El Paso. The letter was an appraisal of the situation of the missions, and an appeal for help—the priests hoped that troops could be sent from New Mexico to help defend their missions against the French. Juan Sabeata was still carrying this letter two years later, when he handed it over to Governor Isidro de Pardiñas at Parral; apparently he did not, in the interim, have occasion to pass near El Paso.

In the spring of 1691, Sabeata was back in Texas. By then, Fray Foncuberta had died. Sabeata picked up two more letters from the remaining missionaries, which he handled with more dispatch, turning them over a few months later to Domingo de Teran, the new governor of Coahuila. Sabeata encountered the governor on the Guadalupe River, along with Fray Damian Mazanet who was once more traveling north to relieve the Tejas missions. Mazanet's account of this expedition is, once more, a source of information concerning the Indian groups encountered on the route north from Coahuila. As they crossed the Rio Bravo, the Spaniards encountered Indians of the Quem, Pacpul, Paac, Ocana, and various other nations which, Mazanet observed, "speak the same language"; all of them can be identified as Coahuiltecans. Beyond this point, he noted more diversity: "From this place to the Techas are other languages. There follow the Indian nations of Catquesa, Cantona, Emet, Cavas, Zana, Tojo, Toaa, and others." [17] These appear, in the main, to be Tonkawans. In the vicinity of San Antonio, there were more Coahuiltecans—Sanpanal, Papanaca, and Apayus—to whom Mazanet distributed rosaries and tobacco. Leaving this point, they moved on through an open landscape, which Mazanet described in positive terms.

> . . . low hills, wooded with live oaks and mesquites, and region very easily traversed . . . Before reaching the river there are other hills . . . the river has much timber—poplars, savins, live oaks, mulberries, and many grape vines. There are many fish, and on the plains numerous prairie chickens . . . Here we found the *rancheria* of the Indians of the Payay nation. This is a very large nation, and the country where they live and have their habitat is very fine. I named this place San Antonio de Padua, because of its being his day [July 13]. [18]

After remaining in that place—the future city of San Antonio, Texas—for two days, the expedition departed, accompanied by the Payay captain, who offered "to guide us as far as the *rancheria* of the Chomanes Indians." A few leagues further to the north, they met the Chomanes (Jumanos) on the road. "We encountered an Indian who was coming on horseback, and he said that the captains of the Choma (Jumano), Cibola, Cantona, Choleme . . . Catqueca, and Caynaya nations were coming to receive us peacefully." [19]

Half a league further on, these captains and other Indians were found, all on horseback; the Franciscans were, as usual, proceeding on foot. When the two parties met, the Indians "all dismounted and saluted us with the greatest courtesy." [20] Juan Sabeata immediately delivered the two letters from the priests whom Mazanet had, the year previously, left in the Tejas missions. Mazanet noted that all of the Indian captains had very small saddles on their horses; he inquired about this, and was told that they had been taken in war from Apaches.

The Spaniards were escorted to the Jumanos' *rancheria* on the Guadalupe River (Map 6, no. 8). Mazanet estimated the total population of this community to be three thousand; it was apparently a mixed population of Jumanos, Cantonas, Catquesas, and others. Damian Mazanet gives us one of the few really vivid descriptions of an encounter with the Jumanos and their allies.

> On the afternoon of our arrival [at the *rancheria*] all of the captains passed in procession, each one with his people. The first was Don Juan Sabeata with his people and nation of Choma Indians; then the captain of the Cantona nation, who led his people and the Chomanes. The said Cantona captain marched in front with a wooden cross, which he said he had kept for many years with great care and veneration . . . Next came the captain of the Cibola nation with his own people and those of the Choleme and Caynaaya nations. The captain marched in front, and carried an image of Our Lady of Guadalupe, which was one of those that had been distributed and given to the captains the previous year . . .
> After these came the captain of the Catquesa nation, who is an Indian named Nicolas, well-versed in the Mexican language, and understanding all that is said to him in Castillian . . . He did the same as the others, namely, advanced at the head of a procession formed in two columns and kissed my habit and hand . . .
> Don Juan Sabeata, the captain of the said Chomenes (whom they call Jumanes) exhibited his commission as governor of the Indians of his nation and of other nations who have joined him. Another Indian of the same nation likewise assumed the title of lieutenant-governor of the said Don Juan Sabeata. Both titles were conferred upon them by the governor of La Viscaya, Don Juan Isidro Pardinas.
> The said nations of Choma, Cibola, and Caynaaya are Indians who live and have their lands on the banks of the Rio del Norte. They likewise border on the Apache Indians, and have wars with them . . . The Indians of the Choma nation are the ones whom in Parral and New Mexico they call Jumanes. Every year they come to the head of the Rio de Guadalupe, and sometimes as far as the Techas. They come to kill the buffaloes, and as soon as cold weather begins, they retire to their own country.[21]

As on earlier occasions, the Jumanos put on a splendid show of piety and devotion for the visiting religious. Juan Sabeata must have felt somewhat gratified to have Spanish missions with military support installed among the nearby Tejas. However, he told Fray Damian that the priests should have come to his people, among whom there were many Christians, who had been baptized in Parral and in New Mexico. He could not, he said, remain on the Guadalupe—"the purpose of his coming was for the buffalos and to bring the pelts."[22] Mazanet told Sabeata that the fathers, who were alone among the Tejas, were in need of the supplies they were taking them. He reasoned, privately, that Sabeata's agreements were "specious, for if they had wished ministers in their country I did not doubt that they would have had them, because the said Indians every year enter El Parral and Paso del Nuevo Mexico."[23]

The Catquezas also tried to persuade the Spanish party to stay with them, passing on rumors to the soldiers to the effect that the Tejas were poor and unhealthy, and that they had stolen clothing, horses, and other possessions from the missions. Mazanet felt uneasy, and moved on two leagues' distance to some waterholes where, in the evening, the captains visited him once more, apparently to mend relations. They brought with them five captive children of the nearby Muruam tribe, whom they turned over to the Spanish captain in exchange for horses.[24]

Spanish Departure from Texas

The tense relationship which apparently developed over time, between the Franciscan missionaries and the Hasinai priests and chiefs, flared when Teran's troops arrived in Tejas territory. After several weeks during which the Spanish soldiers were billeted in the Tejas villages, the *caddi* (chief) ordered the Franciscans to leave his country. In the meantime, Teran had received new orders from Coahuila, instructing him to go on, to explore the country further north.

Some of the missionaries, including Mazanet, departed with the military party, which advanced to the Red River and the Cadohadacho villages before returning to Coahuila. Three friars and a few soldiers lingered at their Tejas mission until late in 1693, waiting for the permission to quit their post to come from the head of their order in Mexico. However, when their departure was demanded by the *caddi*, on pain of death, they finally fled, leaving the mission in flames. The priests reached Monclova in February of 1694, ending for more than a decade the presence of resident Spanish missionaries in Texas. Several soldiers, including one Joseph de Urrutia, deserted or were left behind during the Spaniards' retreat, and remained to join the Indian allies in their wars against the Apaches.

15.

THE VIEW FROM PARRAL

In the spring of 1687, a group of Indians stopped at one of the mission churches at La Junta de los Rios, the confluence of the Rio Conchos and the Rio del Norte, and asked Fray Agustín de Colina, the chief Franciscan missionary in that district, to write a letter. The Indians were Jumano-Cibolos, and they had just returned from a trading expedition to eastern Texas—a round trip of at least twelve hundred miles. There were, they reported to Fray Colina, strange Spaniards coming and going among the Indians in Texas. They requested that the priests write a message to these "Spaniards," which they could carry with them when they returned in the spring. Colina demurred, and suggested that the Indians might instead bring him a letter from those in Texas, to which he would then respond.[1]

As far as we know, no such letter was ever received. But the next year, the Indians once more brought interesting news: a foreigner, a "Moor," was living with one of the tribes and assisting them in wars against their enemies. There was, by then, a wealth of rumors circulating about the foreigners, their ships and houses, and the gifts of hatchets, knives, and other goods which they had given to the Indians. Fray Colina had by this time been forced to abandon his post, due to the insurrection movement which had reached La Junta; he and the other friars, assisted by loyal Indians, took refuge at the mission of San Pedro de Conchos. There, Colina passed on the news from Texas to Captain Juan de Retana, the commander of the presidio.

Subsequently, Retana interrogated a number of Indians in order to obtain more information about the intruders. These word-of-mouth reports, carried from the Texas coast to a distant border post, may have been the first intimations that officials in Nueva Vizcaya received concerning an event which had long been feared—an incursion by a foreign power into the coastal lands claimed by Spain;

a threat to the security, the lands, and the mineral wealth of New Spain. This was an especially frightening thought in the thinly settled frontier regions in which the richest silver deposits were located. Retana obtained what information he could, and drafted an official report to the provincial governor, Juan Isidro de Pardiñas.

The strangers were, as Colina suspected from the beginning, neither Spaniards nor Moors, but Frenchmen, members of the short-lived colony planted at Espíritu Santo by the Marquis de La Salle in the spring of 1685. The French threat had long been a favorite bugaboo in Spanish North America, and the paranoia was intensified by reports of La Salle's successful expedition to the mouth of the Mississippi, where he claimed Louisiana for France in 1682. Having received the unwelcome news of his presence at Espíritu Santo, officials in Parral took action to obtain more information about the French settlement, and to defend their own holdings, if necessary.

On November 2, 1688, Governor Pardiñas dispatched an order for Retana to assemble a company of ninety harquebusiers and as many Indian auxiliaries as he deemed necessary, and to prepare to mount an expedition to the east, beyond the Rio del Norte. Retana was to claim the lands which he entered, in the name of Spain. He was to be accompanied by Fray Juan de Jumeta, a priest who claimed a knowledge of Indian languages. Pardiñas suggested that Retana, assisted by Fray Jumeta, might be able to form an alliance with "any nation of Indians living under an organized government like the Texas Indians, with a king, cacique, or chief whom they obey . . . ," in order to extend Spanish control and to prevent further inroads by the French. Finally, the governor expressed the hope that Retana and his troops could capture one or more of the Frenchmen for interrogation.[2]

After receiving this assignment, Retana ordered his company to assemble. He also sent a message to Juan Sabeata, who was now a Spanish-appointed governor of the Indians around La Junta. It would be his task to lead the Indian auxiliaries and to guide Retana's men into what would surely be, to them, *terra incognita.* Juan Sabeata was officially instructed to remain at La Junta, to await Retana's arrival; however, Sabeata did not wait.

Captain Retana was, evidently, delayed. Before leaving for Texas, he went to lead a punitive campaign against the bands of rebellious Chizos and Tobosos harassing the Spanish settlers around Parral. By the time he arrived at La Junta, Juan Sabeata had long since taken his leave for Texas. Retana eventually sent out scouts, who contacted the Indian governor near the Rio Pecos, east of La Junta. Sabeata was already on his return route, carrying news which rendered the military campaign, for the time being, unnecessary. Sabeata reported to Retana that the French fort had been destroyed by coastal Indians, and that almost all of the Frenchmen were dead. Only a handful survived, who had taken refuge with the Tejas.[3]

The *Autos* at Parral

Some months later, in April of 1689, several of the principals in this episode were summoned to Parral by Governor Pardiñas, to give evidence in an official hearing. Their *autos* (affidavits) were given under oath and translated from the Jumanos' tongue into Mexican and then into Spanish, the language in which they were recorded. This testimony provides a unique body of information relating to the Jumanos at the end of the century, and to their role as intermediaries between the Spanish colony and the Indians of Texas.

A statement signed by Governor Pardiñas, dated April 10, 1689, details the arrival of Juan Sabeata and his followers.

There arrived at the camp of El Parral . . . Don Juan Xaviata [Sabeata], who said that he was governor of the Indians of the Cibolos and Jumanos nations, and Miguel, who said that he was captain of the said nations that reside on the Rio del Norte, and other caciques, who said that they are heathens and that they live at their *rancherias* on the lower Rio del Norte. These, in their usual custom, made obeisance to the said señor governor and promised to obey him.

Through Don Nicolas, governor of the Julime nations . . . and Joseph de Villalba, a Spaniard whom his lordship appointed as interpreter of the Mexican language . . . the said Indians stated that through some Indians who have come to their *rancherias* from this camp [Parral] and from the labor on its hacienda, they have learned of the good opinion that the natives have of the said señor governor. They have desired to see him, and they would have come earlier, but for the fact that the time for going into the interior to the fairs which they conduct with the nations of the upper Rio del Norte, the Texas, and many other Indian nations, prevented them from doing so. They said that recently, on returning from these fairs, they met a captain [Retana] and many Spaniards to whom they made known their desire, and the latter facilitated their journey. They come with great pleasure because the Moors (for thus in their Indian languages do they call the French or foreigners) have been destroyed by the nations of heathen Indians near the place where they were. In testimony of this truth, they bring two sheets of paper which appear to be from some book printed by hand, apparently

in the French language, and a frigate painted on a parchment, with some
written annotations. This they turned over to the said señor governor
tied up in a neckcloth of fine wide lace.

   The said señor governor embraced the Indians and instructed that
they be given lodging and refreshments, and because it was already
late . . . he cited them to appear before him on the following day . . .[4]

The following day, April 11, testimony was taken from the four
Jumano leaders. Pardiñas' instructions stipulated that information
should be requested concerning the distance from Parral to the
lands of the Tejas Indians and to the port of Espiritu Santo; the con-
dition of the road, and the nations which live along it; and, whether
they saw Frenchmen or other foreigners, and what contacts they
had with them. The nature of these inquiries was determined by
the initial information as transmitted by Fray Colina and Captain
Retana.

   Don Juan Xaviata, Indian governor of the Cibolos and Jumanos of the
   Rio del Norte . . . made the oath by God, our Lord, and the sign of the
   cross, under burden of which he promised to speak the truth concerning
   what might be asked of him.[5]

Sabeata's testimony recalled the routine of his working arrange-
ment with Captain Retana. Retana had sent notice telling him to
wait at La Junta "with a sufficient number of bowmen." Since it
was already known that "some men of other countries were, during
the preceding months, approaching in canoes and by land," Sabeata
assumed that the captain would be searching for them. He waited
for several days, but finally learned that Retana had gone to fight
against the Tobosos. "Because it was time to go to their fairs (*ferias
y resgates*) with the Texas Indians and other nations that live along
those rivers," Sabeata finally decided to go ahead, according to custom, and to attempt at the same time to gather news for Retana.

   At a *rancheria* seven days from La Junta, on the "other part" of
the river—evidently the Pecos—Sabeata learned from Miguel, one
of the Jumano captains, that "it was more than three moons since
the arrival there of some men wearing doublets of steel (*jubones de
fierro*)." Having learned this, he and the rest of his company went
on "nearly to the sea." He held the usual trade fairs with the Indians there, and also asked for information about the foreigners. The
Indians indicated that ". . . they had killed all of them, and that only
eight or nine, who had gone . . . to trade with the Texas Indians . . .
had escaped."

A day's travel from that location, at another *rancheria*, the Indians were celebrating the destruction of the fort. Sabeata went from there to "where the Indians called *Texas* are," and found four or five white men who expressed a desire to accompany him to "the country adjacent to the Spaniards." However, after two or three days, they turned back upon learning that there were "many wild Indians"—presumably Apaches—along the way.

The sheets of paper with writing, the picture of a ship, and the lace neck cloth were obtained from a "captain of *rancherias* near the Texas Indians"; there were more, but some were taken by "an Indian who spoke Castillian . . . from near Coahuila."[6]

The Indian Miguel, identified as a captain of the Cibolos, stated that he had been baptized by Fray Agustín de Colina, at La Junta. Since Miguel had been present at meetings with the Frenchmen, he was able to add much of interest to Juan Sabeata's testimony. Miguel's *rancheria* was located ". . . where there are many large cattle called buffalo (*sibolas*), over the killing of which they often have wars with other nations of the upper river (*del rio arriba*) . . ." If, as seems likely, Miguel's *rancheria* was situated on the Pecos (perhaps the same locale as the Jediondo *rancheria* visited by the Lopez–Dominguez de Mendoza expedition), the Apache territory would have been located upriver on this stream.

Miguel had heard, "from others of his nation," about the comings and goings of the foreigners, whom he called *Moros* (Moors). He "traveled for three days' journey to the lower river (*el rio abajo*) and there he got clearer news, for the Indians of that *rancheria* told him that they had been there and had become their friends, that they gave them some hatchets and some glass beads (*cuentas*) . . ." The use of the phrase "lower river," like other geographical references throughout the affidavits, is obscure. In this case, Miguel's destination could have been lower on the Pecos, or a point on the Concho, the "Rio de las Nueces"; the latter is more likely to have been reached by the French exploring parties.

The "Moors," six in number, "came up the river in a canoe"; four others arrived by land. They had with them an Indian translator, and embraced the residents of the *rancheria* as old friends, whom they had contacted before. Miguel saw no reason to distrust these foreigners since "they were like other Spaniards . . . they also had rosaries, and . . . spoke to them of God . . ." They gave the Indians "copper ladles, and some ribbons, table-knives and pocket-knives." According to Miguel, he and others who had done agricultural labor in the Spanish settlements were interrogated about Parral, San Bartolome, and the road linking them. It was after this encounter that

Miguel brought back the report which the mission priests at La Junta passed along to Captain Retana. Subsequently, he accompanied Juan Sabeata on his visit to the Tejas, where they learned of the destruction of the fort.[7]

Two more Cibolos, identified as "heathens," also gave testimony. Cuis Benive indicated that the white men, carrying harquebuses, had come to his *rancheria* on three occasions, at two- and three-month intervals; the fourth time, although expected, they failed to arrive. At that point, he joined Miguel and Juan Sabeata, "to go to the fairs with the other nations and to find out where those people were living." It was he who went, with two companions, to visit the ruined fort; they found it abandoned, with "no living thing except some of the pigs," and returned to inform Juan Sabeata of the fact.[8]

Muygisofac indicated that his *rancheria* "usually has a war every year with the Caribes Indians (Apaches) over the killing of the cattle that they call *sibolas*, which are at certain times of the year between the Rio del Norte and the Nueces River." (This specific geographical reference is of value as a guide to interpretation of the other affidavits.) He, too, had seen the foreigners, "clothed and with harquebuses, arrive by way of the river and by land." They visited several times, and gave them "axes, knives, beads, copper kettles, and sometimes clothing, and made gifts to the women of ribbons and other little things, and for this reason they had warm friendship for them . . ."

Like Miguel, Muygisofac was surprised to learn from Juan Sabeata that the strangers were not to be trusted. He, too, had accompanied Sabeata on his information-gathering mission. They stopped along the way at "various *rancherias*," but got no information until they contacted Indians of the Texas nation who indicated that "the Indians who live in the sierras and those of the sea coast had killed them all."[9]

The "Rio del Norte" and its Environs

Besides the information about contacts with the strangers, or Moors, all of the Indian witnesses gave accounts of the route to the Texas country, locales and settlements along the way, and some of the hazards to be encountered. They uniformly indicated that the road was not long or difficult. According to Juan Sabeata, after leaving the Rio del Norte ". . . there is a sierra, [but] one does not have to climb it, as it has level passes; the rest of the way is level."[10] The distance from La Junta was estimated to be ten to twelve days, if traveling directly; but it might be many more days when stopping

at *rancherias* along the way, to trade or to gather news. Because of
spring and summer rains in Texas, they ". . . set out . . . when the
trees begin to sprout, and return when the leaves are falling."[11]
When rains come, ". . . it is not easy to enter or come out of that
land, because of the flooded rivers and marshes . . ." This was one of
the reasons that Juan Sabeata did not wait for Captain Retana before
leaving La Junta: ". . . after it begins to rain . . . it is not possible to
come out until winter sets in."[12]

The geographical references in the *autos* (reports) are sometimes
confusing, if taken at face value. Most of the locations of Jumano
and other groups are expressed in relation to a complex river system, dominated by the Rio del Norte. This is, of course, the river
known today as the Rio Grande, but it is seen in the context of a
world view which is quite different from that of the twentieth century. And use of the terms *upper* (*arribo*) and *lower* (*abajo*) in reference to the river system would make it appear, on initial reading, as
if the Cibolo settlements were spread along the main valley of the
Rio Grande itself, and that the French traders were advancing along
that stream. This interpretation has confused and misled some historians' efforts to trace the movements of La Salle and his colonists,
but it is erroneous.

It must be realized that neither Jumano nor Spanish familiarity
with the valley of the Rio Grande extended very far downriver
below La Junta de los Rios. Native highways could not have followed the course of the river through the rocky canyons of the Big
Bend region; both the Rio Grande and the Pecos, in their lower
reaches, are deeply canyoned and inaccessible, and would have been
outside the usual routes of travel. We can be sure, however, that all
of the references are to territories and routes with which the Jumano-Cibolos had great familiarity, in which they had lived and
traveled for many years.

Governor Pardiña's statement made reference to two groupings of
Indians—the "nations that reside on the Rio del Norte," and those
"that live at their haciendas on the lower river (*el dicho rio abajo*)."
According to Juan Sabeata's declaration, the "men of other countries," the Frenchmen, approached in canoes, arriving at Miguel's
rancheria, which was located on "the lower river and the other part
of it (*el rio abajo y a la otra parte de el*)."[13] But the Frenchmen,
from their foothold at Espiritu Santo, would surely have ascended
the Colorado of Texas. If La Salle did not immediately recognize the
Colorado as an important route into Mexico, native guides would
soon have pointed out that stream as the main highway toward the

country of the Spaniards. We have already seen that La Salle's explorations were extensive, that they focused on the Robec (Colorado) and Maligne (Brazos), and may have reached as far as the Pecos.

Miguel's *rancheria* was, according to Juan Sabeata's deposition, seven days' travel (sixty-seven leagues, in the translator's estimation) away from La Junta. The conclusion seems obvious that this location was at or near the crossing of the Rio Pecos (Map 6, no. 6). This stream, as a tributary of the Rio Grande, is quite reasonably called the "other part" of the Rio del Norte. The more distant *rancheria* of Muygisofac was located in buffalo country, between the Rio del Norte and the Rio de las Nueces (Map 6, no. 4). The second of these streams is identified as the Concho, a tributary of the Colorado; however, in these texts the river so designated is also referred to as the "lower river" or even the "lower Rio del Norte."

The terminology (as rendered in Spanish) reflects the importance of these rivers and streams for the people who lived and traveled over them. The Rio Conchos, the Rio Grande, above the canyons which begin downstream from La Junta de los Rios, the Pecos, though not necessarily all the way to its confluence with the Rio Grande, and the Colorado, along with its tributary, the Concho, were all part of a single, historically important, native highway system. The Jumano-Cibolo settlements lay along the important segments of this system.

To both Indians and Spaniards, in the late seventeenth century, this land-and-water network of trails was a vital artery. It linked northern Nueva Vizcaya with the Rio Colorado and the world beyond, and provided access to routes over which important goods were transported. By contrast, the Rio Bravo—the Rio Grande below the Big Bend canyon region—was more remote; to all intents and purposes, this lay outside of the regional system.

It might be recalled that late in the century, Alonso de Posada, an educated European, was uncertain about the courses of the many rivers which empty into the Gulf of Mexico. The mouth of the Colorado near Espiritu Santo Bay was variously confused with the Mississippi on the one hand and the Rio Bravo on the other. The Spaniards at Parral, like their Indian neighbors, evidently regarded the Rio del Norte and Rio Colorado as segments of a single large river network. Discontinuous segments of this network were linked by trails. This skewed vision reflects the realities of communication and trade over pathways upon which both Indians and Spaniards were dependent for much of their livelihood. According to the testimony of Juan Sabeata and his captains, the pathways were open and level; this sense of easy access may have contributed to Spanish paranoia when faced with the possibility of foreign invasion.

Juan Sabeata

The dominating figure in these and all other historical records relating to the Jumanos in the last decades of the seventeenth century is Juan Sabeata, the Jumano governor and chief. The first historical notice of Sabeata is seen in the account of the Jumano visit to El Paso, in the autumn of 1683. Sabeata appeared there as the leader of a delegation and the spokesman for a multi-tribal coalition, addressing an appeal to the highest church and state officials.

From 1683 to 1692, Juan Sabeata's presence is reported in locations from Parral to El Paso, to the Hasinai villages near the Gulf coast, and to southern Texas at the border of Coahuila. J. Charles Kelley compiled a calendar of the movements of Juan Sabeata during this period, and concluded that Sabeata made eight crossings of Texas, and many shorter trips between La Junta, Parral, El Paso, and other locations.[14] This is an impressive record, especially since Kelley's data do not cover every year of Sabeata's career as a Jumano leader; it can be assumed that he was equally active in the undocumented years. His comings and goings evidently amounted to an annual itinerary.

Both French and Spanish explorers reported encounters with Juan Sabeata. He is, in fact, one of the first Indians to emerge, in recorded history, as an individual of power and influence. During the 1680's, Sabeata's name became almost synonymous with the Jumanos; he appears dramatically, everywhere that his people are to be found—a flamboyant individual, usually seen on horseback. It would seem that Juan Sabeata was twice given an appointed position as *gobernador* by Spanish colonial authorities: in El Paso in 1683, by Governor Cruzate of New Mexico, and in 1686 (or thereabouts) by Governor Pardiñas of Nueva Vizcaya.

It appears that Juan Sabeata was treated with respect by Indians and Spaniards alike. However, his historical role remains to be defined. In tracing Sabeata's peripatetic movements, Kelley appears to regard him as a typical chief of a nomadic, bison-hunting Plains tribe, and suggests that "there must have been many Sabeatas among the Jumano."[15] Kelly observes that the Jumanos—whom he characterizes as nomads and gossips—were important agents of cultural diffusion. Juan Sabeata's Jumanos did travel extensively and must have been active agents in spreading both material and intellectual culture traits across a large region of North America. However, the picture of Sabeata which emerges from the 1689 *autos* of Parral is hardly that of a typical chief of a hunting tribe. There was only one Juan Sabeata.

Sabeata was a native leader, on a very large scale. He also emerges, in these and other records, as an agent of the colonial administrative hierarchy, and an intermediary in Spanish dealings with the native population at La Junta and further to the east. Sabeata can be seen as a classic example of a contact-period cultural broker, dealing with his own people as a representative of the Spanish colonial government, while also attempting to treat and manipulate that government on behalf of his native constituency. His special status was that of a marginal man, who had interests and influence in both Indian and Spanish spheres, but was not wholly a member of either. At the same time, Sabeata's effectiveness in this complex role appears to be, in large part, a function of a special, liminal, cultural position held by the Jumanos themselves. It was this position that, for a brief period in history, gave Juan Sabeata a unique niche as an intermediary in almost every sphere—economic, military, political, and cultural.

What was Juan Sabeata's constituency? He is repeatedly named as the chief or governor of the Jumano and Cibolo nations. What was the nature and extent of these groups? Were they separate tribes? If so, what was their relationship to one another?

The depositions of the Cibolo caciques make it clear that in the 1680's the Cibolos could be characterized as a tribe in the traditional sense of the word: these men were leaders or prominent members of several local or regional groups, probably best characterized as bands, which occupied separate, though interconnected areas. Of those leaders appearing in Parral, Miguel was the captain of a band which had its *rancheria* some seven days' distance from La Junta on the Rio Pecos. The *rancheria* of Cuis Benive was some distance farther east; it can be seen that he regarded Miguel as his immediate chief. Muygisofac, also a Cibolo, may have lived as far from La Junta as the Rio de las Nueces (Concho); he, of the three Cibolo captains, is most explicit in describing battles for territory fought during the buffalo-hunting season against the Apaches.

In these records and others of the same time period, Cibolo and Jumano often appear linked. The Cibolos are sometimes mentioned, as a group, without reference to the Jumano. However, the Jumanos are almost always found in the company of the Cibolos and/or other groups (Cholome, Caynaya, Catqueza, Cantona, Terco-dame, et al.); they seem hardly ever to have operated alone. Their center of operations in 1689 was at La Junta; they also traveled widely. But it seems unclear whether they had a territorial base of their own, and whether *Jumano* should, at that time, be properly regarded as a tribal designation.

Thus, Juan Sabeata's immediate constituency near La Junta appears to have been the Cibolos, a widely dispersed tribe whose local leaders (caciques or captains) acknowledged him as their overall headman (governor), and the Jumanos, a highly mobile group, perhaps recruited from the Cibolos and other tribes. The Jumanos were traditionally occupied in trade, and were under Sabeata's personal leadership.

However, Governor Pardiñas also treated Sabeata as Governor of the Nations of the North. As traders, the Jumanos made a long annual expedition over a circuit extending from La Junta almost to the Gulf of Mexico. In this enterprise, they were accompanied by members of the Cibolos and other western groups, and they were joined en route by many others, through whose territories they traveled.

It seems clear that, at that point in history, the primary occupation of the Jumanos was trade. They must have engaged in hunting, to obtain their food supply while traveling, and may also have hunted on a large scale during the buffalo season. However, their trade with the Texas tribes regularly brought them furs and pelts, and this trade must have been much more productive and more profitable than hunting per se.

But whatever the scale of the trade, his position in an exchange network can hardly have been the sole reason that Juan Sabeata was appointed governor of the Indians at La Junta. We also find reflected, in the testimony given by Sabeata and others, some hints of his other activities and of his close ties to the Spanish colonial hierarchy by way of the regional commander, Retana.

The Jumanos were entrusted to carry messages between the scattered Spanish installations and, when needed, were sent to more distant locations. There are indications that Juan Sabeata carried the mail; he delivered letters between Parral, La Junta, the Texas country, and Coahuila. Furthermore, the Jumanos and Cibolos served the Spaniards as auxiliary troops and scouts. They were much used by Captain Retana as spies in northern Nueva Vizcaya, gathering information about the movements of the unpacified Indians for the Spanish military.[16] They also served in more distant information-gathering, as exemplified by the expedition to Espiritu Santo Bay.

At La Junta, the Cibolo-Jumano auxiliaries were frequently involved in counter-insurgency operations against the Tobosos, Chizos, and other Indians of the country between Parral and La Junta. The Indians accompanying Retana when he arrived at La Junta from a punitive mission against two Toboso bands were Cibolos and Jumanos.[17] This kind of activity had become quite frequent in the time period represented by the *autos;* within a few years, it would lead to outright war between the Toboso-Chizo bands and Juan Sabeata's followers.

For the time being, however, the Jumanos and Cibolos were part of the colonial system, helping to maintain Spanish authority between Parral and La Junta, bolstering the small military garrison at San Francisco de los Conchos, and protecting the chronically insecure religious mission. As governor of the missionized, pacified, and sedentary Indians of La Junta, Juan Sabeata would also have served as a labor recruiter, with the responsibility for meeting the colonists' demands for workers in the mines and farms further south. There are indications of the involvement of the Indians in these industries in some of the depositions. Remarkably, judging by the testimony of the native captains, the Frenchmen were able to obtain first-hand information about the Spanish industries from Cibolos east of the Pecos, who had spent time as agricultural workers in the region of Parral.

Juan Sabeata's post as a native governor, a position of authority intermediate between the Spanish administration and the native population, would have been parallel to that of Don Nicolas, the Julime governor. The Julime population extended some distance further up to Conchos valley in the direction of Parral, while the Jumanos centered closer to La Junta. The references to Juan Sabeata as Governor of the Nations of the North is a clear recognition of his continuing role as liaison with, and spokesman for, the tribes beyond the territorial limits of Nueva Vizcaya.

The function of the Jumanos as information gatherers is best exemplified in Juan Sabeata's mission (ostensibly on his own initiative, but surely with Retana's tacit acquiescence) into Texas and his return a few months later, bringing a detailed report and material evidence in the form of the artifacts retrieved from the French fort. One key to Sabeata's effectiveness in such a mission was the established network of contacts, originally developed through trade; another may have been the utility of the Jumanos' language as a *lingua franca.* The Jumano tongue would serve in the Texas villages as it would in the *rancherias* between the Rio Grande and the Colorado. It might be noted that the Frenchmen, arriving at the *rancherias* from Ceni territory, were accompanied by interpreters recruited downriver who were able to speak to the Jumano-Cibolos in their own language.

The Jumano-Cibolos of 1688–1689 had been strongly subjected to Spanish cultural influences. Over a century earlier, their ancestors were first drawn into the Spanish economic sphere. Those living at or close to La Junta had become Christians, while those at the more remote *rancherias* remained pagan; this is stated in the *autos* and is reflected in the names of the caciques (as the Frenchmen evidently realized). The influence, direct or indirect, of Catholic missionary teaching is reflected in Spanish loanwords used in native vocabulary, (e.g., *cuentas* for beads) and in the use of the term *Moros* for the foreigners (seen as enemies of the Christians or Spaniards).

Being acquainted with the Franciscan priests of New Spain, Juan Sabeata and the Cibolo captains recognized the regalia of that order among the items pillaged from the French fort. French accounts of the La Salle party's meeting with the Jumanos indicate how strongly hispanicized these Indians had become. Father Douay, as we have seen, was most agreeably surprised by their knowledge of Catholic iconography and ritual behavior. Both the Jumanos and the Cenis who had traveled to the Spanish colonies were in full European dress when encountered by the Frenchmen, who initially mistook them for Spaniards. The Jumanos' apparent lack of fluency in the Spanish language may be, in part, explained by the utility of their own language in trade, and by the considerable amount of time spent on their trade routes and away from La Junta and Parral; it would seem that Spaniards who dealt with the Jumanos learned their language, rather than the reverse.[18]

16.

FIN DE SIÈCLE:
THE JUMANO DIASPORA

In the summer of 1692, Juan Sabeata was finally on his way to deliver Fray Foncuberta's letter to church officials in El Paso, when he received a message that the Satopayogliglas and Sisimbles (Chizos bands) had attacked and killed a number of his followers. He quickly returned south to initiate a campaign against the attackers, but made a detour to turn over the priest's letter at Governor Pardiñas' offices in Parral. Then he traveled to the Rio Conchos to ask the Governor of the Julimes to bring several hundred men to La Junta to support his campaign. The Chizos had attacked, Sabeata told Pardiñas, because the Jumanos would not join in their wars against the Spaniards.[1]

Juan Sabeata, in reminding Pardiñas of his own loyalty and of the hostility of the Chizos, would at the same time have been tacitly soliciting Spanish support, much as he had appealed to Governor Otermin for aid against the Apaches. Captain Retana did take the field, perhaps influenced by Sabeata's appeal (though his first concern was the security of the mines and other Spanish holdings). Early the next year, Retana mounted an all-out campaign against the Chizos, with Julime and Cibolo assistance. By this time, however, Don Nicolas of the Cibolos had been named Governor of the Cibolos, Jumanos, and Nations of the North.[2] Nothing more is heard about Juan Sabeata; it may be that he did not survive the campaign of 1692. He would have been, at this time, roughly sixty years of age.

In 1693, Captain J. F. Marin, the chief military officer of Nueva Vizcaya, prepared a lengthy report concerning relations between that colony's government and the Indian nations, many of which were in revolt. Insurrection had become a chronic state of affairs in northern New Spain, and the expressed attitude of at least one governor was that there was no Indian who did not merit "pain of death."[3] Marin's report was the prospectus of an officer planning a new campaign which was intended either to reduce the Indians on unconditional terms or to "put them completely to the sword."[4]

This report, which roughly reflects locations and alliances of Indian bands and tribes of Nueva Vizcaya and the surrounding areas, does not appear to anticipate the changes then under way. It takes in a very large total area but is most detailed for the first zone, that between Durango and La Junta. Most of the seventy-eight nations included would be, in more general terms, classified as Uto-Aztecans (the Julimes, Conchos, Tobosos, and others extending westward from La Junta toward Sonora) and Coahuiltecans (bands and tribes distributed from La Junta into Coahuila and southern Texas). "So numerous are the barbarous nations that inhabit the provinces," writes Marin, "that influenced by the Cocoimes and Tobosos, they make their expeditions through so many and diverse districts and with such swiftness and cunning that it is impossible . . . to prevent . . . robberies and invasions."[5] It is thus implied, though not explicitly stated, that all of those in this group were hostile.

The second zone includes the Jumanos, along with several others—some of the names recognizable, some not—which may have been bands included in or affiliated with the Jumanos and Cibolos. Others in this zone may be local groups of the Julimes (situated on the Rio del Norte), along with various Coahuiltecans and Tonkawans (further to the east), and finally the Hasinai confederacy (here called *Texas*). This is essentially the network of nations for which Juan Sabeata was the long-time spokesman and with whom he dealt as an Indian governor, on behalf of Spain. "All these nations," asserts Marin, "are more peaceful than warlike, for which reason it should be possible to penetrate with ease into the interior. The Apaches maintain a continuous war with them."[6]

The third zone and the largest in area covers the nations to the north and west of La Junta, including the Sumas, Pimas, western Apaches, and "those of New Mexico." It would seem that the colonial officials, such as Marin, stationed at Parral, had fewer contacts and less intimate knowledge of the tribes in this zone than in either of the other two.[7]

The decade of the 1690's seems in general to have been a time of change. During these years the Jumanos and Cibolos, along with their allies the Julimes, had become in their role as native militia a main support of the Spanish troops in campaigns against the Chiso and Toboso "hostiles." As Christian or "friendly" Indians, the Jumano-Cibolo auxiliaries were originally used as spies and scouts during campaigns into rebel territories. However, in the 1690's Captain Retana also deployed them in battle; orders were repeatedly sent out calling for squads of the friendly Indians to take the field, to surround and close in on the hostiles.[8] Accordingly, a letter from Pardiñas' successor, Gabriel del Castillo, instructs Retana to transmit a command to Governor Don Nicolas of the Cibolos, calling him with his forces to participate in a campaign in which several bands of Chizos will be gathered together and massacred. The women and children are to be taken captive and sent to Parral, where they will no doubt be sold as slaves. "It is contrary to reason not to put the Indians to the sword," Castillo concludes.[9] *Maestro de campo* J. F. Marin is also advised by the governor to make good use of "Indian friends" in police actions, because forty of them can be had for the pay of eight Spanish soldiers.[10]

At about this time, a number of Jumanos and Cibolos were among the native troops drawn from Nueva Vizcaya to fight in Sonora, where joint campaigns were under way against the Apaches and allied tribes. At El Paso in 1693 efforts were focused on the recovery of the New Mexican colony, which Spain had never formally relinquished. All available manpower was drafted for this objective. Native auxiliary forces to be employed in the effort were drawn from the neighboring provinces; among those from Nueva Vizcaya there were possibly a number of Jumanos and Cibolos.

On the eastern frontier of Nueva Vizcaya, a turning point had been reached in Spain's relations with the Nations of the North (the Hasinai and other Indians of Texas). The Jumano liaison and the annual round of trade fairs finally ceased to operate. It is possible that the immediate reason for the cessation of the Jumano trade was, quite simply, the disappearance of Juan Sabeata from the scene. Perhaps with Sabeata's death or retirement from public life there was no other leader with the charisma, knowledge, and audacity to carry out these long and difficult expeditions. However, there are obviously other considerations. Jumano-Cibolo manpower may have been depleted by the military actions in which they were involved on behalf of Spain. The turmoil in the Spanish colonies, the strength and aggressiveness of the Apaches in the Plains, the political decline of the Hasinai, and the increasing decimation of the native population by disease all must have worked against the continuing integrity of the Indians' alliances and patterns of exchange.

The immediate causes and the sequence of events leading to an apparent shift in the Jumanos' own alignments can only be formulated in general terms. The turn-around, in any case, must have begun at about this time. This is the "mystery" which the historian Herbert Bolton singled out for consideration in relation to the Jumanos. He pointed out that when the Spaniards reentered Texas from Coahuila, in 1716, ". . . they found that a noteworthy change had taken place, namely, that the Jumano had become allies of the Apache and enemies of the Spaniards and of the Texas . . ."[11] Bolton documented the gradual incorporation of numerous Jumanos into the regional Apache population between 1716 and 1771. By mid-century, there are scattered references to Indian bands as "Apache-Jumanes," an indication that this process was under way. Bolton's purpose was, simply, to trace the evident disappearance of the Jumanos from the historical record; he did not offer an explanation for what he saw as a dramatic shift in loyalties.

However, reviewing the course of a century of Jumano history, at least one previous shift in loyalties may be recalled—namely, the reversal in Jumano policy toward the colony of New Mexico. From the earliest years of the Spanish presence, a tie between New Mexico and the Jumanos was evident, built on both trade and diplomatic contacts. This relationship was maintained in the face of the continual erosion of Jumano territorial holdings, even though the colony was evidently unwilling to support the Jumanos and their allies against the superior strength of the Apaches. For the Jumanos, the motivation can only have been the market provided by the Spaniards, and the availability of trade goods, which they found at that time in New Mexico.

Following the Pueblo Rebellion of 1680, the Jumanos and their allies attempted to renew the relationship with New Mexico at El Paso, where Juan Sabeata appealed to Spanish economic interests, while also playing on the fear of French penetration into Texas. However, the chronic reluctance or inability of the Spaniards to give effective support to the Indian alliance finally led to alienation of the Jumanos and the outright hostility of Juan Sabeata toward New Mexico. It is impossible to judge whether this rift played any part in precipitating other Indian disaffections, such as the Suma uprising which the Spanish party confronted on their return from Texas to La Junta in 1684. In any case, the fiasco in Texas may have contributed to the growing hostility of Indians all along the Rio del Norte, resulting in a series of local uprisings. After this sequence of events, the Jumanos had become—like the New Mexican Pueblos—potential or de facto allies of the Apaches in rebellion against Spain.

Three years after the break with New Mexico, Juan Sabeata attempted to persuade La Salle and his French colonists to join the Jumanos and their allies in an attack on New Mexico. Perhaps Sabeata dreamed of exterminating Spanish settlements up and down the Rio del Norte. There is no reason to believe that, at that time, the Jumanos were to any degree bound by ties of loyalty to or affection for Spain. However, rather than turn against all Spaniards, Sabeata took refuge in an alliance with the colony of Nueva Vizcaya, utilizing a longstanding Jumano relationship with the Julimes of La Junta de los Rios, as a means to this end.

At the same time, the Jumanos remained close to their eastern allies, the Texas tribes—Caddoan, Tonkawan, and Coahuiltecan—and they continued to act as intermediaries on behalf of this bloc of tribes vis-à-vis Spain, by way of La Junta and Parral. The Indian trade via La Junta may actually have intensified during the years of the Pueblo Rebellion. In fact, it would appear that it was only after the break with New Mexico that the Jumanos became an important power in Nueva Vizcaya and political allies of the colonial administration; this is reflected in the position of Juan Sabeata as an Indian governor. However, identification with the administrative hierarchy of that colony must have committed the Jumanos to an increasing role as scouts and mercenary troops.

Service of the La Junta tribes in police actions against the Chizos and Tobosos may have begun as an extension of a traditional enmity between the villagers and the nomadic bands scattered in the surrounding desert hills. This military function became a growing involvement for the Jumanos and Cibolos, as the desert tribes grew increasingly troublesome. For the Jumanos, a critical point may have been reached when the Sumas and Mansos—related tribes and traditional allies—became participants in the insurrection near El Paso. Both here and at La Junta, where refugee settlements had grown up around several Franciscan missions, the movement was characterized by the Spaniards in religious terms: the Christian Indians were loyal to Spain, while the pagans were seen as the enemy. The Jumanos near La Junta remained loyal.

As early as 1688, certain Jumanos near Eagle Pass had joined the Tercodames, Colorados, Cabezas, and Tobosos in raids against Spanish settlements in Coahuila. Here, along the Texas-Coahuila border, the Jumanos were evidently regarded as part of a coalition of hostile tribes; at the same time, the Jumanos in Nueva Vizcaya continued to serve the interests of the Spanish administration and to carry messages and goods between scattered missionaries and military posts, and the colonial capitals.

It is not difficult to relate the collapse of the trade to changing conditions at both ends of the trade route, as well as in the country in between. When the Jumanos and their allies journeyed to El Paso in 1683, it was already evident that the Apaches, pushing ever further into the Plains, were overrunning the hunting grounds, raiding the horse herds, and attacking the main routes of travel between La

Junta and the Colorado. The Jumano settlements on the Concho and Colorado must have been abandoned within the next few years; the presence of Jumano *rancherias* on the Guadalupe River may reflect a removal from these locations. The southern Plains had increasingly become dominated by the Apaches, and the Rio Colorado tribes—including the Jumanos—were soon to be displaced, as indicated by Posada.[12] The testimony of the Jumano captains, as given in Parral, indicated that the route to eastern Texas was difficult because of conflict with hostile Indians, obviously Apaches, and that annual wars were fought with these Indians during the hunting season.[13] The annual trade expeditions were, however, still in operation. Judging by this native testimony and other evidence, the Jumanos continued to follow their rounds for at least another five to six years; it may be that they continued for as long as they were permitted or, perhaps, encouraged to do so, by Spanish agencies in Nueva Vizcaya.

Apache domination in the South Plains, as well as the growing hostility of the Nations of the North, underlay the termination of Spanish involvement in Texas. However, the end of the Jumano role as middlemen for New Spain may itself have precipitated numerous changes in the political status and affiliations of the native peoples, especially the small tribes and bands in eastern and southern Texas, who would no longer have the security of a wide-reaching network of alliances.

The secret of the Jumanos' ability to come and go through what had become enemy territory may have lain, in part, in knowledge of terrain and skillful leadership by Juan Sabeata and his captains. After all, the Jumanos had long familiarity with the route, and were experienced and knowledgeable in warfare against the Apaches. But it is also likely that they held one critical advantage over their Apache enemies: possession of at least a limited supply of firearms.

Spanish policy was, as a rule, firmly opposed to permitting Indian acquisition of firearms. However, the Jumanos had dealt with the Spaniards longer and more intimately than other native groups. In their special capacity as native militia in Nueva Vizcaya, they may have been issued such weapons. As early as 1684, Juan Sabeata had a musket in his possession, with which he fired a salute to herald the arrival of the New Mexican troops at the Jediondo village on the Pecos.[14] If the Jumanos were, either openly or tacitly, granted an exception to the general prohibition, their ability to pass with relative freedom through Apache-controlled territory can be better understood.

The Jumanos' liaison with Spain, however, was increasingly subject to strain. With the collapse of the trade in Texas, as Apache strength came to prevail both east and west of the Rio Grande, service as mercenary troops may have constituted the main capacity in which the Jumanos and Cibolos remained of value to the Spanish colony. However, their role as mercenaries would eventually alienate them from most of the other Indian nations. Their long-time allies, including the Sumas and Mansos, as well as traditional enemies such as the Chizos, all found themselves increasingly united in opposition to Spanish rule.

In the last decade of the century, some Jumanos may already have come to terms with the Apaches who were, by then, penetrating to the vicinity of La Junta. A rapprochement of this sort did eventually emerge; an exclusive Jumano affiliation with Nueva Vizcaya had become impossible to maintain. When the Hasinai also rose up against the Spanish troops and missions in their lands, their allies—including the Jumanos in Texas—would surely have followed. Thereafter, it would have been pointless for the Jumanos to attempt to maintain the traditional network of relationships. At that juncture, they would choose to join in on the side of their Hasinai trading partners, hoping for an eventual recovery of the trade to rebuild the alliance.

Sometime in the decade of the 1690's, the long expeditions between the Rio del Norte and eastern Texas finally ceased. The Jumanos were now in an anomalous and difficult position. They found themselves, for the first time in centuries, without a network of allies and trading partners. Their numbers were undoubtedly in decline and were fragmented, scattered between eastern Texas and the Rio del Norte.

In central Texas, there were Jumanos in the amalgam of displaced tribes and remnant groups which became known as the *Rancheria Grande*. In fact, it is likely that the basis of this pantribal union, which long continued to struggle against the Apaches, can be found in the earlier trade alliance. A new leader in the native resistance was Joseph de Urrutia, the Spanish officer who had remained in Texas at the time of the Hasinai uprising. It is with good reason that historian Elizabeth John characterized Urrutia as the heir to Juan Sabeata in this capacity. According to John, it was the "resistance which Juan Sabeata worked so hard to organize from his bases at La Junta and on the upper Colorado which Joseph de Urrutia helped to lead during his sojourn among Tonkawas and Xaranames in the 1690's." [15]

By his own testimony, Urrutia commanded ". . . sometimes . . . ten thousand or twelve thousand Indians, sometimes . . . more of the nations where I was . . . [and] of the Pelones and Jumanes. . . ." For seven years, he was their *capitan grande;* he rejoined the Spanish community in San Antonio in 1700.[16] The Pelones were an Athabascan band, perhaps ancestors of the Kiowa Apaches; otherwise, the tribes of the Rancheria Grande seem to have been drawn together by their common enmity for the Apaches. Their relations to Spain were more complex, or perhaps more ambivalent. Like the Jumanos and their allies during the previous century, these Indians continued periodically to appeal for Spanish assistance; at the same time, they would increasingly see their own homelands preempted by Spanish settlers.

In 1716, Spanish friars from Coahuila returned to Texas, to build new missions to accommodate the decimated and refugee tribes beyond the San Antonio River. There were now Apache *rancherias* on the Rio Colorado, not far northwest of San Antonio. As the mission and presidial community grew, Apache raids from that quarter were a major and recurrent problem.

One explanation for this late Apache push toward the southeast is the fact that far away, on their own northwestern frontier, they were now being harassed by the advancing Comanches and Utes. These large tribes soon made an appearance in the South Plains. The Comanches quickly extended their hold to encompass a large territory east and northeast of New Mexico. Around 1730, after pursuing the Apaches from the north, and carving out their own domain in the Plains, the Comanches concluded an alliance with the Wichitas of the Arkansas and Canadian Rivers. This alliance opened the way for French trade goods to enter the region, and effectively blocked any renewed Apache presence north of the Canadian River. Accompanying the Comanches, and claiming a homeland between the Canadian and the Arkansas, the Tanoan-speaking Kiowas also appeared on the scene.

As attacks on camps and homesteads, theft of livestock, and other forms of violence attributed to the Apaches intensified, the remnant Coahuiltecans, Tonkawans, and other Texas aborigines were driven to seek protection in mission settlements around San Antonio and along the Rio del Norte. Both east and west of the Rio del Norte, Apache holdings now extended deep into Mexico. Around La Junta, formerly independent bands and tribes joined forces with, or were incorporated into, the various divisions of the Apaches. It was during this period that there was the first indication of Jumanos allied with the Apaches in southern Texas. The

Jumanos may have been among the last to give up the struggle with their long-time enemies.

> In 1724 an Indian named Geronimo, a native of Santa Elena, Nueva Vizcaya, who came to San Juan Bautista with some Apache, declared that about three years before he had been captured on the Conchos River by the Tovosos [Tobosos], and had lived for a year "among the Tovosos and Jumanes," when he was purchased by some Apache, among whom he lived two years. He also declared that . . . a peace message from San Antonio, Texas, reached the Apache among whom he was living and was read by "two Religious who go . . . among them with the Jumana nation."[17]

This interesting passage, quoted by Bolton, seems to indicate that, as of 1724, certain Jumanos near the Rio del Norte continued, or had resumed, a traditional pattern of passing with immunity between opposing parties—at this date, between Spaniards and Apaches. Apparently their affiliation with the Franciscan order was unbroken. As was the case a century earlier, we see a Jumano party, journeying through Apache territory, accompanied by two Spanish friars.

A Brief Summary: The Jumano Diaspora and Its Aftermath

1. Prior to the Pueblo Revolt of 1680, the Jumanos are seen to be enemies of the Apaches, allies of the Hasinai and other Nations of the North, kinsmen and traditional allies of the eastern Pueblos, and closely tied by trade to Spanish New Mexico.
2. After 1684, relations with New Mexico are severed; possibly as a consequence, the Jumanos strengthen or reestablish a connection at La Junta de los Rios, becoming allied with the Spanish colony of Nueva Vizcaya. Their friendship with the Hasinai confederacy continues and together with their allies they continue to war against the Apaches.
3. In 1686, the Hasinai and their neighbors have their first reported contacts with France. They solicit French aid against the Apaches; the Jumanos, at the same time, ask for help in planning an attack on New Mexico. However, with the backing of Nueva Vizcaya, Jumano trade continues with the Nations of the North, who thus continue an indirect relationship with Spain.
4. In 1693, the Hasinai rebel against Spain; their wars with the Apache continue. The Jumano trade ceases at about the same

time. The Jumanos at La Junta continue to serve Nueva Vizcaya as spies and mercenaries.

5. In 1716, Spain reenters Texas, to reestablish relations with
   the Hasinai and to confront France on the northern frontier.
   But the Hasinai, now increasingly interested in trade with
   France, begin to relocate toward the north. With the collapse
   of the network of alliances, many Tonkawan, Karankawan,
   and Coahuiltecan bands are left in a vacuum or no-man's
   land, between the expanding Spanish colonies, the invading
   Comanches, and the beleaguered Apaches.
6. The Jumano diaspora: (a) Some Jumanos in Texas join with
   the displaced tribes of the Rancheria Grande. (b) Jumanos remaining in south Texas and near La Junta become allied with
   and, eventually, incorporated into the Apache bands of the
   region. (c) Jumano enclaves also remain in the east, possibly
   to become incorporated into the Hasinai or other Caddoan
   groups. (d) In 1719, Apaches report to New Mexico the presence of Jumanos in Wichita territory, on the Arkansas River.
7. The Jumanos' own Tanoan language is, after the diaspora, no
   longer functional as a trade language. Those in the south continue to use Spanish as a lingua franca, along with the Apache
   language. Of those in the north and east, some are assimi-
   lated as Caddoan-speakers and are part of the French trade
   sphere; others may have become the nucleus of an emergent
   people, the Tanoan-speaking Kiowas.
8. In 1746, the Wichitas become allies of the Comanches; it is
   now possible to bypass the Apaches and to renew the Caddoan
   trade with New Mexico. Soon thereafter, the Kiowas appear
   in the South Plains, in locations earlier occupied by their remote kinsmen—or ancestors—the Jumanos.

In a sense, the diaspora, and the virtual disappearance of the Jumanos as a people, can be attributed to Apache success in driving
a wedge into the Plains and occupying the heart of traditional Jumano territories. Beyond this, the polarization of northern and southern divisions of the remnant Jumanos can be seen (as Bolton perceived) as a by-product of the economic and political rivalry between
Spain and France. Those Jumanos drawn into the French trade
sphere, through their traditional friendship with the Caddoan
tribes, became affiliated with or incorporated into the Caddo and/or
Wichita. Of those remaining in the Spanish sphere, some were
eventually identified as Apaches, while others disappeared in the
process of slow genocide of the detribalized Indians of Texas.

PART FOUR

CONTINUITY AND CHANGE IN JUMANO CULTURE

17.

THE JUMANO IDENTITY CRISIS

For almost a century, the question of the identity—or, indeed, the very existence—of an early historic people called *Jumano* has been debated. Historical research has indicated that the Jumanos were geographically scattered, and that their distribution changed over the course of their post-contact history. However, earlier efforts to discern the patterns of Jumano culture and history are, on the whole, inadequate: depending on the area examined, and the amount of information available at a given time, radically different opinions have been formulated, all perhaps partially valid, but all incomplete.

Bandelier believed that the nomadic Jumanos of the plains were offshoots of their sedentary congeners. He was curious about the decline in Jumano fortunes, and linked their disappearance to turbulent events of the seventeenth century: the Pueblo Rebellion and the aggressive expansion of the Apaches. Bandelier's remarks about the Jumanos are insightful but sketchy, since they were never a focus of his researches.

Since Bandelier's time, the relevance of Indian warfare to the "Jumano problem" has been ignored or minimized, despite ample documentary evidence of its impact. Both Hodge and Bolton added information about Jumano provenance and attempted to trace connections among their scattered locales. Hodge called attention to their penchant for nomadism and important role in trade. In retrospect, his efforts to link the Jumanos of the sixteenth century with the modern Wichita seem simplistic. However, the suggestion that there may be a Jumano component in the mix of peoples making up the Wichita confederacy poses an issue which can only be resolved by future research on Caddoan culture history.

Since 1940, interest in Jumano culture and history has been limited by Scholes' premise that some, perhaps many, of the occurrences of this name (in its several cognate forms) are based on either extension or confusion. For example, the name of a particular band or tribe could have been applied to other groups on the basis of superficial similarities of appearance or life-style. Scholes' best contribution may be the insight that the name *Jumano* had both broad or generic, and more limited or specific meanings. However, his suggestion that painting and/or tattooing was the key criterion for the extended usage no longer rings true. Clearly, *Jumano* was not applied, as Scholes implied, to many groups, beyond the limits of New Mexico, who could have been described as *rayados*—painted and/or tattooed peoples.[1]

Bolton had confronted the fragmentation of the Jumanos, late in their history, remarking on the eventual division of their loyalties between two European powers, Spain and France. He also was concerned with their political relations vis-à-vis other Indian groups, including the Caddo and the Apaches. The thrust of Bolton's work could have been extended to analysis of the complex flux of political and economic relationships in which the Jumanos were players. However, subsequent Jumano studies, under the aegis of anthropology, took a different, essentially non-historical, direction.

For much of the twentieth century, American anthropology was typified by a static view of Native American cultures, and made little use of historical documentation.[2] Scholarship in this vein relied heavily on typology and sought to discover order based on structural and distributional patterns. Those anthropologists who pursued the implications of Scholes' solution to the "Jumano problem" relied, as a matter of course, on territorial distribution as a criterion for assessment of tribal identity. This process rests on a pair of unstated assumptions—first, that tribal territories were discrete and exclusive; and, second, that their distribution remained static and virtually unchanging, from aboriginal times up to the reservation period. Neither of these assumptions would be defended by many modern anthropologists. Their effects, however, persist, echoing a traditional antihistoricism of the social sciences, including anthropology.

Operating with territoriality as a criterion, judgements have sometimes been made about ethnic identity on the basis of the locale in which an individual or group is reported, whether in early or recent historical times. We have seen the territorial criterion applied by authors who assigned alternate identities to certain groups which were, in the primary sources, identified as Jumanos. For example, this is the basis for the judgement (by Scholes and later by Forbes) that the Arkansas River Jumanos encountered by Oñate's expedition were, in fact, Wichitas: in later years the region was Wichita territory. Similarly, the Jumanos seen near the mines in northern Arizona have been claimed as either Havasupais or Apaches: the difference simply reflects differing views about the territorical provenance of these two Southwestern tribes. Aside from their geographical situation, in these two cases, there is no *prima facie* reason for assuming that their original identification as Jumanos was in error.

Both Kelley and Forbes focus their attention on the nomadic buffalo-hunting Plains Jumanos, while denying that they had any connection with other groups to whom the name was applied. It cannot be denied that the Plains bands were the central actors in the hunting and trading activities for which the Jumanos were well known. However, historical accounts document a pattern of seasonal movements between Plains and the Rio del Norte villages, frequent visits for trade or for gathering information, and relocations of refugee Plains Jumanos in or near sedentary Jumano villages. These accounts provide clear indications of contacts and relationships among scattered Jumano groups, and between these groups and many other bands and tribes. In the face of such evidence, *a priori* assumptions should not be made about discrete or unique tribal territoriality.

This study began with a working assumption that there was a substantive basis for the recurring Spanish and French references to the Jumanos. Rather than discrediting the primary sources out of hand, it has seemed more reasonable, from the outset, to adopt the premise that the Jumanos were a distinctive and recognizable people, and that there is an authentic common identity reflected in the historical sources. The chronological narrative presented in the foregoing pages constitutes the argument for this position.

Like Scholes, I have concluded that a distinction can be drawn between broader and narrower senses of the name *Jumano*. In my view, the term in its broader sense was a generic name applied to the semi-nomadic to semi-sedentary eastern Tanoans. This was an ethnic population which undoubtedly included a large number of territorially discrete but socially interrelated bands. In the narrower sense, the Jumanos were sometimes seen as removed from territorial and political contexts, and were defined on the basis of a traditional role, in a multi-ethnic regional system; that is, they were seen simply as traders.

The diaspora which followed the Jumanos' loss of territory to Apache encroachment and displacement from their South Plains heartland meant an end to their existence in the broader sense, as a tribe for example. The termination of their activities as traders—also, in part, a consequence of the Apache occupancy of the South Plains—meant an end to the existence of the Jumanos in the narrower sense.

18.

THE TRADE NETWORK

Throughout their extensive area of territorial occupancy, Jumano villages and *rancherias* were positioned along a network of routes which followed natural lines of communication. Although segments of this network can be historically documented, its wider extension and its continuity with prehistoric cultural complexes and trade routes can only be inferred.

One arm of the Jumano network was the Rio del Norte with two of its major tributaries, the Conchos and the Pecos. The Spanish explorers who, in the 1580's, ascended the Conchos to its confluence with the Rio del Norte and proceeded north to New Mexico, were following a well-established native highway. The concentration of farming communities at La Junta de los Rios and the densely populated Pueblo provinces along the upper Rio del Norte were main terminals of the trade routes which extended eastward, across the Plains. There was a sizeable Jumano element at both of these terminals. In both, the Jumano population evidently included permanent residents as well as a seasonal enclave of transhumant nomads. In both areas, also, there were periods in which the numbers of Jumanos were inflated by the arrival of refugees from warfare in the Plains.

The Rio Pecos was another natural highway, with Pecos Pueblo near its northern headwaters. Prior to the arrival of the Apaches, the Rio Pecos must have been an important route for travel between the Southern Plains and the Pueblo provinces. However, the Spanish accounts indicate that a "no-man's land" existed along this river, between the Guadalupe Mountains—an early Apache stronghold—and the agricultural land utilized by Pecos Pueblo.

The mountain trail—a key link in Jumano trade—connected the Rio del Norte, just below La Junta, with the lower Pecos. Some distance downstream from this trail, both rivers have deep canyons and become inaccessible to travellers because of broken terrain;

this was an environmental factor which would have limited travel and trade.[1]

Both east and west, a series of trails linked the Rio Grande system with the headwaters of other rivers and with communities on and near their banks. Outlying Jumano camps or *rancherias* were situated at convenient points for access to these streams. An example of such a Jumano base is the *rancheria* visited by Fray Juan de Salas in 1629. This site lay some 250 to 300 miles east of Santa Fe, in the canyon region of the eastern Llano Estacado. From this base, contact was made and trade was conducted with a number of allied tribes—near at hand, the Apis and Xabatoas, and further to the east, Quivira and Aijados. This Jumano installation in the High Plains of western Texas, abandoned around 1630, gave access to several major river systems, including the Canadian, Red, and Brazos.

Another eastern arm of the extended trade network was the Rio Colorado system. A major Jumano base was located on the Concho (the "Nueces") near its confluences with the Colorado, in west central Texas. This site was the point of contact with a number of tribes—the Tejas, to the east, and many Coahuiltecan, Tonkawan, and other tribes and bands (as listed by Juan Sabeata). The importance of the location probably derived from its attractiveness as the scene of seasonal harvests of pecans, acorns, and other wild plants.

Eventually, the Rio de las Nueces became untenable as the Apaches pushed eastward, and it was finally surrendered around 1690. At about the same time, there is the first mention of a *rancheria* on the upper Guadalupe River, a base for Jumano contact with the Tejas and other eastern tribes (the Cantona, Teao, *et al.*). There was also a Jumano presence at Anacacho Mountain, among Coahuiltecan, Chizos, and other bands (such as the Tercodame, Teimamar, and Manos Prietas). It is not clear whether this was a seasonal camp or a permanent base.[2]

The Commodities of the Trade

Although the general outlines of the Jumano network can be discerned, its limits cannot be precisely defined; furthermore, it may have intersected with or incorporated a number of local and regional exchange systems. The Plains Jumanos participated in a seasonal buffalo hunt, from which they carried meat and other products to the New Mexican and La Junta villages. All of the pueblos were farming communities; some, such as the Zuni and certain Rio Grande villages, were specialized in agriculture, producing surplus crops for trade. This was also the case at La Junta.

The intergroup exchange of staple foods was ancient, and may have existed prior to the development of trade in other, more exotic goods. Such reciprocity between farmers and hunters is a very common type of exchange worldwide. Such a trade in staples also came to exist between Apache bands and their immediate Pueblo neighbors. Like the Jumanos, the Plains Apaches brought products of the hunt to villages in eastern New Mexico, and received both grain and trade goods such as pottery and turquoise.[3]

From the time of their entry into New Mexico, the Spaniards dealt with the Jumanos to obtain buffalo pelts and other goods from the Plains. In this trade, it is clear that the Jumanos operated, in large part, in the role of middleman. At first, the Jumanos brought hides and pelts to New Mexico. Later, after Apache occupancy extended through the High Plains, Spaniards from New Mexico made an annual expedition to the Rio de las Nueces, for peltries and other goods (pearls, pecans, and other foodstuffs). By this time, if not earlier, the Jumanos had become intermediaries between the colonists and the Tejas, or Hasinai confederacy.

At present, it is not possible to make an inventory of the goods circulated in the Jumano trade. This is an aspect of regional culture which will eventually be amplified by the identification and interpretation of archaeological materials. The ethnographically documented fact of local specialization in crafts and production of foodstuffs testifies to the overall importance of trade in and beyond the Southwest. For example, although weaving was practiced in all of the Pueblo provinces, certain communities specialized in textiles. The Hopi men were evidently weavers on a large scale.[4] A distribution route for textiles led from the Hopi villages to the Rio del Norte, and south at least as far as La Junta.[5] The Jumanos' participation in the textile trade is indicated in Luxan's account.

Distinctive pottery styles enable archaeologists to trace the distribution of trade wares of individual villages and provinces. Pottery from the eastern pueblos is especially common at sites in the South Plains.[6] It is suggested that much of this pottery was transported by the Jumanos; in some cases, the vessels may have served as containers for food items or salt.

A trade in bows and arrows was apparently conducted for many years over the route between La Junta and the Rio Colorado. Cabeza de Vaca described trade encounters in which arrows were brought from the west to tuna-harvesting sites near or south of the Colorado; dried or pressed fruit may have been given in exchange, along with trade goods such as sea shells or mescal beans. In prehistory, Kelley finds indications that certain projectile points (Perdiz Stemmed

Points) were made in quantity at La Junta de los Rios, and he associates the distribution of these points with the routes over which the Jumanos moved across Texas.[7] The dynamics of this trade might suggest that residents of La Junta produced a supply of arrows which was stockpiled to be carried by the traders in their annual itinerary. It may be recalled that Juan Sabeata's list of nations included Arrowmakers ("Los que hacen flechas"), while Dominguez de Mendoza noted, among those traveling from La Junta with the Spaniards, Bowmakers ("Los que hacen Arcos").

Thus, it would seem that bows and arrows were a part of the Jumanos' trade for many years, possibly for centuries. Similar patterns of distribution can be inferred for other items, including gourd containers and rattles, metal bells, and possibly peyote, which could have been diffused from northern Mexico to the Southern Plains by way of La Junta de los Rios.[8]

In New Mexico, the Jumano Pueblos were adjacent to extensive salt deposits. Here, it is suggested that the resident Jumano (or Tompiro) population mined and processed salt, while the nomads operated as middlemen. After the conquest, the salt trade continued; the Spanish *encomenderos* exploited Indian labor in extracting and shipping the products of what had been an aboriginal industry, redirected for export to Spanish consumers in Mexico.

Mineral pigments were another natural resource linked with the Jumanos. The most important deposits of copper ores were in Arizona, in the region visited by a number of early Spanish expeditions. Information about the mines may have been obtained as far away as La Junta, by the Espejo expedition. The Jumanos there were knowledgeable about the location of the mining areas; the inference is that their knowledge was acquired through an involvement in the trade in mineral pigments.

Turquoise was perhaps more widely traded than any other Southwestern product. The most important source of turquoise was the Cerrillos mines, near Santa Fe.[9] Mica was also mined and used as temper in pottery making in the northern Pueblos.[10] Mica was traded at least as far as the Rio Colorado, where Cabeza de Vaca observed its use in ritual presentations. In the same region of Texas—perhaps near the eastern limit of the trade in ores and mica from the west— pearls taken from the Rio Concho can be linked definitely with the Jumanos. The pearls attracted Spanish interest, probably as a result of their circulation in native trade. The trade routes brought these goods, and other exotic items from Mexico, New Mexico, the South Plains, and the Gulf coast, into a common sphere of operations.

By the 1680's, if not earlier, the Jumanos were herders, and perhaps breeders, of livestock. They pastured their horse herds in the Plains, between the Pecos and the upper Colorado. The horses were traded to the Tejas, Teao, and other Texas tribes, and even to La Salle's colony on the Texas coast. Late in the century, the Jumano herds were sometimes increased by theft from Apache holdings; the reverse was also true. It was, at least in part, the Apache threat to these herds which in 1683 led Juan Sabeata to appeal for missions and for Spanish military protection.

Spain relied on the Jumanos in her aspirations for economic and political contacts with the Indian confederacies of Texas, Oklahoma, and adjacent areas. Despite the late efforts at direct contacts by Spanish missionaries among the Tejas, the most effective agents in maintaining trade connections and transmitting intelligence appear to have been the Jumanos led by Juan Sabeata. His annual expeditions must have had official sanction in Nueva Vizcaya, since Sabeata was the appointed governor of the Jumanos, Cibolos, and Nations of the North, and provided intelligence to the Spanish captain, Retana.

In its last years, the Jumano trade in Texas conveyed a wealth of Spanish goods—coins and other items of silver, silk, and other fabrics and clothing. It appears that, at that time, the Jumanos were using horses and wagons to transport goods over portions of the La Junta-Texas itinerary.[11]

The impression which emerges from this survey of the Jumanos' activities is that, throughout the Southwest and South Plains, trade was organized and must have involved a high degree of coordination and specialization of function. Foodstuffs, natural resources, and handicrafts were processed and produced in quantity; the goods were accumulated and then transported and stockpiled at a number of trade centers. The Jumanos appear to have functioned, in some cases, as producers (of arrows, salt, pearls, pinon nuts), as warehousers (at La Junta, in the Tompiros, and perhaps elsewhere), and as itinerant transporters of goods. In the Plains, their outlying *rancherias* were, in effect, trading posts, where goods were stored and exchanged, and other goods—most importantly, peltries—were received for transport on the return trip.[12]

19.

FROM HISTORY
TO PREHISTORY

My own efforts to place the Jumanos in a broader diachronic perspective began with an interpretation of population dynamics as
evidenced in the distribution of language-families and phyla.[1] The
ancestors of the Jumanos may have been on the leading edge of a
widespread arid-land adaptation which spread over much of western North America prior to the first millennium B.C. The advances
of this ancient horizon, sometimes called the Desert Culture, may
be tentatively identified with the initial dispersal of a speech community which was to become the Aztec-Tanoan language phylum.

Aztec-Tanoan, the largest contiguous group of related languages
in the Southwest, consists of sister families, Uto-Aztecan and
Tanoan. Uto-Aztecan is the larger, and inclines to a more western
distribution, extending from the Great Basin through the Sonoran
Desert to central Mexico; there are twenty-six languages, including Nahuatl, Huichol, Yaqui-Mayo, Tarahumara, Pima-Papago, Ute,
and Shoshoni-Comanche. Tanoan survives today as a much smaller
family which falls into four sub-families inclining farther to the
east. Three of these (Tiwa, Tewa, and Towa), located on or near the
upper Rio Grande, include Pueblo communities such as Taos, San
Juan, Isleta, and Jemez; the fourth consists of the Kiowa tribe of
the Plains.

The separation between ancestral Uto-Aztecan and Tanoan speech
communities began at least five thousand years ago; the barrier of
the Grand Canyon could have marked the original point of separation or decreased contact within what was originally a contin-
uum of widely dispersed bands of desert foragers. As they expanded
through western America, the Aztec-Tanoans must have incorporated or displaced a more ancient population, perhaps the descendants of an original migration into the continent. The widely scattered and highly diversified languages of the Hokan phylum may

represent remnants of these aborigines; one such group is the Coahuiltecan family of southern Texas and northern Coahuila.

Comparisons of Uto-Aztecan languages indicate that the ancestral population broke into separate northern and southern divisions as long ago as 4000 B.P. Internal diversification within Tanoan seems shallower, with the separation of the three New Mexican sub-families estimated at between 2000 and 2500 B.P. This would suggest a long period of existence of a cohesive, geographically contiguous speech community. The fourth branch of the family, Kiowa, appears to be an exception, and is thought to have separated from the rest of the Tanoan-speakers at a somewhat earlier date.[2]

I have argued that the Jumanos spoke a Tanoan language, and were probably affiliated with the Tiwa subfamily.[3] Manso and Suma are, like Jumano, long extinct, and their languages are unrecorded; however, it now appears that they were part of the same grouping. With these inclusions, the Tanoan bloc inhabited much of New Mexico, the valley of the Rio del Norte at least as far south as La Junta, and the deserts of northern Chihuahua as far west as Casas Grandes. In addition, the territories occupied by the Jumano bloc extended east of the Rio del Norte and the Pecos to include the Llano Estacado and the upper valley of the Rio Colorado of Texas. Thus, the total area which can be ascribed to the late prehistoric, pre-Apachean Tanoans was far greater than the holdings of the remnant Tanoan groups of recent history.[4]

The Rio del Norte was the central axis for the settlement and early movements of the Tanoan peoples. Cultural diversification followed, as a variety of microenvironments were explored and occupied. The rivers and streams, with a relative abundance of plants and animals, supported a denser population than arid, less productive locations. East of the Rio del Norte, the ancestors of the Jumanos found their way across the hills separating that river and the Pecos and entered the South Plains. All of the bands must have been nomadic to a degree, moving seasonally to harvest piñon nuts, cactus fruit, and acorns and to maintain access to water. But even at this time there was differentiation between bands located in river valleys and those in the arid hinterlands. With access to different resources, scattered bands were able to maintain ties through the exchange of foodstuffs and other goods. Stretches of territory away from watercourses or springs served only for occasional hunting, and would have been neither occupied nor defended on a permanent basis. In the South Plains, the eastern Tanoans entered a region which was accessible—after centuries of desertification—primarily as seasonal hunting territory.

When agriculture spread through the Southwest, between four thousand and fifteen hundred years ago, growing crops became an option for communities with adequate and reliable access to water. The earliest ceramic horizon along the western borders of the South Plains, and very likely the beginning of plant cultivation and sedentary life, is associated with an extension of a major cultural horizon, the Mogollon, which made its appearance in southern Arizona, New Mexico, and western Texas during the first millennium B.C. Culturally, the Jumanos appear to have a close connection with the Jornada branch of the Mogollon, whether by descent from what may have been an immigrant population, or by cultural contact and diffusion.[5]

By A.D. 100, corn, beans, and squash were grown as staple crops in the upper valley of the Rio del Norte. As agricultural productivity increased, the population of the oasis areas grew, and permanent villages were established. Increased social complexity along the river valley is reflected in the linguistic diversity found there, with a number of distinct languages and dialects concentrated in a restricted geographical area.

The cultural gap between oasis and desert dwellers may have increased, as the farming population adopted a more stable life-style, increased in numbers, and instituted new forms of political organization, land tenure, and legal forms. However, it is in the natural complementarity between farmers and hunter-gatherers that the trading and exchange relations of the Jumanos and their neighbors had their origin. A number of possible scenarios for this development might be posited:

(1) Originally independent farming and foraging tribes came into contact and initiated an exchange of products, either peacefully or as the outcome of initial hostilities. They eventually developed a mutual dependency on trade, and became political allies.

(2) Within a single regional population, cultural diversification evolved in a series of microenvironments. As some groups adopted farming, their numbers increased. The foraging groups increased their hunting activities to meet an increased demand for meat and hides. Ritual prestations progressed to trade, both in prestige goods and in staple commodities.

(3) A widespread regional population of hunter-gatherers adopted extensive agriculture. As farming was intensified in oasis areas, the gardens in marginal and less favorable areas were abandoned. These groups intensified their hunting, in order to trade for agricultural staples.

I believe that the history of the Jumanos and their neighbors and trading partners may include elements of all three of these scenarios. The first would be atypical of events affecting related Tanoan groups; it would better apply to the Apaches, who migrated into the South Plains and confronted entrenched and sometimes resistant Tanoan farmers.

As to the second scenario, there may have been Tanoan-speaking hunter-gatherers who occupied the High Plains and followed a nomadic pattern from the beginning. The ancestors of the Kiowa could have moved into the Plains at this time, if linguists' estimates of the antiquity of the separation of Kiowa from the rest of Tanoan are realistic.

In any case, it is the third scenario which is the most suggestive in relation to the Jumanos, in the overall context of Western prehistory. There are archaeological[6] traces of an early eastern extension of the Jornado branch of the Mogollon, taking agriculture well beyond its later limits, in historic times. In the first millennium A.D. variants of the Jornada were found as far east as Tule Canyon in western Texas; along the middle Pecos in eastern New Mexico; and, farther to the south, along the Rio Grande as far as La Junta de los Rios.[7] The distribution of these regional foci appears to parallel the scattered locations later identified with the Jumanos.

Jornada cultures fall into northern and southern divisions and a number of regional variants. In the earlier phases, semi-sedentary horticulture is generally indicated, with substantial reliance on foraging as well. However, by around A.D. 900 to A.D. 1000, permanent horticultural villages, showing a mixture of Anasazi and Mogollon tradition, developed along the southern Rio del Norte. This culture continued to expand southward as far as La Junta, where by A.D. 1200 it replaced or absorbed the earlier occupation.[8]

At about A.D. 900, also, there were small horticultural villages along the middle Pecos. Jelinek made a detailed survey of the prehistory of this area, extending roughly from Santa Rosa to Carlsbad, New Mexico. He indicates that, from the beginning, the closest cultural ties were with the Southwest; ceramic evidence, from circa A.D. 800, links the valley with the Jornada Mogollon tradition.[9] Agriculture, beginning at about this time, was limited to the riverbanks and depended on spring flooding from the melting snows of the Sangre de Cristo Mountains. In succeeding phases, ceramic trade wares indicate contacts with the eastern Anasazi tradition, and specifically with the Gran Quivira area, as indicated by distinctive Chupadero Black-on-White pottery; these trade wares increase markedly after A.D. 1200.

The most intensive farming, and evidently the densest population, comes roughly between A.D. 1000 and A.D. 1200. The type of rectangular, slightly excavated houses, clustered in small villages, also suggests eastern Anasazi influences. The main subsistence pursuit was farming; game was evidently scarce along the Pecos. During this period, according to Jelinek, any cultural activity on the neighboring Llano Estacado was "an eastward extension of the Pecos Valley phases."[10] This might suggest that the middle Pecos folk were making periodic hunting trips onto the Llano Estacado.

Between A.D. 1250 and A.D. 1350, there was a fundamental change in middle Pecos subsistence. Farming was abandoned, with a rapid transition to intensive bison hunting. Evidently there was a slight increase in moisture and a spread of grasslands around and near the Pecos, followed by an expansion of buffalo herds—which, at the same time, were on the increase in the Great Plains. In short, the Middle Pecos people became full-time hunters and adopted a nomadic way of life. This way of life "continued in the Middle Pecos area for a short period before leading them elsewhere, undoubtedly out onto the High Plains." On the basis of their cultural connections with the middle and northern Rio Grande, Jelinek reasons that the residents of the Middle Pecos were Tanoan in language affiliation. He also suggests that they may have been the group ancestral to the Kiowa tribe of later history.[11]

One point of interest in the cultural history outlined by Jelinek is his conviction that it was not crop failure, but increased opportunity for hunting, which caused the Pecos Valley residents to abandon their farms. However, he also notes that their farming was marginal and probably was quite susceptible to late summer flooding; this may have been a precipitating factor. There is nothing in Jelinek's reconstruction to indicate that warfare or hostile relations with their neighbors played a role in destabilizing the Middle Pecos way of life. He remarks, however, that this stretch of the Pecos remained depopulated up to historic times, as attested by Luxan and other early documentary sources.[12]

Neither does Jelinek suggest that full-time buffalo hunting was supplemented by trade. However, it seems possible that the long-existing trade relations between the Middle Pecos people and the eastern Pueblos were maintained and even intensified, as hunting brought an increase in the supply of game. Their nomadic movements, then, would have led them over a seasonal round between hunting grounds on the Llano Estacado and the villages of their Tanoan kin—perhaps even to Gran Quivira, site of the Pueblo of the Jumanos. The wide distribution of Jornada Brownware ceramics in the Llano Estacado throughout the late prehistoric period

(A.D. 1200–1600) identifies the affiliation of this area with the Northern Jornada; trade wares also indicate an active trade with the eastern Pueblos of New Mexico, which are archaeologically classified in the southeastern Anasazi tradition.[13]

Archaeological studies in the Tompiro province, which includes the Gran Quivira site, confirm the frontier character of this region. Gordon Vivian, who directed excavations at Gran Quivira National Monument in 1951, found that the earliest habitations in the area were pithouses, dated circa A.D. 600–700.[14] Ceramics were predominately Jornada Brownwares. Other artifacts also indicated an affiliation with the Jornada centers located some distance to the south. By Basketmaker III times, some three centuries later, Anasazi features were in greater evidence: "the peoples of the Gran Quivira villages . . . were as much like the Anasazi Pueblos of the Rio Grande as they were like the Jornada Mogollon to the south."[15]

Vivian accepts the judgement of F. Wendorf and E. K. Reed[16] that the early sedentary population of the Rio Grande valley was Tanoan in linguistic identity. Based on the colonial documents, Vivian also judges that the language of the Jumanos was similar to that of their Piro neighbors, and thus also related to the more progressive Rio Grande Tanoans.[17]

As time went on, additional Pueblo traits were accepted in the Gran Quivira area, and Rio Grande pottery types outweighed the Jornada tradition. Around 1200, however, the distinctive Chupadera Black-on-White style emerged, as a local derivative of the Anasazi tradition.[18]

The Southern Jornada area, south of Gran Quivira, became depopulated some time between 1300 and 1400. Vivian follows Mera[19] in judging not only that the original source of the Gran Quivira population was in the Jornada Brownware people, but also that this population was eventually joined by a second wave, which migrated northward at the time of the depopulation. The migration, Vivian suggests, might account for the growth of the large population centers such as Gran Quivira.[20] Vivian has little to say about Gran Quivira as a trade center, though he notes the presence of some Caddoan-style pottery. He does indicate that there was a symbiotic relationship between the Jumanos of Gran Quivira and certain nomadic groups, based on the exchange of agricultural produce for meat and hides.[21]

It may be that the influx of migrants, of which Vivian speaks, was actually precipitated by Athabascan movements into the Guadalupe Mountains region. The first nomadic groups which came to trade were undoubtedly Jumanos—perhaps descendants of the earlier middle Pecos people. By the 1660's, of course, the Apaches had also begun to make their presence directly felt at the Jumano Pueblos.

After A.D. 1450, the Jornada population of the southern Rio Grande valley contracted to two locations, one around El Paso and the other at La Junta de los Rios. Robert Campbell identifies these river valley populations as "Jumanos or Sumas."[22] La Junta was a point of direct contact between river valley agriculturalists and South Plains nomads. Kelley's study of the prehistory of this region was originally influenced by the work of Scholes and Mera,[23] and reflects Scholes' formulation of the "Jumano problem." Accordingly, Kelley explicitly denies that the Plains Jumanos who traded at La Junta had any connection with those in the Tompiro Pueblos.[24]

Kelley's use of *Patarabueyes* to designate the population of several villages at La Junta muddies over distinctions within what was evidently a complex clustering of peoples. According to the historical accounts, the villages were divided along language lines. One of the divisions had westward connections, linking La Junta with the Concho and other Uto-Aztecan groups; the other extended along the Rio del Norte and had eastward connections, to the outlying Jumanos of the Rio Pecos.[25] The earlier terms—e.g., Gallegos' Cabri and Amotomanco—followed this linguistic distinction, while *Patarabuey* was a Spanish designation applied to the entire resident population of the region.

Kelley is concerned with distinguishing and identifying archaeological traces of the nomadic and sedentary cultures, and with documenting the extensive trade at this crossroads area. There is a continuity of population, from the La Junta focus of circa A.D. 1200–1400, through the subsequent Concepcion and Conchos foci, both of which show evidence of a Spanish presence; some of the village sites are still occupied. In all three of the archaeological foci, there is evidence of a Plains trade, which Kelley attributes to the Jumanos.[26]

No ceramics were produced in the La Junta villages. Early trade wares are of El Paso Polychrome and other Southwestern types, while in the Concepcion focus, red wares showing a startling resemblance to Mogollon types predominate. There are also occasional sherds from the Allen focus of eastern Texas, identified with the historic Hasinai—a "striking confirmation of the reported trade relations maintained by the Jumanos."[27] Iron tools and other Spanish artifacts begin in the Concepcion focus; during the Conchos focus, Spanish-style pottery and religious artifacts indicate a missionary presence.

Patarabuey village architecture was pueblo-like, with flat-roofed rectangular houses built of poles, covered with adobe plaster; the floors were excavated, from a few inches to several feet in depth. Houses were either clustered or arranged in rows; the number of houses and the evidence of cooperative planning in their construction and placement increase in the later foci. As a minority type, there are also " . . . circular houses that occur as oddities at all periods."[28] These "alien-looking" structures appeared to have circular to oval floors, with a large number of small support posts, and each is bordered by a ring of backed-up gravel and larger stones. They are variously interpreted as storage houses, sweat lodges, or "pit-houses built in the fields"; alternatively, they " . . . may represent the habitations of some group such as the Jumanos."[29]

Although the La Junta situation remains open to differing interpretation, I suggest that it was analogous to that at the Tompiro Pueblos. In both regions, there was a mixed population of permanent residents (Tompiro/Jumano in one case, Julime/Jumano in the other), in contact with a transient population of itinerant Plains Jumanos. In both regions, the permanent residents may have worked to provision and stockpile goods (e.g., salt-mining or arrow-making) as part of the trade operations.

The circular house floors which Kelley discovered at La Junta seem remarkably similar to those typical of the Cielo Complex, described by Robert J. Malouf as "beehive-like arrangements . . . or wickiups thatched with grasses and brush or covered with deer and bison skins."[30] The Cielo Complex is "a Late Prehistoric-to-Protohistoric forager complex found in the Texas Big Bend and in northern Chihuahua," which Malouf ascribes to the Jumanos and Cibolos of the early historical documents.[31] The type site, Cielo Bravo, lies at the edge of the La Junta culture area, a few miles below the mouth of the Rio Conchos.

Archaeological materials, according to Malouf, " . . . confirm that foraging peoples of the Cielo Complex were prehistorically coeval and interactive with semi-sedentary agriculturalists of the La Junta phase in the Big Bend . . . [T]hey appear to have traveled in bands of from six to thirty-five people, and to have occasionally come together on the Rio Grande for purposes of exchange and other activities."[32] He observes that, except for their dwellings and the absence of ceramics at these sites, their material remains are much like those at La Junta.

It is evident that pottery did occasionally reach La Junta from the east; more commonly, however, it was imported from the west. The Jumanos, in any case, did not conduct substantial trade in ceramics at this port of call. It is bows and arrows which have been indicated as items exported in quantity from La Junta to the eastern tribes. Kelley also suggests that La Junta was a center for the production of arrows;[33] this is consistent with Malouf's finding of an abundance of Perdiz points and preforms at Cielo Bravo and other Cielo complex sites.[34]

Kelley suggests that the Toyah Phase, a late prehistoric cultural horizon with a distribution from northern Chihuahua to the South Plains and central and southern Texas, is closely associated with the Jumanos or later history.[35] Malouf makes a similar suggestion: both Toya and Cielo lithic assemblages "are indicative of a Plains bison-hunter technology and tool kit," very possibly to be identified as the Jumanos.[36] For both of these assemblages, the Perdiz point is characteristic.

It is the late Prehistoric period on the Llano Estacado that poses the greatest challenge and holds the greatest promise in relation to the Jumanos. Between, roughly, A.D. 1400 and A.D. 1600 a series of cultural assemblages have been defined, under a variety of names. Among these are the Garza and Tierra Blanca Complexes of Texas, the Wheeler and Edwards Complexes of Oklahoma, and the Antelope Creek Phase of the Texas and Oklahoma panhandles.[37] All of these show semi-nomadic to semi-sedentary residence patterns and indicate a high degree of dependence on buffalo hunting. All evidently had strong contacts with the Southwest, evidenced by distinctive pottery types, obsidian, turquoise, and other trade materials. Any or all of these groups could be Tanoans, the descendants of eastern Jornada populations.

Comparing archaeological complexes with the accounts of exploration in the South Plains, Judith Habicht-Mauche has recently suggested that sites identified with the Tierra Blanca Complex, clustered in the headwaters of the Red River, approximate the geographical range of the Querechos of the Coronado expedition. She identifies this complex with the Plains Apaches. Habicht-Mauche also proposes that Garza Complex sites, on and near the upper Brazos, are the remains of the Teyas encountered in the region by the Coronado expedition. She identifies the Teyas with the Jumanos, later encountered by Zaldivar in the same region; however, she judges the Jumanos to have been Caddoan, ancestral to the Wichita.[38]

Habicht-Mauche's identification of these archaeological cultures is reasonable, though one may differ with her view of the Jumanos' ethnic affiliation. I have already argued that the Teyas are to be identified with the Plains Jumanos, and thus were a Tanoan (rather than a Caddoan) group. It will be recalled that the Castañeda narrative described the Teyas as a people with close ties to the eastern Pueblos. A preponderance of trade in this direction is indicated in Garza complex sites by a concentration of ceramics from the Salinas region. The Tierra Blanca people may have been Apaches, as Habicht-Mauche suggests; conceivably, they could have been a second Jumano band, with trading contacts with the northern Pueblos as indicated by northern Rio Grande tradewares.

It is clear that the Garza folk were, like the historic Jumanos, very actively engaged in trade. Garza Complex assemblages include, according to Habicht-Mauche, Chupadero Black-on-White and Jornada Brownwares which indicate ties with the Salinas Pueblos, and also pottery types such as Edwards Plain which point to contacts with Caddoan-affiliated cultures in Oklahoma. There are quantities of obsidian, turquoise, and western marine shells. Habicht-Mauche indicates that some Garza sites on Blanco Canyon are large, with substantial deposits, representing "semi-sedentary base camps or villages."[39]

One of these, the Floydada Country Club site, studied by J. Word, exhibits features especially suggestive of intertribal contacts. Word believes that the site was not permanently occupied, but that several groups with differing cultural affiliations camped repeatedly in different areas of the site, presumably for the purpose of trade. Based on lithic materials and ceramic samples, it is his interpretation that the dominant Garza component, group A, represents a nomadic people who hunted bison and produced dried meat and processed hides. This group evidently traded extensively with the eastern Pueblos. Group B is associated with Mogollon peoples between El Paso and mid-eastern New Mexico, while group C is identified, tentatively, as Caddoan.[40] This site could represent one of the bases, or trading posts, where Jumanos dealt with their trading partners; it could also have been a point of rendezvous of northern and southern Jumano bands, seen in groups A and B.

Timothy Baugh, whose work focuses on Caddoan prehistory, has posited the existence of a "Southern Plains Macroeconomy."[41] This designates an exchange system of late prehistoric times, which involved the interaction of Pueblo and Plains Caddoan groups. I agree with Baugh that the Pueblo-Plains interaction sphere can be best interpreted as a macro-system. However, I would argue that the system operated through the agency of a third party, the Jumanos, who contributed both as hunters and as intermediaries in trade.

As Baugh indicates, the exchange system was disrupted and transformed, first by the arrival of the Apaches, and later by the Spanish conquest.[42] I suggest that Apache bands, entering into competition for trade goods with the Jumanos, began to impose exclusive bipartite trade partnerships on the Pueblo villages and effectively blocked their access to other Plains tribes. Thus, the Apaches replaced the Jumanos in trade with the Pueblo groups, but did not serve the same linking function in a larger sphere of operations. Therefore, when the Jumano trade died, the South Plains became a marginal zone, peripheral to the Pueblos, to northern Mexico, and to the Caddoan tribes on the east. It was no longer a zone of trade and communication, linking these diverse areas, as had been the case for centuries past.

NOTES

Preface

1. Robert G. Campbell, "Some Possible Kiowa Origins," p. 15.
2. Francisco Pimentel, *Cuadro Descriptivo de las Lenguas.*
3. John P. Harrington, "Notes on the Piro Language," p. 593.
4. Nancy P. Hickerson, "The Linguistic Position of Jumano," p. 324; "Jumano: the Missing Link in South Plains History," p. 7.
5. France V. Scholes and H. P. Mera, "Some Aspects of the Jumano Problem."
6. I have approached this problem in two recent papers: Nancy P. Hickerson, "Ethnogenesis in the Great Plains: Jumano to Kiowa?" and "Kiowa: the Resurgence of Tanoan in the South Plains."

Introduction

1. In the Spanish and French documents, the name appears in a variety of forms, including Humano, Humana, Jumana, Xumana, Chouman, and Sumana.
2. In 1888, a Tewa Indian told Adolph Bandelier that some thirty years earlier, he was visiting the Comanches in Texas when Jumanos (Humanesh) came to trade with them (Adolph F. Bandelier, *The Southwestern Journals of Adolph F. Bandelier*, edited by C. H. Lange, C. L. Riley, and E. M. Lange, 4:54). The putative date, circa 1858, is at least seventy years later than any other reference.
3. Adolph F. Bandelier, *Final Report of Investigations among Indians of the Southwestern United States* 1:93.
4. Ibid., pp. 168–169.
5. Frederick W. Hodge, ed., *Handbook of American Indians North of Mexico*; Frederick W. Hodge, "The Jumano Indians," *Proceedings of the American Antiquarian Society*, n.s. 20:249–268.
6. F. W. Hodge, "Jumano," in F. W. Hodge, ed., *Handbook of American Indians North of Mexico* 1:636.
7. F. W. Hodge, "The Jumano Indians," *Proceedings of the American Antiquarian Society*, n.s. 20:258.

8. Ibid., p. 268.
9. Herbert Bolton, "The Jumano Indians in Texas, 1650–1771," *Texas Historical Association Quarterly* 15:66–84.
10. Ibid., p. 84.
11. Carl O. Sauer, "The Distribution of Aboriginal Tribes and Languages in Northwestern Mexico," *Ibero-Americana* 5.
12. Ibid., p. 68.
13. France V. Scholes and H. P. Mera, "Some Aspects of the Jumano Problem," 6:269–299.
14. Ibid., p. 275.
15. Ibid., p. 285.
16. Ibid., p. 285.
17. Ibid., pp. 291–299.
18. Gordon Vivian, *Gran Quivira: Excavations in a 17th Century Jumano Pueblo*, p. 8.
19. Stuart J. Baldwin, *A Brief Report on the Piro-Tompiro Archaeology and Ethnohistory Project, 1981 Field Season.*
20. J. Charles Kelley, *Jumano and Patarabueye: Relations at La Junta de los Rios.*
21. Kelley's choice of the term might be criticized, since *Patarabuey* was apparently a pejorative term which the Spanish colonists applied indiscriminately to the Indians around La Junta.
22. J. Charles Kelley, "Juan Sabeata and Diffusion in Aboriginal Texas," *American Anthropologist* 57:981–995.
23. W. W. Newcomb, Jr., *The Indians of Texas*, pp. 226–227.
24. Jack Forbes, "Unknown Athapaskans: The Identification of the Janos, Jocome, Suma, Manso, and Other Indian Tribes of the Southwest," *Ethnohistory* 6:145.
25. Ibid., p. 144.
26. George Parker Winship, trans. and ed., *The Journey of Coronado, 1540–1542*, pp. 215–216.

1. The Travels of Cabeza de Vaca

1. Alvar Nuñez Cabeza de Vaca preferred to use the metronymic, which was, according to family tradition, a title of honor awarded to a maternal grandfather by the King of Navarre.
2. Cabeza de Vaca's narrative was first published in Zamora in 1541 under the title *Relacion (Relation)*; in later editions it became known by the more familiar title *Naufragios (Shipwrecks)*. Both the *Relation* and the *Joint Report* are included in Fanny Bandelier, trans., *The Narrative of Alvar Nuñez Cabeza de Vaca.* Cyclone Covey, trans. and ed., *Cabeza de Vaca's Adventures in the Unknown Interior of America*, is a translation of the relation, with commentary and references to the *Joint Report* interspersed in the text. C. Hallenbeck, *Alvar Nuñez Cabeza de Vaca: The Journey and*

Route of the First Europeans to Cross the Continent of North America, 1534–1536, has been especially useful for the account given here.

3. Cabeza de Vaca, in Covey, trans. and ed., *Adventures,* p. 64.

4. Efforts have been made to estimate this distance by referring to the commodities of the trade. Hallenbeck, *Journey,* pp. 128–129, indicates the western tributaries of the Trinity River as a source of red ochre and suggests that Cabeza de Vaca wintered there. Hallenbeck also thinks that Cabeza de Vaca may have traveled inland as far as the Red River of Oklahoma. Such speculations are inconclusive and almost irrelevant; since Cabeza de Vaca was part of a trade network, he probably did not extract the ochre himself, and did not necessarily travel to the point of origin.

5. Covey, trans. and ed., *Adventures,* pp. 67–68.

6. Covey indicates, incorrectly, that this is the fruit of the mesquite tree. The mescal bean is the seed of the Texas Mountain Laurel (*Sophora secundiflora*). Its use in ritual was widespread prior to the diffusion from Mexico of the use of peyote (Weston La Barre, *The Peyote Cult*). Among historic Indians, the Tonkawa used the mescal bean in rituals associated with deer hunting.

7. Ives Goddard, "The Languages of South Texas and the Lower Rio Grande," in *The Native Languages of North America,* edited by L. Campbell and M. Mithun, p. 356.

8. Cabeza de Vaca, in Covey, trans. and ed., *Adventures,* pp. 80–81.

9. Ibid., p. 63.

10. Cabeza de Vaca, by his own statement, became a trader after his first year (1528–1529) among the coastal Indians; it was in this capacity that he left the islands for the mainland, early in 1530. Beyond that point, he does not give a clear chronological account of his activities. Covey (*Adventures,* p. 67) estimates that he spent twenty-two months as a trader; Hallenbeck (*Journey,* p. 129) calculates the period as three years.

11. Hallenbeck (*Journey,* pp. 245–306) discusses the earlier theories of Bancroft, Bandelier, Davenport and Wills, and others, and also presents his own. Krieger's is perhaps the most influential recent attempt to trace the Spaniards' route across the continent (Alex D. Krieger, "The Travels of Alvar Nuñez Cabeza de Vaca in Texas and Mexico, 1534–1536," in *Homenaje a Pablo Martinez del Rio en al XXV Aniversario de los Origines Americanos,* pp. 459–474).

12. Cabeza de Vaca, in Covey, trans. and ed., *Adventures,* p. 80.

13. Hallenbeck (*Journey,* pp. 147–151) traced the distribution of several species of prickly pears (tunas), and indicated that the Spaniards could have visited large thickets in the vicinity of San Antonio. According to Campbell and Campbell (*Historic Indian Groups of the Choke Canyon Reservoir and Surrounding Area, Southern Texas,* p. 14), the largest thickets were located further south, near the Nueces River.

14. Fanny Bandelier, *Narrative,* p. 228.

15. Cabeza de Vaca, in Covey, trans. and ed., *Adventures,* p. 101.

16. Hallenbeck, *Journey,* p. 169; Carl O. Sauer, *Sixteenth Century North America,* pp. 119–120.

17. Hallenbeck, *Journey,* p. 165.
18. Cabeza de Vaca, in Covey, trans. and ed., *Adventures,* p. 104.
19. Ibid., p. 104.
20. Ibid., p. 104.
21. Ibid., p. 105.
22. Fanny Bandelier, *Narrative,* p. 238.
23. Hallenbeck, *Journey,* p. 178.
24. Cabeza de Vaca, in Covey, trans. and ed., *Adventures,* p. 108.
25. Fanny Bandelier, *Narrative,* p. 240.
26. Cabeza de Vaca, in Covey, trans. and ed., *Adventures,* p. 109.
27. Ibid., p. 112.
28. Ibid., pp. 113–114.
29. Hallenbeck, *Journey,* pp. 184–185.
30. Cabeza de Vaca, in Covey, trans. and ed., *Adventures,* pp. 115–116.
31. Ibid., p. 116.
32. Fanny Bandelier, *Narrative,* p. 251.
33. Ibid., p. 122.

2. Explorations by Way of the Western Corridor

1. Percy M. Baldwin, "Fray Marcos de Niza and His Discovery of the Seven Cities of Cibola," *New Mexico Historical Review* 1:204–205.
2. Ibid., pp. 206–207.
3. See Carl O. Sauer, "The Road to Cibola," *Ibero-Americana* 3, for a geographer's commentary on Fray Marcos' claims and an assessment of his accomplishments.
4. Carroll L. Riley, *The Frontier People.* Riley has traced and mapped this and other major trade routes between Mexico and the Pueblo provinces as of 1500.
5. Pedro de Castañeda, "Account of the Expedition to Cibola," in G. P. Winship, trans., *The Journey of Coronado, 1540–1542,* pp. 40–41.
6. There has been much scholarly interest in, and disagreement about, the route of the Coronado exploration of the Plains. This is discussed by Herbert E. Bolton (*Coronado: Knight of Pueblos and Plains*); David Donoghue ("The Route of the Coronado Expedition in Texas," *New Mexico Historical Review* 44:77–90); W. C. Holden ("Coronado's Route Across the Staked Plains," *West Texas Historical Association Yearbook* 20 [1940]: 3–20); and Carl O. Sauer ("The Road"); among others.
7. Castañeda, "Account," in Winship, trans., *Coronado,* pp. 64–66.
8. Ibid., p. 111.
9. For example, Jack Forbes believes that the Jumanos were a division of the Apache; he suggests that the Teyas " . . . probably were . . . Lipan or Jumano Apaches" (Forbes, *Apache, Navajo, and Spaniard,* p. 15).
10. This is the position of Albert H. Schroeder ("A Re-analysis of the Routes of Coronado and Oñate," *Plains Anthropologist* 7 (1962): 2–23). Schroeder is willing to accept a suggestion by Bolton that the Teyas were Jumanos, but he qualifies this with an indication that these were Canadian

River Jumanos, whom he identifies as "Plains Caddoans" ("Re-analysis," *Plains Anthropologist* 7:20).

11. According to Bolton (*Coronado*, p. 250), ". . . before the coming of the Spaniards, the word Texas, variously spelled by the early writers, had wide currency among the tribes of eastern Texas and perhaps over a larger area; its usual meaning was 'friends,' or, more technically, 'allies'. . . ." Swanton quotes this passage at greater length, ending with the comment that this ". . . was not a specific term for the Hasinai, but became such by accident" (John R. Swanton, *Source Material on the History and Ethnology of the Caddo Indians*, pp. 3–5).

12. Castañeda, in Winship, trans., *Coronado*, pp. 67–76.

13. Ibid., p. 108.

14. Ibid., pp. 111–112.

15. Juan Jaramillo, in Winship, trans., *Coronado*, pp. 312–322.

16. Waldo Wedel, "Archaeological Remains in Central Kansas . . . ," *Smithsonian Miscellaneous Collections*, 101 (1942): pp. 7–8, 22.

17. Carl O. Sauer, *Sixteenth Century North America*, p. 142.

18. Coronado, in Winship, trans., *Coronado*, p. 218.

3. Opening the Central Corridor

1. J. Charles Kelley, who did an archaeological study at La Junta in the 1930's, was able to locate and map at least six village sites which could be positively identified with the villages mentioned in early historical records (J. Charles Kelley, *Jumano and Patarabueye: Relations at La Junta de los Rios*).

2. The main source of information on the Rodriguez-Chamuscado expedition is the Relation of Hernan Gallegos, preserved in the *Archivo General de Indias* (AGI). An English translation is included in George P. Hammond and Agapito Rey, eds., *The Rediscovery of New Mexico, 1580–1594*, pp. 67–114. The same volume contains shorter reports, letters, etc., by Gallegos, Bustemente, and other participants in the expedition. The Declaration of Pedro de Bustemente, one of the eight soldiers, is included in H. E. Bolton, ed., *Spanish Exploration in the Southwest*, pp. 142–150.

3. The most important account of the Espejo expedition is the Journal of Diego Perez de Luxan from the AGI, included in Hammond and Rey, eds., *Rediscovery*, pp. 153–212. The shorter report of Antonio de Espejo and several of Espejo's letters are included in the same volume, pp. 213–231. Espejo's report is also reprinted in Bolton, ed., *Spanish Exploration*, pp. 168–192.

4. Luxan, in Hammond and Rey, eds., *Rediscovery*, p. 169.

5. Ibid., pp. 158–159. Since the term did not distinguish between these two distinct population groups, it is unfortunate that Kelley (*Jumano and Patarabueye*) has chosen to use *Patarabueye* as a cultural designation for only one of them.

6. Gallegos, in Hammond and Rey, eds., *Rediscovery*, p. 73.

7. Ibid., pp. 73-74.

8. Luxan, in Hammond and Rey, eds., *Rediscovery*, p. 159.

9. Ibid., pp. 160-161.

10. Ibid., p. 161.

11. Ibid., p. 164.

12. Ibid., p. 166.

13. Ibid., p. 167.

14. Introduction to Hammond and Rey, eds., *Rediscovery*, p. 8.

15. Joseph P. Sanchez, *The Rio Abajo Frontier, 1540–1692*, p. 4.

16. Gallegos, in Hammond and Rey, eds., *Rediscovery*, p. 76.

17. George P. Hammond and Agapito Rey, eds., *Obregon's History of 16th Century Explorations in Western America*, pp. 317, 338.

18. Gallegos, in Hammond and Rey, eds., *Rediscovery*, p. 79.

19. Ibid., p. 79.

20. Luxan, in Hammond and Rey, eds., *Rediscovery*, p. 168.

21. Espejo, in Hammond and Rey, eds., *Rediscovery*, pp. 217–218.

22. Luxan, in Hammond and Rey, eds., *Rediscovery*, p. 169.

23. Espejo, in Hammond and Rey, eds., *Rediscovery*, p. 218.

24. Luxan, in Hammond and Rey, eds., *Rediscovery*, p. 206.

25. Ibid., pp. 207–209.

26. Ibid., p. 209.

27. Ibid., pp. 209–210.

28. Ibid., p. 210.

29. Ibid., p. 211.

4. The Illegal *Entrada* of Castaño de Sosa

1. Gaspar Castaño de Sosa, in Hammond and Rey, eds., *Rediscovery*, p. 256. Castaño's account must be used with caution, due to the failure to give adequate indications of distances, time intervals, or landmarks; also, there may be significant omissions of information about natives encountered, since the journal downplays slavetaking and other depredations which may have occurred.

2. Ibid., p. 256; the editors' note cites Jack D. Forbes, "Unknown Athapaskans," who identified the Indians as *Jumano Apaches*. If the Indians were actually Tepehuanos, their presence on the lower Pecos would attest to the wide use of the native roads by trade and, perhaps, hunting parties.

3. Castaño, in Hammond and Rey, eds., *Rediscovery*, pp. 260–261.

5. Juan de Oñate and the Conquest of New Mexico

1. Translations of the important documents for Oñate's conquest of New Mexico and his governorship are collected in G. P. Hammond and A. Rey, eds., *Don Juan de Oñate: Colonizer of New Mexico, 1595–1628*.

Some of the same are found in H. E. Bolton, ed., *Spanish Exploration* and Scholes and Mera, "Some Aspects," pp. 269–299. Most of the originals are in the Archive of the Indies in Seville.

2. The road opened by Zaldivar, according to Oñate, would "shorten the previously known road by sixty leagues and bypass the warlike Patarabueyes Indians . . ." (Hammond and Rey, eds., *Oñate*, p. 384). This rebellion, which evidently involved the Jumanos at La Junta, could well have contributed to the early rebelliousness among the Jumanos in New Mexico—assuming that there was communication between these regions.

3. Juan Gutierrez Bocanegra, in Bolton, ed., *Spanish Exploration*, p. 225.

4. Ibid., p. 226.

5. Ibid., p. 230.

6. Scholes and Mera, "Some Aspects," p. 276.

7. Ibid., p. 277.

8. Don Juan de Oñate, in Bolton, ed., *Spanish Exploration*, pp. 233–234; see also Scholes and Mera, "Some Aspects," p. 276.

9. Oñate, in Hammond and Rey, eds., *Oñate*, p. 351.

10. Scholes and Mera, "Some Aspects," pp. 277–278.

11. Ibid., p. 278.

12. Ibid., p. 278.

13. Ibid., pp. 278–279.

14. See Stuart J. Baldwin, "A Brief Report on the Piro-Tompiro Archaeology and Ethnohistory Project," for a discussion of the identification of historic and prehistoric sites.

15. According to Hackett, Farfan's party proceeded "over the route previously taken by Espejo" (Charles Wilson Hackett, trans., *Historical Documents Relating to New Mexico, Nueva Vizcaya, and Approaches Thereto, to 1773* 3:211).

16. Oñate, in Bolton, ed., *Spanish Exploration*, p. 240. This is the location which is generally accepted; however, the distance traveled would be over two hundred miles, seemingly a greater distance than indicated by Espejo's and Farfan's accounts, and requiring, as Bolton remarks, that Farfan's league be calculated at around six miles. For a detailed analysis of the routes and location of the mines, see Katherine Bartlett, "Notes upon the Routes of Espejo and Farfan to the Mines in the Sixteenth Century," *New Mexico Historical Review* 17:21–36.

17. Oñate, in Bolton, ed., *Spanish Exploration*, p. 241.

18. Ibid., p. 242.

19. This is Bandelier's identification, cited by Bolton, ed., *Spanish Exploration*, p. 242. Yavapai, or some other division of Yuman, seems the most likely possibility. Bartlett ("Notes," p. 32) makes the same suggestion.

20. Oñate, in Bolton, ed., *Spanish Exploration*, p. 242.

21. Ibid., p. 244.

22. Ibid., p. 245.

23. Oñate, in Bolton, ed., *Spanish Exploration*, p. 253.

24. Rodriguez, in Hammond and Rey, eds., *Oñate*, p. 864.

25. Ibid., p. 865.

26. Ibid., p. 866.

27. Ibid., pp. 866-867.

28. Oñate, in Bolton, ed., *Spanish Exploration*, p. 262.

29. Valverde y Mercado, in Bolton, ed., *Spanish Exploration*, pp. 872-877.

6. The Jumanos at the Dawn of History

1. The general configuration of the Jumano's trading system is discussed later.

2. *Patarabueyes* could be a Spanish coinage, possibly meaning "Ox-feet" or "Ox-kickers"; more likely, it could be a Spanish rendering of an unknown native term.

3. Scholes and Mera, "Some Aspects," pp. 276-285. Schroeder reviews the history of exploration of the Salinas region, as well as the issue of linguistic identity of the pueblos ("The Language of the Saline Pueblos—Piro or Tewa?," *New Mexico Historical Review* 39:235-249).

4. Archaeologists have debated the identification of the ruins of Gran Quivira as either historic Tabira or Cueloce; the latter seems to be indicated (S. Baldwin, *Brief Report;* Gordon Vivian, *Gran Quivira*).

5. George E. Hyde, *Indians of the High Plains*, pp. 11-12.

6. W. W. Newcomb and T. N. Campbell, "Southern Plains Ethnohistory," in D. D. Wyckoff and J. L. Hofman, eds., *Pathways to Plains Prehistory*, pp. 35-38.

7. Oñate, in Bolton, ed., *Spanish Exploration*, p. 257.

8. Ibid., p. 258.

9. Valverde, in Hammond and Rey, eds., *Oñate*, p. 841.

10. Oñate, in Bolton, ed., *Spanish Exploration*, p. 257.

11. Valverde, in Hammond and Rey, eds., *Oñate*, p. 841.

12. Ibid., p. 841.

13. Ibid., p. 866.

14. Thus, the witness Juan de Leon indicated that in New Mexico there were "one or two pueblos of Rayado people" (Ibid., p. 850). Here, *Rayado* is clearly a reference to the Jumano pueblos.

7. New Mexico in the 1620's

1. John L. Kessell, *Kiva, Cross, and Crown*, p. 95.

2. Alonso de Benavides, in F. W. Hodge, G. P. Hammond, and A. Rey, eds., *Fray Alonso de Benavides' Revised Memorial of 1634*, p. 68.

3. The development of a Spanish trade in buffalo pelts indicates the establishment of trade links with the Plains Indians; the eastern Apaches dealt in pelts and other buffalo products, as did the Jumanos. Piñon nuts—extremely valuable in trade—could be gathered near the Pueblo villages; they were also brought in from greater distances, along with cactus and other fruits. Salt was obtained from the salt ponds located near the Jumano

pueblos. By inference, it would appear that the Jumanos were deeply involved in the procurement and transportation of these commodities, which were a common source of extra income for appointed officials in colonial New Mexico.

4. Benavides, in Hodge, Hammond, and Rey, eds., *Benavides 1634*, p. 69.

5. Ibid., pp. 99–100.

6. Ibid., p. 81.

7. Ibid., p. 66.

8. Benavides, in Mrs. E. E. Ayer, trans., "The Memorial of Fray Alonso de Benavides, 1630," *Land of Sunshine* 13:285.

8. Fray Juan de Salas' Mission to the Jumanos

1. The earlier *Memorial* had been in circulation since the seventeenth century, and had been translated into many languages. Mrs. E. E. Ayer, trans., "The Memorial of Fray Alonso de Benavides, 1630," *Land of Sunshine* 13:227–290, 345–358, 435–444; 14:39–52, 131–148, 227–232, includes extensive notes by F. W. Hodge. Also, P. P. Forestal, trans. and ed., *Benavides' Memorial of 1630*.

2. The existence of the later *Memorial* was only suspected until it was discovered in the Vatican archives in 1909; it was not published until 1945 (Hodge, Hammond, and Rey, eds., *Benavides 1634*). This volume also includes other writings by Benavides and the Memorial of Estevan de Perea.

3. Benavides, in Ayer, trans., "Memorial," *Land of Sunshine* 13:281.

4. Ibid., 13:285.

5. Ibid., 13:439–441.

6. Ibid., 13:438–439.

7. Ibid., 14:46.

8. Ibid., 14:46.

9. Ibid., 14:46.

10. Ibid., 14:137.

11. Ibid., 14:137.

12. Ibid., 14:137.

13. Ibid., 14:137–138.

14. Ibid., 14:138.

15. Ibid., 14:138.

16. Ibid., 14:138.

17. Ibid., 14:139.

18. Ibid., 14:139.

19. Benavides, in Hodge, Hammond, and Rey, eds., *Benavides 1634*, p. 136.

20. Ibid., p. 136.

21. Ibid., p. 138.

22. Ximenez Samaniego, *Relacion de la Vida de la V. Madre Sor Maria de Jesus*, pp. 132–133; Charles W. Hackett, ed., *Pichardo's Treatise on the Limits of Louisiana and Texas* 2:485–492.

23. Hackett, ed., *Pichardo's Treatise* 2:466.

24. Samaniego, *Relacion*, p. 34.

25. Benavides, in Hodge, Hammond, and Rey, eds., *Benavides 1634*, pp. 140–141.

26. Ibid., p. 141.

27. Hackett, ed., *Pichardo's Treatise* 2:469.

28. Sanchez, *Rio Abajo*, p. 88.

29. Note the Indians' statement that the woman preached to each of them "in their own tongue" (Ayer, trans., "Memorial," *Land of Sunshine* 14:46).

30. Benavides, in Hodge, Hammond, and Rey, eds., *Benavides 1634*, p. 94.

31. Ibid., p. 94.

32. Ibid., p. 94.

33. Benavides, in Ayer, trans., "Memorial," *Land of Sunshine* 14:139–140.

34. Benavides, in Hodge, Hammond, and Rey, eds., *Benavides 1634*, p. 315.

35. N. P. Hickerson, "The Jumanos and Trade in the Arid Southwest," unpublished paper.

36. N. P. Hickerson, "The Linguistic Position of Jumano," *Journal of Anthropological Research* 44:311–326.

37. F. W. Hodge, "The Jumano Indians," *Proceedings of the American Antiquarian Society* 20:249–268; H. E. Bolton, "The Jumano Indians, 1650–1771," *Texas Historical Association Quarterly* 15:66–84; J. C. Kelley, *Jumano and Patarabueye*, p. 20.

38. The account in the 1630 Memorial reflects an assumption that the missionaries would return to reduce the Indians, build churches, etc. (Ayer, trans., "Memorial," *Land of Sunshine* 14:139). By the time he composed the later work, he had evidently been apprised of the failure of these efforts (Hodge, Hammond, and Rey, eds., *Benavides 1634*, pp. 98–99).

39. F. V. Scholes, "The Supply Service of the New Mexican Missions in the Seventeenth Century," *New Mexican Historical Review* 5:97.

40. Fray Augustin de Vetancurt, *Teatro Mexicano* 3:261.

9. The Jumanos at Mid-Century

1. The essential documents on the Tompiro province during this period are collected in Hackett, ed., *Historical Documents*, vol. 3. Other valuable sources include F. V. Scholes, "Documents for the History of the New Mexican Missions in the Seventeenth Century," *New Mexican Historical Review* 5:93–115, 186–210, 386–404; Scholes and Mera, "Some Aspects," Hodge, Hammond, and Rey, eds., *Benavides 1634*; and Sanchez, *Rio Abajo*.

2. Kessell, *Kiva, Cross, and Crown*, p. 170.

3. Albert H. Schroeder, "Pueblos Abandoned in Historic Times," in W. C. Sturtevant, ed., *Handbook of North American Indians* 9:236–254. Dozier's estimates are generally lower, but show similar overall tendencies (*The Pueblo Indians of North America*, pp. 121–125).

4. Benavides, in Hodge, Hammond, and Rey, eds., *Benavides 1634*, pp. 65–67.

5. Vetancurt, *Teatro Mexicano*, p. 261.

6. The *Mesa Jumanes* is a northern extension of Chupadero Mesa, which forms the southern rim of the Estancia Valley in central New Mexico.

7. The source of confusion about the personnel of these missions appears to be Posada, who, writing in 1686, mentioned only the expedition of 1632 to the Nueces, which he incorrectly credited to Salas and Ortega (Alfred Barnaby Thomas, ed., *Alonso de Posada Report, 1686*, p. 26). See the biographical data in Hodge, Hammond, and Rey, eds., *Benavides 1634*, pp. 281–283.

8. Bolton, "The Jumano Indians," pp. 68–74. Some scholars (e.g. Kelley, *Jumano and Patarabueye*) have found it reasonable to discount indications of distance and geographical location, and to conclude that these two expeditions traveled over the same itinerary and reached the same Jumano camp. This simplifies the picture of Jumano territoriality, and stabilizes their situation in relation to the Apaches. If the 1629 location were the same as that in 1632—a site which Jumanos occupied for most of the century—then it might be claimed that they never occupied the high plains east of New Mexico, and evidence for their wars and loss of territory to the advancing Apaches would seem less compelling. This inclination to oversimplification appears to reflect a static view of tribes with fixed territorial limits; it is not justified, in view of compelling evidence for the late entry of the Apaches into the South Plains, and the clear indications of constant shifts in location and changes in the relations between these groups during the seventeenth century.

9. Benavides, in Hodge, Hammond, and Rey, eds., *Benavides 1634*, pp. 98–99.

10. Ibid., p. 164.

11. Ibid., p. 97.

12. Posada, in Thomas, ed., *Posada Report*, p. 26.

13. Ibid., pp. 26–27.

14. Ibid., pp. 28–29. Identification of none of these groups is certain, even the Tejas (Hasinai), since the exact limits and political composition of the confederacy which was apparently at that time under Hasinai leadership is not well understood. The identity and exact geographical locations of the others—all of which changed over time—remain a mystery.

15. Ibid., pp. 27–28.

16. Ibid., p. 29.

17. Ibid., pp. 29–30.

18. Scholes and Mera, "Some Aspects," p. 288.

19. Hodge, Hammond, and Rey, eds., *Benavides 1634*, p. 265. Archaeological excavations at Gran Quivira have identified the ruins of both of these churches.

20. Hackett, ed., *Historical Documents* 2:161.

21. Hackett, ed., *Historical Documents* 3:206.

22. Ibid., p. 135.

23. Scholes and Mera, "Some Aspects," p. 285.

24. Hackett, ed., *Historical Documents* 3:143.

25. Scholes and Mera, "Some Aspects," p. 298.

26. Benavides, in Hodge, Hammond, and Rey, eds., *Benavides 1634*, p. 66.

27. Scholes and Mera, "Some Aspects," p. 283.

28. Hackett, ed., *Historical Documents* 3:143. It is evident that the "Indians of Cuarac" included Jumano refugees, settled there a quarter-century earlier, and their descendants.

29. Ibid., pp. 271–272.

30. Hackett, ed., *Historical Documents* 2:201.

31. Scholes and Mera, "Some Aspects," p. 284.

32. At El Paso, in 1909, John P. Harrington ("Notes on the Piro Language," *American Anthropologist* 11:563–594) found a few individuals who acknowledged Piro descent, though the Piro language had ceased to be spoken at least sixty years earlier; culturally and linguistically, they were indistinguishable from the Tiwa, with whom they shared a common self-identification as *Indian*. For all, Spanish was the dominant language. Harrington's queries about the Suma were unproductive; nor is there any indication of knowledge of the Manso or Jumano. The community of Isleta del Sur, today a part of the El Paso metropolitan area, still retains its Tiwa identity; Spanish is the prevailing language.

10. The Pueblo Rebellion of 1680 and Its Aftermath

1. Anne E. Hughes, *The Beginnings of Spanish Settlement in the El Paso District*, pp. 306–307. Hughes covers the settlement of El Paso and the beginnings of missionary efforts on the lower river. For the Tompiro pueblos in the 1660's and 1670's, the most useful source is Hackett, ed., *Historical Documents* 2.

2. Vetancurt, "Chronica," in Hughes, *Beginnings*, p. 310.

3. Hughes, *Beginnings*, p. 314.

4. The Jano are one of several tribes or bands which merged with, or were absorbed by, the Apaches at an early date. Forbes (*Apache, Navajo, and Spaniard*) is inclined to believe that most of these—including the Jumano—were Athabascan in language, and thus historically related to the Apache. Although I have argued (Hickerson, "The Linguistic Position of Jumano") against his general position, which indicates that Athabascan groups were both more numerous and more ancient in the southwest than is generally accepted, Forbes may be correct in identifying Jano as an early western division of Apachean.

5. Carl Sauer, "The Distribution of Aboriginal Tribes and Languages in Northwestern Mexico," *Ibero-Americana* 5:68.

6. This was the population of the east bank of the Rio Grande, opposite and upstream from La Junta. The name Cibolo may be identified with a Tanoan term for *cattle* (or buffalo), c.f. Kiowa tsæ-bo (John P. Harrington,

Vocabulary of the Kiowa Language, p. 210), and thus is perhaps the source of Cabeza de Vaca's designation of this Jumano band as the "Cow Nation" (Covey, ed., *Adventures,* pp. 115–116).

11. The Expedition to the Rio de las Nueces

1. Bolton, ed., *Spanish Exploration,* pp. 284–285. Dominguez de Mendoza's journal, translated and edited by Bolton, is the most important documentary source for this episode; of several secondary accounts of the expedition, the most detailed is that of Carlos Castañeda (*Our Catholic Heritage in Texas,* vol. 2).

2. Fray Nicolas Lopez, in Hackett, ed., *Pichardo's Treatise* 2:354.

3. Don Domingo Gironza Petris de Cruzati, in Hackett, ed., *Pichardo's Treatise* 1:137–138.

4. Ibid., pp. 138–139.

5. Lopez, in Hackett, ed., *Pichardo's Treatise* 2:350.

6. Vetancurt, in Hackett, ed., *Pichardo's Treatise* 2:328.

7. Lopez, in Hackett, ed., *Pichardo's Treatise* 2:350.

8. These were probably divisions of the Julime, perhaps those identified in 1693 as the Oposne, Polacme, Posalme, Conejo, Cacalote, Mesquite, and Topalcome (Marin, in Hackett, ed., *Historical Documents* 3).

9. Dominguez de Mendoza, in Bolton, ed., *Spanish Exploration,* p. 320.

10. Hernan Martin Serrano translated Juan Sabeata's petition to Governor Gironza (Hackett, ed., *Pichardo's Treatise* 1:137) and is also listed among Dominguez de Mendoza's company of volunteers, designated as the official translator (Bolton, ed., *Spanish Exploration,* p. 337). The identification with Captain Hernan (or Hernando) Martin of the 1650 expedition means that he would have been a man of advanced years in 1683–1684; however, according to Fray Angelico Chavez (*Origins of New Mexico Families in the Spanish Colonial Period,* p. 224), Hernan Martin Serrano, seventy-four, was "healthy and active" at the time of the Pueblo Rebellion. Martin is indicated to be a resident of El Paso, and fluent in the Jumano language; both of these facts suggest that he may have made a long career of dealing with these Indians.

11. Dominguez de Mendoza, in Bolton, ed., *Spanish Exploration,* pp. 320–322.

12. Ibid., p. 325.

13. Ibid., p. 326.

14. Ibid., p. 327.

15. Ibid., p. 331.

16. Ibid., pp. 330–331.

17. Castañeda, *Catholic Heritage* 2:321.

18. Dominguez de Mendoza, in Bolton, ed., *Spanish Exploration,* p. 331.

19. Ibid., pp. 331–332.

20. Ibid., p. 333.

21. Ibid., p. 335.

22. Ibid., p. 340.

23. Ibid., pp. 336-337.

24. The Piros were not listed by name by either Juan Sabeata or Dominguez de Mendoza; they must have been among the native auxiliaries whom the Spaniards recruited at El Paso. The Piros were, however, close kin of the Jumanos, with whom they were long associated in trade in the southern pueblos of New Mexico.

25. Dominguez de Mendoza, in Bolton, ed., *Spanish Exploration,* p. 339.

26. Ibid., p. 338.

27. Ibid., p. 338.

28. Ibid., pp. 338-340.

29. Dominguez de Mendoza, in Hackett, ed., *Pichardo's Treatise* 2:337.

30. Dominguez de Mendoza, in Bolton, ed., *Spanish Exploration,* p. 339.

31. Ibid., p. 342.

32. Ibid., p. 339.

33. See Bolton, ed., *Spanish Exploration,* pp. 313-319; John Francis Bannon, *The Spanish Borderlands Frontier, 1513-1821,* p. 99; Castañeda, *Catholic Heritage* 2:311-328; and Elizabeth H. John, *Storms Brewed in Other Men's Worlds,* pp. 174-180.

34. Lopez, in Hackett, ed., *Pichardo's Treatise* 2:355.

35. Lopez, in Cesario Fernandez Duro, *Don Diego de Peñalosa y su Descubrimiento del Reino de Cuivira,* p. 69.

36. Lopez, in Hackett, ed., *Pichardo's Treatise* 2:356.

12. Alonso de Posada's Report: The Jumano World in 1685

1. The Peñalosa affair is treated by many historians. Fernandez Duro (*Don Diego de Peñalosa*) assembled a collection of documents, including Posada's report and a selection of documents from the Lopez–Dominguez de Mendoza expedition; some of these have already been cited (2.5). The most complete edition of Posada's report is that translated and edited by Thomas (*Posada Report*). The impact on New Mexico of Peñalosa's reign as governor, and its aftermath, is treated by Sanchez (*Rio Abajo*).

2. The meaning of the terms *Quivira* and *Teguayo*—often linked, as the names of important Indian "kingdoms"—can not be clearly defined; both seem to have had a semilegendary appeal, connected with the Spanish search for riches. Quivira can usually be identified as the country along, and north of, the Arkansas River near—and perhaps extending to—the eastern bank of the Mississippi (as in Posada's reference to the "Great River," in Thomas, ed., *Posada Report,* p. 33); the tribes were predominantly of the Caddoan language family, later identified as the Wichita. Teguayo (or Tagago) is more difficult to localize; it was sought by the earliest Spanish expeditions, but its provenance seems to have moved further to the north as exploration pushed in that direction. Posada locates Teguayo in the northwest, near the Sierras Nevadas, and suggests that it borders Quivira at its northern extreme—effectively, he presumes that it is there,

in *terra incognita*. It seems possible that this was actually a name given to the extensive territory in the Plains formerly occupied by Indians of the Tanoan family—the Jumano, in the inclusive sense—in late prehistoric times, before the entry of the Apache into the southwest and South Plains; this territory would have reached from the Rio Grande, at the west, to the western limits of the Caddoan tribes (*Quivira*). See n. 4, Chap. 19.

3. Charles II of Spain was an incompetent; the first *cedula* would have been dispatched during the ten-year regency of his mother, Maria Anna of Austria; the second, after Charles took the throne. It is not important to the present discussion to know who, or which ministry, dispatched the *cedula* requesting information on the state of affairs in the colony.

4. Thomas, ed., *Posada Report*, pp. 16–17.

5. Posada, in Thomas, ed., *Posada Report*, pp. 25–26.

6. A similar confusion is seen in the account of the exploration of the Plains led by Oñate's second in command, Vicente de Zalvidar, in 1599. After a reference to the ". . . great river to the east, in the direction of Florida" (evidently the Arkansas or the Mississippi), the narrator indicates that "[we] all understand this to be the famous Rio de la Magdalena which flows into Florida, and that this was the route followed by Dorantes, Cabeza de Vaca, and the negro . . ." (Bocanegra, in Bolton, ed., *Spanish Exploration*, p. 224).

7. Posada, in Thomas, ed., *Posada Report*, pp. 32–33.

8. The fact that this river, actually the Mississippi, was thought to reach the sea at the Bay of Espiritu Santo may be of some significance in view of the confusion surrounding the location there of La Salle's colony, presumably by error, when the announced destination was the mouth of the Mississippi (see 3.1). It might be noted that the actual Spanish designation of the Mississippi, as used by the chroniclers of the Coronado expedition, was the "Great River of the Holy Spirit" (Espiritu Santo) (Castañeda, in Winship, ed., *Coronado*, p. 114).

9. Posada, in Thomas, ed., *Posada Report*, p. 36.

10. Posada's reference is puzzling because the name *El Cuartelejo* is usually applied to an Apache stronghold northeast of New Mexico, in western Kansas. Thomas suggests, as a possible explanation, that there are lines missing from the report at this point in the discussion of Apache locations (Thomas, ed., *Posada Report*, p. 39). However, Posada's discussion seems quite coherent, and it seems likely that he is using the phrase in a generic sense; however, it is still somewhat puzzling that, as Thomas notes, he does not use the term when discussing the northeastern borders of the Apache realm.

11. Posada, in Thomas, ed., *Posada Report*, p. 40.

12. Ibid., p. 41.

13. Ibid., p. 49.

14. Ibid., p. 51.

15. Ibid., p. 56.

16. Ibid., pp. 56–57.

13. La Salle's Colony: The French Connection

1. On the disagreement about La Salle's intentions, see John Bartlett Brebner, *The Explorers of North America,* p. 272; Francis Parkman, *The Discovery of the Great West: La Salle,* pp. 276–288; and John, *Storms,* p. 163.

2. Isaac Joslin Cox, ed., *The Journeys of Rene Robert Cavelier Sieur de La Salle* 2:245.

3. Joutel's narrative seems to indicate that there was a disagreement between Beaulieu and La Salle, who identified the Bay of the Holy Spirit after five days of exploring the coast (in Cox, ed., *Journeys* 2:2). Considering the evident confusion already seen in Posada's view of the continent, it seems possible that Beaulieu actually believed the bay to be the mouth of the Mississippi.

4. In Cox, ed., *Journeys* 1:275.

5. Ibid., pp. 278–279.

6. Ibid., pp. 279–280.

7. Ibid., pp. 280–281.

8. Douay, in Cox, ed., *Journeys* 1:231.

9. Ibid., pp. 232–233.

10. Ibid., p. 233.

11. Ibid., pp. 233–234.

12. Douay, in Hackett, ed., *Pichardo's Treatise* 1:237. The distance of two days' journey probably refers to the location of settlements in or near the valley of the Rio del Norte, and their distance from the Spaniards at El Paso.

13. Joutel, in Cox, ed., *Journeys* 2:93–94.

14. Douay, in Cox, ed., *Journeys* 1:236–237.

15. Ibid., pp. 239–240.

16. Joutel, in Cox, ed., *Journeys* 2:115.

17. Ibid., p. 115.

18. Ibid., pp. 117–118.

19. Ibid., pp. 133–135.

20. Ibid., p. 162.

21. Douay, in Cox, ed., *Journeys* 1:240.

22. Cavelier, in Cox, ed., *Journeys* 1:290.

23. Hyde, *Indians of the High Plains,* pp. 43–44.

14. Approaches from Coahuila

1. Bosque, in Bolton, ed., *Spanish Exploration,* p. 291.

2. Ibid., p. 298.

3. Ibid., p. 297.

4. Ibid., pp. 299–300. Throughout, Bosque followed a convention of recording the name of the band or tribe as the surname of the headman.

5. T. N. Campbell, "Coahuiltecans and their Neighbors," in William C. Sturtevant, ed., *Handbook of North American Indians*, vol. 9: *The Southwest*, pp. 345–350.

6. Bosque, in Bolton, ed., *Spanish Exploration*, pp. 304–308.

7. Joseph Francisco Marin, in Hackett, ed., *Historical Documents* 2: 393–395.

8. Forbes, "Unknown Athapaskans," *Ethnohistory* 6:142–143.

9. Massanet, in Bolton, ed., *Spanish Exploration*, p. 354.

10. Ibid., p. 355.

11. Ibid., p. 356.

12. According to J. Charles Kelley's calculations ("Juan Sabeata and Diffusion in Aboriginal Texas," *American Anthropologist* 57:981–995), Juan Sabeata had come from Sacatsol (Sierra Dacate) just prior to meeting Captain Retana near the Pecos in 1687; it is likely, then, that he was among the Chomenes seen there by Massanet's emissary.

13. Massanet, in Bolton, ed., *Spanish Exploration*, pp. 356–357.

14. Ibid., p. 366.

15. De Leon, in Bolton, ed., *Spanish Exploration*, p. 389.

16. Ibid., p. 403.

17. Massanet, in Hackett, ed., *Pichardo's Treatise* 2:136.

18. Ibid., p. 136.

19. Ibid., p. 137.

20. Ibid., p. 137.

21. Ibid., pp. 137–139.

22. Ibid., p. 139.

23. Ibid., p. 139. Fray Damian might have doubted, if he had been told, the efforts that Juan Sabeata had already expended in vain efforts to obtain ministers!

24. Ibid., pp. 139–140. The Muruam, mentioned here, may be the Mariamnes of Cabeza de Vaca's narrative.

15. The View from Parral

1. Juan de Retana, in Hackett, ed., *Historical Documents* 2:241.

2. Juan Isidro de Pardiñas Villar de Francos, in Hackett, ed., *Historical Documents* 2:251–255.

3. Retana, in Hackett, ed., *Historical Documents* 2:257–259. Although not so indicated, it is possible that Retana delayed his own departure, and covertly delegated Juan Sabeata to gather information and to take prudent action, if necessary.

4. Pardiñas, in Hackett, ed., *Historical Documents* 2:261.

5. Juan Sabeata, in Hackett, ed., *Historical Documents* 2:263.

6. Ibid., p. 267.

7. Miguel, in Hackett, ed., *Historical Documents* 2:271.

8. Cuis Benive, in Hackett, ed., *Historical Documents* 2:275–277.

9. Muygisofac, in Hackett, ed., *Historical Documents* 2:283.

10. Sabeata, in Hackett, ed., *Historical Documents* 2:267.

11. Cuis Benive, in Hackett, ed., *Historical Documents* 2:275.

12. Miguel, in Hackett, ed., *Historical Documents* 2:273.

13. Sabeata, in Hackett, ed., *Historical Documents* 2:262.

14. Kelley, "Juan Sabeata," *American Anthropologist* 57:981.

15. Ibid., p. 987.

16. Retana, in Hackett, ed., *Historical Documents* 2:257–259.

17. Cuis Benive, in Hackett, ed., *Historical Documents* 2:277.

18. Although Juan Sabeata's testimony was given through interpreters, there are indications that he sometimes did use the Spanish language, and he surely also spoke "Mexican"—though not, perhaps, as well as Nicolas, the Julime governor, who served as translator in Parral.

16. Fin de Siècle: The Jumano Diaspora

1. Pardiñas, in Hackett, ed., *Historical Documents* 2:285–287.

2. Retana, in Hackett, ed., *Historical Documents* 2:329; Forbes, *Apache, Navajo, and Spaniard*, p. 223; John, *Storms*, p. 194. Although its primary sense is geographical, the term *Nations of the North* was used for years by the Spanish colonies to refer to Plains tribes, primarily the Caddoan confederacies and their allies. By extension, in some contexts, it can be taken as a cover term for the coalition opposing the Apaches.

3. Don Lope de Sierra de Ozorio, in Hackett, ed., *Historical Documents* 2:213.

4. This phrase recurs many times in correspondence between governors and their military commanders; e.g., Hackett, ed., *Historical Documents* 2:299, 347.

5. Joseph Francisco Marin, in Hackett, ed., *Historical Documents* 2:391.

6. Ibid., p. 395.

7. Ibid., p. 395.

8. Retana, in Hackett, ed., *Historical Documents* 2:331.

9. Gabriel del Castillo, in Hackett, ed., *Historical Documents* 2:351.

10. Agustín Herbante del Camino, in Hackett, ed., *Historical Documents* 2:375.

11. Bolton, "The Jumano Indians," *Texas Historical Association Quarterly* 15:80; see above, 2.5.

12. Posada, in Thomas, ed., *Posada Report*, p. 36; see above, 2.6.

13. Muygisofac, in Hackett, ed., *Historical Documents* 2:277; see above, III.3.

14. Mendoza, in Bolton, ed., *Spanish Exploration*, p. 331; see above, 2.5.

15. John, *Storms*, p. 193.

16. Ibid., p. 192.

17. Geronimo, in Bolton, "The Jumano Indians," *Texas Historical Association Quarterly* 15:80.

17. The Jumano Identity Crisis

1. Nancy P. Hickerson, "The Linguistic Position of Jumano," *Journal of Anthropological Research* 44:3:315.

2. Although labeled "historical particularism," the American school of anthropology founded by Franz Boas had the reconstruction of baseline pre-European Indian cultures as its dominant theme. The date of the baseline period might be as early as the fifteenth century in the Caribbean, or as late as the twentieth in Arctic America. William Sturtevant contrasts the perspectives of history and anthropology as follows: "Most generally, the word 'history' refers to what is past, both static phenomena or stages, and changes over time . . . Historians recognize that historiography involves the selection of some facts over others, and the attribution of meaning or significance to the facts selected. . . . Anthropologists, on the other hand, are much more explicitly concerned with classifying, typologizing, and generalizing . . ." W. C. Sturtevant, "Anthropology, History, and Ethnohistory," *Ethnohistory* 15:1–2.

18. The Trade Network

1. It is not suggested that there was no communication between the middle Pecos and the lower river, but that the transport of goods would have been difficult; it was not a main route.

2. Kelley treats this as a separate group of "Eagle Pass Jumanos" and questions whether they were a "detached division of the Jumanos" or an "entirely different and unrelated group." J. C. Kelley, *Jumano and Patarabueye: Relations at La Junta de los Rios*, p. 37.

3. The Apache trade at Taos and Picuries Pueblos was witnessed during Zaldivar's exploration of the Plains in 1599.

4. The fact that Hopi men, rather than women, practiced weaving may reflect professionalization of the craft in this province.

5. Note Espejo's mention of woven textiles carried by travellers near La Junta, probably as trade goods.

6. J. Habicht-Mauche, "Coronado's Querechos and Teyas . . . ," pp. 10–12; "Evidence for the Manufacture of Southwestern-Style Culinary Ceramics on the Southern Plains," in Spielman, *Farmers, Hunters, and Colonists*, p. 52.

7. J. C. Kelley, "Juan Sabeata and Diffusion in Aboriginal Texas," *American Anthropologist* 57:992; also, *Jumano and Patarabueye*, p. 139.

8. Griffin indicates that peyote was in use in religious ceremonies conducted at La Junta at about this time. Griffin, "A North Mexican Nativistic Movement, 1684," *Ethnohistory* 17:103–109; also *Indian Assimilation in the Franciscan Area of Nueva Vizcaya*.

9. Turquoise was mined at Cerillos, near Santa Fe, in prehistoric times. (W. H. Holmes, "Turquoise," in F. W. Hodge, ed., *Handbook*, vol. 2, pp. 841–842). According to Schroeder, residents of San Marcos and other

Pueblo villages worked these mines until the Pueblo Rebellion of 1680. (A. H. Schroeder, "Pueblos Abandoned . . . ," in W. H. Sturtevant, ed., *Handbook of North American Indians,* vol. 9, p. 247).

10. "They [Rio Colorado Indians] brought out and presented us: beads, ochre, and some little bags of mica." Covey, *Adventures,* p. 104. Cabeza de Vaca referred to the mineral as both "silver" and "pearl"; Covey follows Hallenbeck and Bandelier in identifying it as mica. Note also the use of ochre in ceremonial prestation.

11. For the Jumanos' use of horses and wagons, see Hackett *Historical Documents* 3, pp. 257–259.

12. Brief glimpses of this arm of the trade are seen in the narratives of Castañeda and Castaño de Sosa.

19. From History to Prehistory

1. This approach is developed at greater length in Hickerson, "Jumano: the Missing Link in South Plains History," *Journal of the West* XXIX: 4:7–9.

2. Lexicostatistical dating places the separation of Kiowa from the Rio Grande Tanoans at between 2.5 and 4 millennia B.P. Hale and Harris, "Historical Linguistics and Archaeology," in Sturtevant, *Handbook of North American Indians* 9:171.

3. Hickerson, "The Linguistic Position of Jumano," *Journal of Anthropological Research* 44:317–318.

4. Early Spanish documents repeatedly refer to a "Kingdom of Teguayo," or "Gran Teguayo," usually said to be near or to border on Quivira. Hyde suggested that this name was a reference to the territory of the early Apaches. (Hyde, *Indians of the High Plains,* p. 25). However, it may now be suggested that it originally denoted the extensive pre-Apachean holdings of the Jumanos in the Plains, which would have bordered on Quivira in the vicinity of the Canadian-Arkansas River system. A number of references to Teguayo are compiled in Hackett, *Pichardo's Treatise,* 2:500–530.

5. According to archaeologist R. Campbell, "The term Jumano appears to have been applied by the New Mexican Spanish for more than two centuries to most of the historic descendants of the Northeastern Jornada." R. Campbell, "Possible Kiowa Prehistoric Origins," p. 15.

6. Hickerson claims no expertise in archaeology. The following observations are based on a cursory reading of selected studies, anticipating that a definitive identification of prehistoric Jumano cultural foci will eventually be made by more qualified scholars.

7. R. Campbell, "Some Possible Kiowa Origins," pp. 12–13.

8. Ibid., p. 13.

9. Jelinek, *A Prehistoric Sequence in the Middle Pecos Valley, New Mexico,* p. 143.

10. Ibid., p. 155.

11. Ibid., p. 162.

12. Ibid., p. 22.
13. Ibid., pp. 160–161.
14. Vivian, *Gran Quivira*, p. 142.
15. Ibid., p. 143.
16. Wendorf and Reed, "An Alternative Reconstruction of Rio Grande Prehistory," *El Palacio* 62:3:160–161.
17. Ibid., pp. 10–11.
18. Ibid., p. 145.
19. Scholes and Mera, "Some Aspects of the Jumano Problem," p. 292.
20. Vivian, *Gran Quivira*, p. 146.
21. Ibid., p. 151.
22. R. Campbell, "Possible Kiowa Prehistoric Origins," p. 13.
23. Kelley, *Jumano and Patarabueye: Relations at La Junta de los Rios*, p. ix.
24. Ibid., pp. 8–9.
25. Hickerson, "The Linguistic Position of Jumano," *Journal of Anthropological Research* 44:317–318.
26. Kelley, *Jumano and Patarabueye: Relations at La Junta de los Rios*, p. 129.
27. Ibid., p. 83.
28. Ibid., p. 55.
29. Ibid., pp. 74, 81, 82.
30. Malouf, "The Cielo Complex," p. 3.
31. Ibid., p. 6; Malouf, "Commentary," p. 21.
32. Malouf, "The Cielo Complex," p. 6.
33. Kelley, *Jumano and Patarabueye*, p. 129.
34. Malouf, "Commentary," pp. 10, 13.
35. Kelley, *Jumano and Patarabueye*, p. 143.
36. Malouf, "Commentary," p. 17.
37. Hofman, "Protohistoric Culture History," pp. 91–100.
38. Habicht-Mauche, "Coronado's Querechos and Teyas," pp. 14–18.
39. Ibid., p. 13.
40. Word, "The 1975 Field School of the Texas Archaeological Society," *Bulletin of the Texas Archaeological Society* 60:100.
41. Baugh, "Ecology and Exchange," p. 122.
42. Ibid., p. 125.

BIBLIOGRAPHY

Anderson, Melville B. *Joutel's Journal of La Salle's Last Voyage.* New York: Burt Franklin, 1896.

Ayer, Mrs. E. E., trans. "The Memorial of Fray Alonso de Benavides, 1630." *Land of Sunshine* 13 (1900): 227–290, 345–358, 435–444; 14 (1901): 39–52, 131–148, 227–232.

Baldwin, Percy M. "Fray Marcos de Niza and His Discovery of the Seven Cities of Cibola." *New Mexico Historical Review* 1 (1926): 193–223.

Baldwin, Stuart J. *A Brief Report on the Piro-Tompiro Archaeology and Ethnohistory Project, 1981 Field Session: Excavation and Archaeological Survey in the Abo Pass Area.* Ms. Department of Archaeology, University of Calgary. 1981.

Bandelier, Adolph F. *Final Report of Investigations among Indians of the Southwestern United States.* 2 vols. Papers of the Archaeological Institute of America, vols. 3 and 4. Cambridge, Mass. 1890–1892.

———. *The Southwestern Journals of Adolph F. Bandelier.* vol. 4. Edited by C. H. Lange, C. L. Riley, and E. M. Lange. Albuquerque: University of New Mexico Press, 1984.

Bandelier, Fanny, trans. *The Narrative of Alvar Nuñez Cabeza de Vaca.* Barre, Mass.: Imprint Society, 1972 [1906].

Bannon, John Francis. *The Spanish Borderlands Frontier, 1513–1821.* Albuquerque: University of New Mexico Press, 1970.

Bartlett, John R. "The Language of the Piro." *American Anthropologist* 11 (1909): 426–433.

Bartlett, Katherine. "Notes upon the Routes of Espejo and Farfan to the Mines in the Sixteenth Century." *New Mexico Historical Review* 17 (1942): 21–36.

Baugh, Timothy G. "Culture History and Protohistoric Societies in the Southern Plains." In *Memoir 21: Current Trends in Southern Plains Archaeology,* edited by Timothy G. Baugh, 167–187. Special issue of *Plains Anthropologist* 1986.

———. "Ecology and Exchange: the Dynamics of Plains-Pueblo Interaction." In *Farmers, Hunters, and Colonists: Interaction between the Southwest and the Southern Plains,* edited by Katherine A. Spielman, pp. 107–127. Tucson: University of Arizona Press, 1991.

Black, Stephen L. "South Texas Plains." In *From the Gulf to the Rio Grande: Human Adaptation in Central, South, and Lower Pecos Texas*, edited by Thomas R. Hester et al., 17–76. Arkansas Archaeological Survey Research Series no. 33. Fayetteville: Arkansas Archaeological Survey, 1989.

Bloom, L. B. "Fray Estevan de Perea's *Relacion*." *New Mexico Historical Review* 8 (1933): 211–235.

———. "The Chihuahua Highway." *New Mexico Historical Review* 12 (1937): 209–216.

Bolton, Herbert E. *Coronado: Knight of Pueblos and Plains*. Albuquerque: University of New Mexico Press, 1949.

———. "Entries on Tawehash and Wichita." In *Handbook of American Indians North of Mexico*, edited by F. W. Hodge. Bureau of American Ethnology, Bulletin 30. Washington, D.C.: Government Printing Office, 1907–1910.

———. *The Hasinais: Southern Caddoans as Seen by the Earliest Europeans*. Norman: University of Oklahoma Press, 1987.

———. "The Jumano Indians in Texas, 1650–1771." *Texas Historical Association Quarterly* 15 (1911): 66–84.

———, ed. *Spanish Exploration in the Southwest, 1542–1706*. New York: Scribner, 1908.

Brebner, John Bartlett. *The Explorers of North America*. Garden City: Doubleday & Co., 1955 [1933].

Bronitsky, Gordon. "Indian Assimilation in the El Paso Area." *New Mexican Historical Review* 62 (1987): 151–168.

Brooks, Robert L. "Village Farming Societies." In *From Clovis to Comanchero: Archaeological Overview of the Southern Great Plains*, edited by Jack L. Hofman et al. *Arkansas Archaeological Survey Research Series* 35 (1989): 71–90.

Bullock, Alice. *Living Legends of the Santa Fe Country*. Santa Fe: Sunstone Press, n.d.

Campbell, L., and M. Mithun, eds. *The Languages of Native America*. Austin: University of Texas Press, 1979.

Campbell, Robert G. Some Possible Kiowa Origins. Unpublished manuscript. 1983.

Campbell, T. N. "Coahuiltecans and their Neighbors." In *Handbook of North American Indians*, edited by William C. Sturtevant, vol. 10. Washington, D.C.: Smithsonian Institution, 1979.

———. "Espinosa, Olivares, and the Colorado Indians, 1709." *Sayersville Historical Association Bulletin* 3 (1983): 2–6, 15–16.

———. *Ethnohistoric Notes on Indian Groups Associated with Three Spanish Missions at Guerrero, Coahuila*. Center for Archaeological Research, University of Texas at San Antonio, Report #3, 1979.

———. "Name all the Indians of the Bastrop Area." *Sayersville Historical Association Bulletin* 7 (1986): 7–10.

Campbell, T. N., and T. J. Campbell. *Historic Indian Groups of the Choke Canyon Reservoir and Surrounding Area, Southern Texas*. Center for Archaeological Research, University of Texas at San Antonio, 1981.

Castañeda, Carlos. *Our Catholic Heritage in Texas,* vols. 1–5. Austin: Von Boeckmann-Jones, 1936.

Chavez, Fray Angelico. "Genizaros." In *Handbook of North American Indians,* edited by W. C. Sturtevant, vol. 10. 198–200. Washington, D.C.: Smithsonian Institution, 1983.

———. *Origins of New Mexico Families in the Spanish Colonial Period.* Santa Fe: Historical Society of New Mexico, 1954.

Connor, Seymour V. "The Mendoza-Lopez Expedition and the Location of San Clemente." *West Texas Historical Association Yearbook* 45 (1969): 3–29.

Covey, Cyclone, ed. *Cabeza de Vaca's Adventures in the Unknown Interior of America.* New York: Collier Books. 1961.

Cox, Isaac Joslin. *The Journeys of Rene Robert Cavalier Sieur de La Salle,* Vol. 1 & 2. New York: Allerton Book Co., 1922.

Davis, Irvine. "The Kiowa-Tanoan, Keresan, and Zuni Languages." In *The Languages of Native America,* edited by L. Campbell and M. Mithun. Austin: University of Texas Press, 1979.

———. "Linguistic Clues to North Rio Grande Prehistory." *El Palacio* 66 (1959): 73–84.

Dearen, Patrick. *Castle Gap and the Pecos Frontier.* Fort Worth: Texas Christian University Press, 1988.

Di Peso, Charles C. "Prehistory: Southern Periphery." In *Handbook of North American Indians,* edited by W. C. Sturtevant, vol. 10. 152–161. Washington, D.C.: Smithsonian Institution, 1983.

Dittert, Alfred E., Jr., and Fred Plog. *Generations in Clay: Pueblo Pottery of the American Southwest.* Flagstaff: Northland Publishing, 1980.

Donahue, William H. "Mary of Agreda and the Southwest United States." *The Americas* 9, no. 1 (1953): 291–314.

Donoghue, David. "The Route of the Coronado Expedition in Texas." *New Mexico Historical Review* 44 (1969): 77–90.

Dozier, Edward P. *The Pueblo Indians of North America.* New York: Holt, Rinehart, and Winston, 1970.

Encyclopaedia Britannica, 15th ed., s.v. "Agreda, Maria de."

Eoff, J. Dexter. "The Jumano: a Phantom Tribe?" *West Texas Association Yearbook* 40 (1964): 16–27.

Fernandez Duro, Cesareo. *Don Diego de Penalosa y su Descubrimiento del Reino de Cuivira. Informe presentado a la Real Academia de la Historia.* Madrid, 1882.

Fewkes, J. Walter. "The Pueblo Settlements near El Paso, Texas." *American Anthropologist* 4 (1902): 1.

Foote, Cheryl. "Spanish-Indian Trade along New Mexico's Northern Frontier in the Eighteenth Century." *Journal of the West* 24 (1985): 22–33.

Forbes, Jack D. *Apache, Navajo, and Spaniard.* Norman: University of Oklahoma Press, 1960.

———. "The Appearance of the Mounted Indian in Northern Mexico and the Southwest, to 1680." *Southwestern Journal of Anthropology* 15 (1959): 189–212.

———. "Unknown Athapaskans: the Identification of the Janos, Jocome, Suma, Manso, and Other Indian Tribes of the Southwest." *Ethnohistory* 6, no. 2 (1959): 97–159.

Ford, Richard I. "Inter-Indian Exchange in the Southwest." In *Handbook of North American Indians*, edited by William C. Sturtevant, vol. 10. 711–722. Washington, D.C.: Smithsonian Institution, 1983.

Forestal, Peter P., ed. *Benavides' Memorialo of 1630.* Washington, D.C.: Academy of American Franciscan History, 1954.

Goddard, Ives. "The Languages of South Texas and the Lower Rio Grande." In *The Native Languages of North America*, edited by L. Campbell and M. Mithun, pp. 355–389. Austin: University of Texas Press, 1979.

Griffin, William B. "A North Mexican Nativistic Movement, 1684." *Ethnohistory* 17 (1970): 95–116.

———. *Cultural Change and Shifting Populations in Central Northern Mexico.* University of Arizona, Anthropological Papers 13. Tucson, 1969.

———. "Indian Assimilation in the Franciscan Area of Nueva Vizcaya." University of Arizona, Anthropological Papers 33. 1979.

———. "Some Problems in the Analysis of the Native Indian Population of Northern Nueva Vizcaya." University of Arizona, Anthropological Papers 38. 1981.

———. "Southern Periphery: East." In *Handbook of North American Indians*, edited by W. C. Sturtevant, vol. 10, 320–342. Washington, D.C.: Smithsonian Institution, 1983.

Griffith, William J. *The Hasinai Indians.* Middle American Research Institute, Philosophical and Documentary Studies, vol. 2, no. 3. New Orleans: Tulane University, 1954.

Gunnerson, Dolores A. *The Jicarilla Apache.* De Kalb: Northern Illinois University Press, 1974.

Habicht-Mauche, Judith A. "Coronado's Querechos and Teyas in the Archaeological Record of the Texas Panhandle." *Plains Anthropologist* 37: 247–259. 1992.

Hackett, Charles W., ed. *Historical Documents Relating to New Mexico, Nueva Vizcaya, and Approaches Thereto, to 1773*, vols. 1–3. Collected by A.F.A. Bandelier and F. Bandelier. Carnegie Institution of Washington, Pub. 330, 1922, 1926, 1937.

———. *Pichardo's Treatise on the Limits of Louisiana and Texas*, vols. 1–5. Austin: University of Texas Press, 1931, 1934, 1946.

Haines, Francis. "The Northward Spread of Horses among the Plains Indians." *American Anthropologist* 40 (1938): 429–436.

Hale, Kenneth, and David Harris. "Historical Linguistics and Archaeology." In *Handbook of North American Indians*, edited by William C. Sturtevant, 9. 170–177. Washington, D.C.: Smithsonian Institution, 1979.

Hallenbeck, Cleve. *Alvar Nuñez Cabeza de Vaca: The Journey and Route of the First European to Cross the Continent of North America, 1534–1536.* Glendale, Calif.: Arthur C. Clark, 1940.

Hallenbeck, Cleve, and J. Williams. *Legends of the Spanish Southwest.* Glendale, Calif.: Arthur C. Clark, 1938.

Hammond, George P. "The Search for the Fabulous in the Settlement of the Southwest." In *New Spain's Far Northern Frontier,* edited by D. J. Weber. Albuquerque: University of New Mexico Press, 1979.

Hammond, George P., and Agapito Rey. *Don Juan de Oñate: Colonizer of New Mexico, 1595–1628.* Coronado Historical Series 5 & 6. Albuquerque: University of New Mexico Press, 1953.

———. *Obregon's History of 16th Century Explorations in Western America.* Los Angeles: Wetzel Publishing, 1928.

———. *The Rediscovery of New Mexico, 1580–1594.* Albuquerque: University of New Mexico Press, 1966.

———. "The Rodriguez Expedition to New Mexico, 1581–1582." *New Mexico Historical Review* 2 (1927): 239–248.

Harper, Elizabeth Ann (see John, E.A.H.). "The Taovayas Indians in Frontier Trade and Diplomacy, 1719 to 1786." *Chronicles of Oklahoma* 31 (1953): 268–289.

Harrington, John P. "Notes on the Piro Language." *American Anthropologist* 11 (1909): 563–594.

———. "Southern Peripheral Athabascan Origins, Divisions, and Migrations." Smithsonian Institution, Miscellaneous Collections 100 (1940): 503–532.

———. "Vocabulary of the Kiowa Language." Bureau of American Ethnology, Bulletin 84. Washington, D.C.: Smithsonian Institute, 1928.

Haskell, J. Loring. *Southern Athapaskan Migration, A.D. 200–1750.* Tsaile, Ariz.: Navajo Community College Press, 1987.

Heimsath, C. H. "The Mysterious Woman in Blue." In *Legends of Texas,* edited by J. F. Dobie. Hatboro, Penn.: Folklore Associates, 1964.

Hickerson, Nancy P. "The Decline and Fall of the Jumano Trade Empire." Paper read at the annual meeting of the American Anthropological Association, Washington, D.C. 1989.

———. "Ethnogenesis in the Great Plains: Jumano to Kiowa?" Paper read at the annual meeting of the American Association for the Advancement of Science, Chicago, Ill. 1991.

———. "The Jumano and Trade in the Arid Southwest." Paper read at the annual meeting of the Western Social Science Association, Denver, Col. 1988.

———. "Jumano: the Missing Link in South Plains History." *Journal of the West* 29, no. 4 (1990): 5–12.

———. "Kiowa: the Resurgence of Tanoan in the South Plains." Paper read at the annual meeting of the American Anthropological Association, San Francisco, Calif. 1992.

———. "The Linguistic Position of Jumano." *Journal of Anthropological Research* 44, no. 3 (1988): 311–326.

Hodge, Frederick W. "The Jumano Indians." *Proceedings of the American Antiquarian Society,* n.s. 20 (1911): 249–268.

Hodge, Frederick W., ed. *Handbook of American Indians North of Mexico.* Bureau of American Ethnology, Bulletin 30. Washington D.C., Govt. Printing Office, 1907–1910.

Hodge, Frederick W., G. P. Hammond, and A. Rey, eds. *Fray Alonso de Benavides' Revised Memorial of 1634.* Albuquerque: University of New Mexico Press, 1945.

Hofman, Jack L. "Land of Sun, Wind, and Grass." In *From Clovis to Comanchero: Archeological Overview of the Southern Great Plains,* edited by Jack L. Hofman et al. Arkansas Archeological Survey Research Series 35 (1989): 5–14.

———. "Protohistoric Culture History on the Southern Great Plains." In *From Clovis to Comanchero: Archaeological Overview of the Southern Great Plains,* edited by Jack L. Hofman et al. Arkansas Archaeological Survey Research Series 35 (1989): 91–99.

Holden, W. C. "Coronado's Route Across the Staked Plains." *West Texas Historical Association Yearbook* 20 (1944): 3–20.

Hughes, Anne E. "The Beginnings of Spanish Settlement in the El Paso District." University of California Publications in History, vol. 1, no. 3 (1914).

Hyde, George E. *Indians of the High Plains.* Norman: University of Oklahoma Press, 1959.

Jelinek, Arthur L. "A Prehistoric Sequence in the Middle Pecos Valley, New Mexico." Museum of Anthropology, Anthropological Papers 31. Ann Arbor: University of Michigan, 1967.

John, Elizabeth H. (see E. A. Harper). *Storms Brewed in Other Men's Worlds.* College Station: Texas A & M Press, 1975.

———. "An Earlier Chapter of Kiowa History." *New Mexico Historical Review* 60, no. 4 (1985): 379–397.

Jones, Oakah L., Jr. *Low Paisanos: Spanish Settlers on the Northern Frontier of New Spain.* Norman: University of Oklahoma Press, 1979.

———. *Nueva Vizcaya: Heartland of the Spanish Frontier.* Albuquerque: University of New Mexico Press, 1988.

Jorgenson, Joseph. *Western Indians.* San Francisco: W. H. Freeman, 1980.

Kelley, J. Charles. "Factors Involved in the Abandonment of Certain Peripheral Southwestern Settlements." *American Anthropologist* 54 (1952): 356–387.

———. "Juan Sabeata and Diffusion in Aboriginal Texas." *American Anthropologist* 57 (1955): 981–995.

———. *Jumano and Patarabueye: Relations at La Junta de los Rios.* Museum of Anthropology, University of Michigan, Anthropological Papers 77, 1986.

———. "Jumano Indians." In *The Handbook of Texas,* edited by Walter Prescott Webb, H. Bailey Carroll, and Eldon S. Branda. Austin: Texas State Historical Association, 1952.

———. "Notes on Julimes, Chihuahua." *El Palacio* 56 (Dec. 1949): 358–361.

———. "Review of C. Hallenbeck, 1939." *New Mexico Historical Review* 15 (1940): 79–81.

Kendrick, T. D. *Mary of Agreda: The Life and Legend of a Spanish Nun.* London: Routledge and Kegan Paul, 1967.

Kenner, Charles L. *A History of New Mexican–Plains Indian Relations.* Norman: University of Oklahoma Press, 1969.

Kessell, John L. *Kiva, Cross, and Crown: the Pecos Indians and New Mexico, 1540–1840.* Albuquerque: University of New Mexico Press, 1987.

Kingston, Mike, ed. *1988–1989 Texas Almanac.* Austin: Texas Monthly Press, 1987.

Krieger, Alex D. "The Travels of Alvar Nuñez Cabeza de Vaca in Texas and Mexico, 1534–1536." In *Homenaje a Pablo Martinez del Rio en el XXV Aniversario de los Origines Americanos,* Mexico City: Instituto Nacional de Antropologia e Historia, 1961. pp. 459–474.

Kubler, George. "Gran Quivira-Humanas." *New Mexico Historical Review* 14 (1939): 418–421.

La Barre, Weston. *The Peyote Cult.* Hamden, Conn.: Shoestring Press, 1964.

Lange, Charles H. "Relations of the Southwest with the Plains and Great Basin." In *Handbook of North American Indians,* edited by W. C. Sturtevant, vol. 9, 201–205. Washington, D.C.: Smithsonian Institution, 1979.

Lutes, Eugene. "A Marginal Prehistoric Culture of Northeastern New Mexico." *El Palacio* 66, no. 2 (1959): 59–68.

Malouf, Robert J. "The Cielo Complex: Archaeological Evidence of the Jumano and Jumano-Apache in the Texas Big Bend." Paper presented at Chiricahua and Mescalero Apache Conference, Truth-or-Consequences, New Mexico, Nov. 9, 1990.

———. "A Commentary on the Prehistory of Far Northeastern Chihuahua, the La Junta District, and the Cielo Complex." Unpublished manuscript. 1990.

Margry, Pierre. *Decouvertes et etablissements des Français dans l'Ouest et dans le Sud de l'Amerique Septentrionale (1613–1754),* vol. 3. Recherche des Bouches du Mississipi. Paris, 1875–1883.

Martin, Paul S. "Prehistory: Mogollon." In *Handbook of North American Indians,* edited by W. C. Sturtevant, vol. 9, pp. 61–74. Washington, D.C.: Smithsonian Institution, 1979.

Miller, Robert Ryal, ed. "New Mexico in Mid-Eighteenth Century: a Report Based on Gov. Velez Capuchin's Inspection." *Southwestern Historical Quarterly* 79 (1975–1976): 166–181.

Naylor, Thomas H. "The Extinct Suma of Northern Chihuahua: Their Origin, Cultural Identity, and Disappearance." *Artifact* 7, no. 4 (1969): 1–14.

Newcomb, W. W., Jr. *The Indians of Texas.* Austin: University of Texas Press, 1969.

Newcomb, W. W., and T. N. Campbell. "Southern Plains Ethnohistory: a Re-examination of the Escanjaques, Ahijados, and Cuitoas." In *Pathways to Plains Prehistory: Anthropological Perspectives of Plains Natives and Their Pasts,* edited by Don G. Wyckoff and Jack L. Hofman. Oklahoma Anthropological Society, Memoir 3. 1982.

Orozco y Berra, Manuel. *Geografia de las Lenguas y Carta Etnografica de Mexico.* Mexico City: J. M. Andrade y F. Escalante, 1864.

Parkman, Francis. *The Discovery of the Great West: La Salle.* Edited by William R. Taylor. New York: Rinehart and Co., Inc., 1956.

Pimentel, Francisco. *Cuadro Descriptivo de las Lenguas.* Mexico City: J. M. Andrade y F. Escalante, 1862–1865.

Pond, K. E. "Mary of Agreda." In *The New Catholic Encyclopaedia* I: 212–213. New York: McGraw-Hill, 1967.

Powell, J. W. "Indian Linguistic Families North of Mexico." Bureau of American Ethnology, Annual Report no. 7. 1891.

Reed, Eric K. "The Greater Southwest." In *Prehistoric Man in the New World*, edited by J. Jennings and E. Norbeck. Chicago: University of Chicago Press, 1964.

Riley, Carroll L. "Early Spanish-Indian Communication in the Greater Southwest." *New Mexico Historical Review* 46 (1971): 285–314.

———. *The Frontier People: the Greater Southwest in the Protohistoric Period.* Albuquerque: University of New Mexico Press, 1987.

Riley, Carroll L., and Joni L. Manson. "The Cibola-Tiguex Route: Continuity and Change in the Southwest." *New Mexico Historical Review* 58 (1983): 347–367.

Salinas, Martin. *Indians of the Rio Grande Delta.* Austin: University of Texas Press, 1990.

Samaniego, Joseph Ximenez. *Relacion de la Vida de la V. Madre Sor Maria de Jesus.* Madrid, 1759.

Sanchez, Joseph P. *The Rio Abajo Frontier, 1540–1692.* Albuquerque: The Albuquerque Museum, 1987.

Sauer, Carl O. "The Discovery of New Mexico Reconsidered." *Ibero-Americana*, no. 3., 1932.

———. "The Distribution of Aboriginal Tribes and Languages in Northwestern Mexico." *Ibero-Americana* no. 5; Berkeley, Calif., 1934.

———. "The Road to Cibola." *Ibero-Americana*, no. 3, 1932.

———. *Sixteenth-Century North America: The Land and the People as Seen by the Europeans.* Berkeley: University of California Press, 1971.

Scholes, France V. "Documents for the History of the New Mexican Missions in the Seventeenth Century." *New Mexican Historical Review*, 5 (1930): 93–115, 186–210, 386–404.

———. "The Supply Service of the New Mexican Missions in the Seventeenth Century." *New Mexico Historical Review* 5 (1930): 93–115.

Scholes, France V., and H. P. Mera. "Some Aspects of the Jumano Problem." Carnegie Institution, Contributions to American Anthropology and History, 6 (1940): 269–299.

Schroeder, Albert H. "A Re-analysis of the Routes of Coronado and Onate into the Plains in 1541 and 1601." *Plains Anthropologist* 7 (1962): 15: 2–23.

———. "The Language of the Saline Pueblos—Piro or Tiwa?" *New Mexico Historical Review* 39 (1964): 235–249.

———. "Pueblos Abandoned in Historic Times." In *Handbook of North American Indians*, edited by W. C. Sturtevant, vol. 9, 236–254. Washington, D.C.: Smithsonian Institution, 1979.

————. "Spanish Entradas, the Big Houses, and the Indian Groups of Northern Mexico." *Artifact* 7 (1969): 4: 15–22.

Simmons, Alan H. "The Formative Period-Neolithic Archaeology in the Southwest." In *Human Adaptations and Cultural Change in the Greater Southwest*, edited by Alan H. Simmons et al., *Arkansas Archeological Survey Research Series* 32 (1989): 75–128.

Simmons, Marc. "History of Pueblo-Spanish Relations to 1821." In *Handbook of North American Indians*, edited by W. C. Sturtevant, vol. 9, pp. 178–193. Washington, D.C.: Smithsonian Institution, 1979.

Sjoberg, Andree F. "The Culture of the Tonkawa, a Texas Indian Tribe." *Texas Journal of Science* 3 (1953): 281–304.

Smith, Ralph A., trans. "Account of the Journey of Benard de la Harpe, Discovery Made by Him of Several Nations Situated in the West." *Southwestern Historical Quarterly* 62 (1958): 525–541.

Spielman, Katherine A., ed. *Farmers, Hunters, and Colonists: Interaction between the Southwest and the Southern Plains.* Tucson: University of Arizona Press, 1991.

Stevens, A. Ray, and William M. Holmes. *Historical Atlas of Texas.* Norman: University of Oklahoma Press, 1989.

Stewart, Omer C. "Peyotism and Mescalism." *Plains Anthropologist* 24, (1979): 297–309.

Sturtevant, William C., ed. "Archaeology, History and Ethnohistory," *Ethnohistory* 17, no. 3 (1968): 1–51.

————. *Handbook of North American Indians*, vol. 4: Indian-White Relations. Washington, D.C.: Smithsonian Institution, 1988.

————. *Handbook of North American Indians*, vol. 9: The Southwest. Washington, D.C.: Smithsonian Institution, 1979.

————. *Handbook of North American Indians*, vol. 10: The Southwest. Washington, D.C.: Smithsonian Institution, 1983.

Swaggerty, William R. "Indian Trade in the Trans-Mississippi West to 1870." In *Handbook of North American Indians*, edited by W. C. Sturtevant, vol. 4, pp. 351–774. Washington, D.C.: Smithsonian Institution, 1983.

Swanton, John R. *Source Material on the History and Ethnology of the Caddo Indians.* Bureau of American Ethnology, Bull. 123. 1942.

————. *The Indian Tribes of North America.* Bureau of American Ethnology, Bull. 145. Washington, D.C. 1952.

Tainter, Joseph A., and Frances Levine. "Cultural Resources Overview: Central New Mexico." Albuquerque: USDA Forest Service, Southwestern Dist., 1987.

Tanner, Helen Hornbeck. "The Land and Water Communication Systems of the Southeastern Indians." In *Powhatan's Mantle: Indians in the Colonial Southeast*, edited by Peter H. Wood, Gregory A. Waselkov and M. Thomas Hatley. Lincoln: University of Nebraska Press, 1989.

Thomas, Alfred Barnaby, ed. *Alonso de Posada Report, 1686.* The Spanish Borderlands Series, IV. Pensacola: Perdido Bay Press, 1982.

Vehik, Susan C. "Onate's Expedition to the Southern Plains: Routes, Desti-
nations, and Implications for Late Prehistoric Cultural Adaptations."
Plains Anthropologist 30 (1985): 13–33.

Vetancurt, Fray Augustin de. *Teatro Mexicano: Descripcion Breve de los
Sucessos Exemplares de la Nueva-Espana en el Nuevo Mundo Occiden-
tal de las Indias,* vol. 3. Chronica de la Provincia del Santo Evangelio.
Edited by Jose Porrua Turanzas. Coleccion Chimalistac 10. Madrid,
(1698) 1961.

Vivian, Gordon *Gran Quivira: Excavations in a 17th Century Jumano
Pueblo.* U.S. National Park Service, Archeological Research Series no. 8.
1979.

Voegelin, C. F., and F. M. Voegelin. *Map of North American Indian Languages.* American Ethnological Society/Rand McNally & Co, 1966.

Wagstaff, R. M. "Coronado's Route to Quivira: 'The Greater Weight of the
Credible Evidence.'" West Texas Historical Association Yearbook 42
(1966): 137–166.

Wallace, Ernest, and E. A. Hoebel. *The Comanches: Lords of the South
Plains.* Norman: University of Oklahoma Press, 1952.

Wedel, Waldo R. "Archaeological Remains in Central Kansas and Their
Possible Bearing on the Location of Quivira." Smithsonian Miscellaneous Collections 101, 7 (1942): 1–24.

———. *Prehistoric Man on the Great Plains.* Norman: University of Oklahoma Press, 1974.

Wendorf, F., and E. K. Reed. "An Alternative Reconstruction of Rio Grande
Prehistory." *El Palacio* 62 (1955): 5–6, 131–165.

Williams, J. W. "New Conclusions on the Route of Mendoza, 1683–1684."
West Texas Historical Association Year Book 38 (1961): 111–134.

Winship, George Parker, trans. and ed. *The Journey of Coronado, 1540–
1542.* New York: Allerton, 1904.

Wolf, Eric. "The Virgin of Guadalupe: a Mexican National Symbol." *Journal of American Folklore* 71 (1958): 34–39.

Woodbury, Richard B., and Ezra B. W. Zubrow. "Agricultural Beginnings
2000 B.C.–A.D. 500." In *Handbook of North American Indians,* edited by
W. C. Sturtevant, vol. 9, pp. 43–60. Washington, D.C.: Smithsonian Institution, 1979.

Worcester, D. E. "The Spread of Spanish Horses in the Southwest." *New
Mexico Historical Review* 19 (1944): 225–232.

Word, James H. "The 1975 Field School of the Texas Archaeological Society." *Bulletin of the Texas Archaeological Society* 60 (1991): 57–106.

INDEX

Cabris, 35–36, 65. *See also* Julimes
Caddoan language family, xi, xviii, 24, 27, 71, 202;
Caddoes, xx, xxviii, 24, 73, 99, 172, 179, 208, 229; "Turk" identified as, 22. *See also* Hasinais; Cenis; Tejas
Caguates, 16–17, 38–39, 66. *See also* Cibolos
Camino Real, 85
Campbell, Robert G., vii, 226
Campbell, T. N., 71, 178
Canadian River, xxv, 23, 53, 60, 70, 100
Cancey, 71
Canoatino, 170–171
Cantor, Juan, 26, 32–33, 43
Capoques, 4, 5
Castañeda, Pedro de, 25–26, 27, 228
Castaño de Sosa, Gaspar, 45–49, 67
Castillian language, 190
Castillo, Alonso del, 3–18, 19
Castillo, Diego del, 110–112
Cavelier, M., 161–164, 168, 171, 172
Cenis, xiii, 164–166, 168–170, 172, 174, 198. *See also* Hasinais
Chamuscado, Francisco Sanchez, 31–33, 37–38, 41, 42–44, 50
Chihuahua, xi, xvi, xix, xxv, 12, 47. *See also* Nueva Vizcaya
Chihuahua Trail, 12
Chilili, 78
Chisos, 140, 179, 187, 199–200
Chizos. *See* Chisos
Chizos Mountains, xxvi
Chupadero pottery, xxi, 223, 225
Cibolos, 16–17, 38, 189–191, 195–198, 199. *See also* Caguates; Sumanas; Jediondos
Cicuye, 22, 28. *See also* Pecos Pueblo
Cielo archaeological complex, 227–228
Clemente, Don Esteban, 120–121
Coahuila, xiii–xiv, 47, 127, 175–176, 181–183, 203, 206

Coahuiltecan Indians, 127, 176, 178, 200, 203
Coahuiltecan language family, 8, 178, 220–221
Colina, Fray Agustín de, 186–187, 189
Colorado River (of Texas), xiii, xviii, xxv, xxviii, 8–11, 30, 67, 139, 143, 150–151, 164, 167–168, 170–171, 192–193, 216; Rio Colorado tribes, 204. *See also* Robec River
Comanches, 206–208
Concho River, xviii, 8, 11–12, 14, 66–67, 108, 110, 114, 137–138, 149–150, 193, 216; Jumano settlement on, 111–113. *See also* Rio de las Nueces; Rio de las Perlas
Conchos, xx, 30, 33–34, 43
Conchos River. *See* Rio Conchos
Coronado, Francisco Vasquez de, xxvi, 19, 21–29, 37, 40, 44, 51, 53, 71, 101, 150
Cruzate, Gironza Petris de, 126–129, 131, 133, 138, 140, 159, 194
Cueloce, 54, 55, 68–69, 117. *See also* Las Humanas; Jumano Pueblos
Cuis Benive (Cibolo-Jumano Indian), 191, 195
Cuitoas, 111, 113, 152

Davis Mountains, xxvi, xxviii; trail through, 12, 30, 42, 67, 68, 135
Devil's River, 46
Diablo Mountains, 16
Diaspora, Jumano, 207–208, 213–214
Diseases, among native population, 15, 103–104
Dominguez de Mendoza, Juan, 112, 125–126, 132–143, 144, 159
Dorantes, Andres, 3–18, 19, 27
Dorantes, Estevan. *See* Estevan
Douay, Father Anastasius, 166, 167–168, 169, 170, 171, 198